D1195781

NEW KNOWLEDGE IN THE BIOMEDICAL SCIENCES

PHILOSOPHY AND MEDICINE

Editors:

H. TRISTRAM ENGELHARDT, JR.

Kennedy Institute of Ethics, Georgetown University, Washington, D.C., U.S.A.

STUART F. SPICKER

University of Connecticut Health Center, Farmington, Conn., U.S.A.

VOLUME 10

NEW KNOWLEDGE IN THE BIOMEDICAL SCIENCES

Some Moral Implications of Its Acquisition, Possession, and Use

Edited by

WILLIAM B. BONDESON

University of Missouri-Columbia, Columbia, Missouri

H. TRISTRAM ENGELHARDT, JR.

Kennedy Institute of Ethics, Georgetown University, Washington, D.C.

STUART F. SPICKER

University of Connecticut Health Center, Farmington, Connecticut

JOSEPH M. WHITE, JR.

St. Paul Hospital, Dallas, Texas

D. REIDEL PUBLISHING COMPANY

DORDRECHT : HOLLAND / BOSTON : U.S.A.

LONDON : ENGLAND

Library of Congress Cataloging in Publication Data

Main entry under title:

New Knowledge in the biomedical sciences.

(Philosophy and medicine ; v. 10)
Outgrowth of proceedings of the Seventh Transdisciplinary
Symposium on Philosophy and Medicine, held May 18–20, 1978,
in Columbia, Mo.
Includes index.
1.   Medical ethics—Congresses.   2.   Medical innovations—
Moral and religious aspects—Congresses.   I.   Bondeson, William B.,
1938–   .   II.   Trans-disciplinary Symposium on Philosophy and
Medicine (7th: 1978: Columbia, Mo.)   III.   Series.
R724.N48   174'.2   81–15834
ISBN 90–277–1319–7   AACR2

Published by D. Reidel Publishing Company,
P.O. Box 17, 3300 AA Dordrecht, Holland.

Sold and distributed in the U.S.A. and Canada
by Kluwer Boston Inc.,
190 Old Derby Street, Hingham, MA 02043, U.S.A.

In all other countries, sold and distributed
by Kluwer Academic Publishers Group,
P.O. Box 322, 3300 AH Dordrecht, Holland.

D. Reidel Publishing Company is a member of the Kluwer Group.

Printed in The Netherlands

EDITORS' ACKNOWLEDGEMENT

On the occasion of the publication of Volume 10 of the series, *Philosophy and Medicine*, the Editors wish to acknowledge their gratitude to those persons who generously offered their energies and talents to this on-going research enterprise. In addition to the extensive list of contributors to the Series, innumerable colleagues provided their able assistance, many doing so without compensation except for the knowledge and satisfaction that they were participating in a scholarly endeavor whose primary purpose was and is to establish a new subdiscipline — the philosophy of medicine — on a firm foundation, and to sustain future scholarship and enhance medical practice by making significant research available to future generations of readers.

In addition to the many authors, editors, research assistants, office staffs, and the staff and executive offices of D. Reidel Publishing Company at Dordrecht, Holland and Hingham, Massachusetts, the Editors wish publicly to thank their family members who made sacrifices in various ways in the service of the Editors' ever-present deadlines. We offer a very special word of appreciation to Susan Engelhardt and Mark and Frances Spicker.

TABLE OF CONTENTS

SECTION V / BIOMEDICAL ETHICS AND ADVANCES IN BIOMEDICAL SCIENCE

SECTION VI / CONCLUSIONS AND REFLECTIONS: PRESENT AND FUTURE PROBLEMS

EDITORIAL PREFACE

The spectacular development of medical knowledge over the last two centuries has brought intrusive advances in the capabilities of medical technology. These advances have been remarkable over the last century, but especially over the last few decades, culminating in such high technology interventions as heart transplants and renal dialysis. These increases in medical powers have attracted societal interest in acquiring more such knowledge. They have also spawned concerns regarding the use of human subjects in research and regarding the byproducts of basic research as in the recent recombinant DNA debate. As a consequence of the development of new biomedical knowledge, physicians and biomedical scientists have been placed in positions of new power and responsibility. The emergence of this group of powerful and knowledgeable experts has occasioned debates regarding the accountability of physicians and biomedical scientists. But beyond that, the very investment of resources in the acquisition of new knowledge has been questioned. Societies must decide whether finite resources would not be better invested at this juncture, or in general, in the alleviation of the problems of hunger or in raising general health standards through interventions which are less dependent on the intensive use of high technology. To put issues in this fashion touches on philosophical notions concerning the claims of distributive justice and the ownership of biomedical knowledge. These issues, along with questions of the moral accountability of physicians and biomedical scientists, of the ownership of new knowledge, and of the propriety of employing expensive new technology rather than less expensive preventive health interventions, occasioned the symposium that produced this volume.

Over the last three years, this volume has taken shape through the revision of the proceedings of the Seventh Transdisciplinary Symposium on Philosophy and Medicine, held May 18, 19, and 20, 1978. In addition to many essays maturing over that period, new ones have been added. The history of gradual development was augured by the rescheduling of the original symposium from March 2, 3, and 4, 1978, due to a prodigious snowstorm that struck the Midwest and left philosophers, physicians, historians, and others stranded in various surrounding cities, unable to reach Columbia, Missouri. We would like to thank all who contributed so generously to the development of this symposium. Here we can mention only a few: Joseph Bien, Elizabeth Dickhaus, Charles G. Lobeck, Herbert W. Schooling, Louis Jolyon West, and Armon F. Yanders. We are also very grateful to the many institutions which supported this symposium: the Department of Philosophy and the School of Medicine of the University of Missouri-Columbia; the Institute on Human Values in Medicine and the Society for Health and Human Values under National Endowment for the Humanities grant no. EH-10973-74-365; the Education and Research Fund of the American Medical Association; D. Reidel Publishing Company; the Graduate School, Provost for Academic Affairs, and the Development Fund for the University of Missouri-Columbia.

Numerous individuals have helped generously during this time with their energy, labor, time, and suggestions in the development of the proceedings of a symposium into this volume. We wish especially to thank Jane L. Backlund, Mary Ann Gardell, Jude Payne, and Danialle Weaver. Through their aid and that of many others, old essays have been revised and new essays written. For assistance in this area we would particularly like to thank the series editorial assistant, S. G. M. Engelhardt. They have all, each in her own way, contributed to the successful completion of this volume.

March 2, 1981   WILLIAM B. BONDESON
                                                         H. TRISTRAM ENGELHARDT, JR.
                                                         STUART F. SPICKER
                                                         JOSEPH M. WHITE

H. TRISTRAM ENGELHARDT, JR.

INTRODUCTION

The acquisition of new knowledge is troubling because it can bring us to recast our understanding of ourselves and of our condition. Such changes are often disturbing. One need only think of the reception of Nicholaus Copernicus's and Galileo Galilei's heliocentric view, or of Charles Darwin's theory of evolution; the pursuit of knowledge has social costs associated with the alteration of an established worldview (though it surely has benefits as well). The investment in the acquisition of new knowledge also deflects social energies and goods from the solution of medical problems with current technologies, to the pursuit of new technological solutions. When biomedical knowledge is sought, there is also the question of whether one should seek the development of preventive or curative medicine. And the question arises as to the prerogatives of those who possess expert knowledge on these issues. Thus, the acquisition of new knowledge, as well as its presence, raises moral issues concerning what exchanges of what social goods for what biomedical goals are proper, and under what circumstances. As a consequence, this volume addresses the role of the physician as moral arbiter, the status of medical knowledge as a social product, the question of the costs involved in acquiring new medical knowledge, the use of cost-benefit calculations in the resolutions of such choices, the questions of distributive justice that underlie such choices, and the problems in employing an engineering model in resolving the biomedical quandaries raised by new medical knowledge. Possession and acquisition of new biomedical knowledge is never innocent of occasions for ethical reflections and analyses.

It is because we are an action-oriented, progress-presuming culture that knowledge has its morally problematic character for us. Our culture is, as in Cicero's phrase for revolutionaries, "eager for new things", *novis rebus studens*. We have come to expect changes in our understanding of nature and ourselves. We live and practise medicine in the expectation of imminent breakthroughs. The realization that our resources are finite has not dislodged us from that attitude. It has caused us to address the consequences of having god-like expectations, though finite capacities. We have, therefore, set upon the tasks of giving priority to partially realizable goals. New knowledge requires that we acknowledge a problematic involving macro-allocations (i.e., assigning

William B. Bondeson, H. Tristram Engelhardt, Jr., Stuart F. Spicker and Joseph M. White, Jr. (eds.), New Knowledge in the Biomedical Sciences, xi–xviii.

resources to various avenues for the pursuit of particular biomedical knowledge goals, versus other biomedical knowledge goals, as well as other social
goals), and involving micro-allocations (i.e., assigning the benefits of new
biomedical knowledge to some individuals rather than others). New biomedical knowledge, or even the expectation of new biomedical knowledge,
can bring us to reconsider accepted hierarchies of values and understandings
of distributive justice.

New biomedical knowledge, or the expectation of new biomedical knowledge, is especially intrusive, for it bears upon the destiny of our physical and
psychological integrity. It allows us new lifeplans or permits us to return to
old ones that we had abandoned. One might think of the implications of
the technologies upon which we, as a culture, are already dependent. For
example, the development of inexpensive and effective contraceptive methods
has engendered a contraceptive ethos which supports the very character of
modern industrial societies in which women are full participants in the work-
force, while fully sexually active, and while holding population growth at a
replacement level. Modern medical technology has fostered the sexual ethos
around which the social patterns of modern industrial society have been
organized. Biomedical knowledge and the technologies it sustains are silently
and powerfully active in fashioning the human condition. It is because of
the implications new biomedical knowledge has for our society and for
understanding the human condition that it is explored by the essays of this
volume.

The volume opens with an historical examination of the physician's role
as a moral arbiter in American life. As John Duffy's sketch shows, medicine
in the early 19th century arrogated a position of moral power because of its
actual weakness as a science and technology. As a consequence, the medical
profession came to emphasize the importance of character more than the
possession of specialized knowledge. In addition, medicine used its moral
position to protect established cultural viewpoints with regard to women, the
status of blacks, and the significance of sexuality. The profession employed its
position as the putative possessor of knowledge and expert skills in order to
maintain prevailing cultural values. Also, as when advocating the prohibition
of abortion in the 19th century, medicine acted in part to secure the position
of regular practitioners against that of irregulars, including abortionists. Medicine has thus not been simply a disinterested moral arbiter. Nor has it used
its claims to special knowledge in a fashion free of cultural prejudices. As the
other essays in this volume suggest, these problems are perennial, surely not
restricted to medicine. They hinge on the difficulty of discerning the character

of the moral element in decisions concerning new knowledge and technology, and of deciding who should participate in such decisions, and in what ways. As Duffy demonstrates, such analyses are difficult, for decisions regarding biomedical knowledge involve not only the economic well-being of society, but that of the professions as well.

If the medical profession has often failed to liberate us from our cultural prejudices, one might, as Samuel Gorovitz suggests, be suspicious of medicine's current claim of rights to moral leadership or to playing special roles regarding the use of new medical technology. Indeed, Gorovitz argues that in moral matters physicians have no particular authority or expertise. One would not therefore expect them to make a special contribution as *moral* arbiters to developing policies for new medical knowledge, though one would expect physicians to be able to anticipate some of the kinds of problems new knowledge might raise. Further, any attempt to play the role of a moral arbiter is confounded by the lack of a prevailing moral consensus. We no longer live (if we ever did) in communities fashioned by one religious, metaphysical, or even ideological view of the good life, where moral arbiters might have a generally recognized standing. This lack of consensus makes it difficult to approach one of the major issues raised by new medical technology, namely, whether it is worth investing further money in research to acquire such knowledge.

As Nicholas Rescher indicates, there has been a marked increase in the over-all resource costs of realizing new scientific findings. It is costing ever more to make new breakthroughs, for it appears that the easy-to-find inexpensively discoverable breakthroughs have already been made. Much like the search for gold in a well-scoured area, the nuggets that were lying loose to be found at the surface have long since been collected. The acquisition of new biomedical knowledge, as the acquisition of more of the precious metal, requires digging deeper with ever more expensive equipment. In the case of the research for new knowledge, this appears to involve ever more individuals than in the past. Rescher asks whether the investment in such costly research is justified. And, if so, on what grounds. He addresses the same issue with regard to the use of technologically sophisticated therapies.

His analyses provide a challenge to what have been for the most part the unquestioned undertaking of medical research. Rescher asks (1) whether the expense in manpower and resources should not bring us to redeploy those resources from research to therapy, (2) whether the expense of high technology intervention should not move us to invest instead in lower technology therapy and especially in preventive medicine, and (3) whether the costs involved in health care should bring us to abandon the maxim "only the very best is good enough". As Richard Zaner shows in his commentary, these questions become ever more acute as we recognize the limitations on our resources and the possibility of having an economy in which there is no longer appreciable and continued growth. Responses to Rescher's challenges may indeed move us as a society not only to abandon the ambitious hopes of perpetual medical progress, but also to restrict our use of the sick role, thus medicalizing fewer of our complaints. We may come to use our knowledge in less expensive and intrusive ways and to seek new medical knowledge that would lead to a greater and more efficacious distribution of benefits.

In his essay, Tom Beauchamp faces Rescher's question of the assessment of new medical technologies by proposing the use of a cost-benefit analysis in making decisions concerning the use of such technologies. He argues for the use of a preference rule utilitarian analysis, which attempts to maximize the realization of individual preferences. Beauchamp holds such an analysis can, for example, be employed to decide the extent to which preventive medicine should be supported at the expense of personal health care, or to determine the levels of allowable exposure in the work-place to carcinogens, such as benzene. In short, Beauchamp shows that the choice of policies of investment in biomedical research and in high technology treatment, and of public policies concerning risks of cancer, are open to rational analysis. Through such analysis he envisages the development of public policies regarding how much of our resources should be allocated to biomedical research, to high technology medicine, to routine clinical services, to preventive medicine, and to classes of individuals under each of those rubrics. These issues thus raise philosophical questions regarding distributive justice. Further, the use of new knowledge in establishing relations between work-place risks and rules for work-place safety involves questions about the proper grounds for creating such standards for avoiding risks to health and life. The resolution of these questions will depend on notions of proper exchanges of deaths and illnesses for profit (of the worker, the company, and society) and of who should participate in creating the standards for such exchanges – philosophical issues turning on basic notions of autonomy, ownership, and justice. As indicated, Beauchamp approaches these through the general analytical framework of a preference utilitarianism.

Individual preferences with regard to programs in biomedical research, personal health care, and preventive medicine will be influenced, however, by public perceptions of medical science and of the value of physicians. In part, the very presence of bioethical reflection and of bureaucratic concerns with medicine will alter the efficiency with which biomedical research can be undertaken, thus affecting both the calculations concerning the productivity of biomedical research and the preferences of individuals regarding biomedical research. Physicians and biomedical scientists have also contributed, as Professor Towers indicates, to misperceptions by either forwarding or not correcting unrealistic expectations of miracle breakthroughs. Misperceptions have also grown from popular television dramas, and from the advertisements of patent medicine that appeal to tests in hospitals which "establish" their efficacy or to their being "doctor-recommended". A consequence has been a cult of high-technology medicine that supports, among other things, high-technology therapy of individuals far beyond that point at which such medical technology would be useful, leading both to unjustified costs as well as to indignities to those treated.

Mary Rawlinson, in commenting on the papers of Beauchamp and Towers, stresses the need to provide an adequate theory of distributive justice in order to frame satisfactory cost-benefit analyses. That is, cost-benefit analyses must include costs with respect to, and in terms of, different senses of fairness. One would need, in addition, to consider the moral interests in providing new advances in biomedical research and employing expensive new technologies. Beyond that, one would need to decide on the scope of one's moral obligations. Some theories of justice may force one to adopt an international, not simply national, set of interests. One might therefore lower the priority one would assign to Western high-technology medicine. Instead, one might be more concerned with diminishing malnutrition, developing inexpensive and effective contraception, as well as pursuing more knowledge concerning non-Western diseases, such as schistosomiasis and malaria, than with less frequent Western diseases.

Issues of distributive justice also raise the question of the right to pursue and control biomedical knowledge, while the question of cost-benefit analysis raises the issue of determining the most productive models for scientific inquiry. Gerald Weissmann argues that scientists produce best when moved by the intrinsic beauty and allure of science, rather than by social impetus, direction, and control. He holds, in fact, that restrictions on the pursuit of new knowledge should, as far as possible, be avoided. The scientist, as the artist, must have liberty to pursue his or her own visions. In contrast, Marx Wartofsky emphasizes the social nature of medicine, biomedical research, and biomedical knowledge. Since biomedical knowledge is a social product, Wartofsky concludes that it should be viewed as social property, and therefore should be placed squarely under social control. However, Kenneth Schaffner contends that only a pragmatic multi-level analysis of the moral intuitions occasioned by biomedicine will give an adequate account of the moral issues involved. The questions raised by Weissmann and Wartofsky lead, so he argues, to acknowledging that biomedical undertakings have a value-laden, complex structure. There is a rich interplay of internal and external factors, including moral and non-moral values, as well as psychological and social forces, in the development of new biomedical knowledge.

In the second to last section of the volume, Arthur Caplan develops this point through a critique of prevailing bioethical analyses of ethical questions occasioned by new biomedical technology. He argues that the approach by ethicists to biomedicine has failed to take account of the complexity of the puzzles that biomedicine occasions: they have over-simplified the task. As a result, the standard view of bioethics has forwarded bioethical analyses on the model of undertakings in engineering. The presumption has been that the task is simply one of applying basic moral principles to new situations. As a consequence, so Caplan argues, current bioethics is often very similar to what had been the received view in the philosophy of science, namely, that the endeavor of science is in principle organizable in an axiomatized, deductive manner. So, too, bioethics appears to be a deductive system requiring only application. However, the complexity that ethical reasoning must face in order to take account of those moral issues raised by new biomedical knowledge cannot be fully appreciated with such an approach. One of the many difficulties resides in the fact that one can, in many circumstances, find competing bases for moral theorizing. If this is the case, bioethics cannot simply function as an enterprise in moral engineering, for the initial and crucial difficulty will be that of problem definition. One will first need to determine the· moral and empirical content. Moreover, the content will depend upon views of what should count as the central moral issues and the relevant empirical data. Caplan suggests that bioethics will need to proceed empirically and inductively in framing its analyses of biomedicine. Further, as Laurence McCullough indicates in commenting on Caplan, one would need to turn to the examination of underlying principles in ethics and in public policy in order to address adequately the issues raised by new biomedical knowledge.

In the concluding section, Ross Kessel, Mary Ann Gardell, William Bondeson, and Stuart Spicker provide a review of the issues raised by this volume's essays. Ross Kessel gives grounds for optimism, suggesting that promising modes for public policy responses have developed in overseeing the acquisition of new medical knowledge (e.g., the National Commission for the Protection of Human Subjects of Biomedical and Behavioral Research, and its successor, the President's Commission for the Study of Ethical Problems in Medicine and Biomedical and Behavioral Research), and that current problems and costs in achieving new medical breakthroughs may not, in principle, differ from those in the past. In short, medical progress may indeed continue somewhat as before. This point is developed by Mary Ann Gardell, who argues that the diversity of costs and real benefits of new medical technology show that there is not one sense of optimal treatment. Moreover, the increased power of medicine presses us to define "optimal".

Here one theme of the volume is underscored. New medical knowledge is always potential or actual medical power. Knowledge is sought in clinical medicine in order to increase the therapeutic and prognostic power of medicine. The basic medical sciences are thus more correctly auxiliary sciences. They are pursued as medical sciences because they are potentially useful in achieving the goals of medicine. This point is made more generally by William Bondeson, who contrasts the Aristotelian view of knowledge as understanding, with the modern view of knowledge drawn from Bacon and Hobbes, that knowledge is power. Moreover, it is a power developed by society with social costs and therefore open to societal assessment. As Stuart Spicker argues, these views of medical knowledge, its nature and its promises, have altered the character of our everyday life-world. The healthy and the ill live in the hope of new knowledge and of new breakthroughs. The very sense of our experience has been radically reconstituted by and through a host of new expectations, some of which are unreasonable.

New knowledge in the biomedical sciences is always laden with public policy implications. It is never simply knowledge, but knowledge with possible consequences for better health or for ameliorating the effects of disease, with possible social costs and benefits, and with consequences that underscore problems in our theories of distributive justice. In addition, new knowledge is often developed as a response to explicit social policy and therefore has greater public policy consequences. We now explicitly frame societal choices about investment in common goals concerning the pursuit of biomedical knowledge. The possession of new medical knowledge, or the likelihood of acquiring such knowledge, has a place in the calculations of public policy makers. It is this increasing social saliency of biomedical knowledge that raises special concerns regarding the role of those who acquire and possess it, the grounds for allocating scarce resources for its acquisition, and the criteria for assessing its impact upon society.

As this volume will show, these social and public policy concerns have complex conceptual presuppositions. Moreover, the significance of new biomedical knowledge can be understood only against background views about distributive justice and the social character of biomedical knowledge. Determining which biomedical technologies are appropriate for development involves us in complex choices, the philosophical analysis of which these essays undertake.

Washington, D.C.   H. TRISTRAM ENGELHARDT, JR.
March 16, 1981

SECTION I

THE PHYSICIAN AS MORAL ARBITER

JOHN DUFFY

THE PHYSICIAN AS A MORAL FORCE IN AMERICAN HISTORY

Before discussing the profession of medicine it may be well to point out that professionalization is itself a fairly recent development. While doctors, lawyers, professors, and other university-trained individuals have existed in Western society for many centuries, the concept of a highly organized group possessing specialized knowledge and backed by a legally sanctioned monopoly is relatively new. In the American colonial period, neither law nor medicine could properly be called organized professions. Entrance into both of these fields was open to anyone, regardless of qualifications. In the case of medicine the first few tentative efforts to establish licensure laws had only limited success, and opposition to such proposals intensified in the early 19th century with the rise of Jacksonian democracy. All measures by local and state medical societies to require minimum educational standards for entrance into medicine were looked upon askance by legislators convinced that physicians were simply seeking a legal monopoly to improve their financial position. Thus by the 1850's the few existing state licensure laws were completely swept away. Even the ministry, a profession long the prerogative of the educated class, felt the impact of the egalitarian spirit. Both the Great Awakening in the colonial period and the Revival Movement of the early 19th century emphasized emotionalism and revealed religion and led to a multiplication of religious sects. In so doing they opened the ranks of the ministry to all who felt inspired by the Holy Spirit.

While the lawyers had their legal codes, constitutions, and statutory laws and ministers were backed by sanctified writings, rituals, and moral codes, the physicians in the early 19th century could find little to agree upon. The traditional humoral theory and its modifications had given way in the previous two hundred years to various other theories, none of which provided a satisfactory basis for medical practice. By this time all areas of Western society, science, industry, and technology, were steadily advancing, but medicine lagged far behind. The few major discoveries in medicine seemed of little value to the general practitioner. Little was known of physiology and its related fields, which meant that there was virtually no understanding of the constitutional and degenerative disorders, and, until the role of pathogenic organisms and their vectors was discovered later in the century, the great

3

William B. Bondeson, H. Tristram Engelhardt, Jr., Stuart F. Spicker and Joseph M. White, Jr. (eds.), New Knowledge in the Biomedical Sciences, 3–21.

epidemic and endemic killer diseases were completely incomprehensible.

While the new scientific methodology led to discarding traditional theories, unfortunately not enough scientific knowledge existed to provide medicine with an alternative. In frustration and despair, the profession intensified its debates over medical theories and applied its traditional therapeutics — bleeding, purging, vomiting, sweating, and blistering — even more drastically. Already skeptical about these heroic forms of treatment, the public was further disenchanted by the constant quarreling and bickering among the doctors, and in consequence the prestige of the profession steadily diminished. At the same time the physician's status was little improved by the rise of proprietary medical schools which added only the thinnest veneer of academic training and a nominal doctor's degree to the basic apprenticeship system.

The public quarrels between members of medical societies and between individual physicians are all too well documented to need further elaboration. Ironically, the area in which physicians made their greatest contribution to social progress, public health, initially contributed to public distrust of the profession. In the 19th century the major argument among doctors and informed laymen alike concerned the nature of infectious diseases. Were they specific contagions brought in from the outside which might be excluded or controlled by quarantine and isolation measures or were they spontaneously generated in putrefying organic matter? When the early municipal health boards sought to prevent epidemic outbreaks by ordering the removal of infected patients to isolation hospitals or pesthouses, they often encountered opposition from the physicians. For example, in 1795, during a yellow fever outbreak in New York City, the Health Commissioner complained of the lack of cooperation from "many if not most" of the profession. In response to this complaint, President John Charleton of the local medical society reported that most of the society's members did not believe the disease to be contagious ([10], pp. 27–29, 35–37).

In 1862 the City Inspector for New York City responded to a call for sanitary reform by explaining that his greatest difficulty came from the medical profession. He had sought their enlightened counsels, he wrote, but had vainly looked for harmony among them. This chronic disagreement had compelled him to look elsewhere for help, he declared, for he had "to deal with facts, while more learned medical expounders have been busy with theories" [9]. Twenty years later *The New York Times*, in reporting that a group of physicians had met to support some proposed public health measures, commented: "The fact that this is the first time the medical profession have come together in this city to urge the public to take measures to avert the causes of disease is sufficient evidence of their opinion as to the urgency of the crisis" [26]. Understandably, when New York City established a permanent health department in 1866, the law specified that the majority of members of the Board of Health should be laymen. A board consisting largely of physicians, it was generally agreed, would be rendered ineffective by their disputations.

Since professional standing requires public recognition of a highly specialized knowledge on the part of the profession, physicians for most of the 19th century were in an unenviable position. Beset by irregular practitioners such as homeopaths, hydropaths, and eclectics whose therapeutic methods often achieved greater success than their own, and confronted by a highly skeptical public, doctors were almost compelled to fall back upon the moral authority inherent in medicine. Throughout history, medicine and religion had gone hand in hand until the secularization of Western society brought a measure of separation. Had medicine been able to keep abreast of the general advance of knowledge, no harm would have ensued, but, as noted, such was not the case. Consequently the medical profession was forced to emphasize the importance of character rather than the possession of specialized knowledge. Doctors envisioned themselves as dedicated men akin to ministers and philanthropists. In 1786 Dr Benjamin Rush, in a lecture on "The Influence of Physical Causes upon the Moral Faculty", argued that advances in science and taste had strengthened the moral faculty and contributed to the rising spirit of humanity. He than went on to discuss the impact of such factors as climate, diet, idleness, excessive sleep, the eloquence of the pulpit, music, and the role of medicine [31, 38]. While Rush was hardly a typical physician, he had a profound influence upon an entire generation of American doctors. In 1845, a highly favorable review was given of the Reverend H. A. Boardman's publication, *The Claims of Religion upon Medical Men*. The good minister had written that physicians enjoyed the confidence and affection of the community along with the clergy and concluded, to the delight of the doctors, that no group of citizens was more prompt to abate social evils, establish public charities, foster schools, and promote "judicious schemes for the substantial improvement of society" [24]. Towards the end of the century, the *Cincinnati Lancet-Clinic* editorialized: "In the settlement of great sociological questions affecting the masses of people . . . none are so well prepared to cope as the learned physicians of the country." The moral force and temperament of physicians, the editorial continued, made them "the natural antagonists of the crimes of avarice . . . " [20].

Despite the profession's exaggerated claim to moral leadership, its lack of

professional respectability meant that it was in no position to have any profound influence upon society during the 19th century. Moreover, with one
or two exceptions, physicians generally supported the prevailing mores and
attitudes. Thomas Bonner, in his study of social and political attitudes of
midwestern physicians from 1840 to 1940, noted that they were generally
conservative but reflected the changing times. For example, doctors supported
many of the popular reform movements of the 1840's, and they also shared
the general enthusiasm for change during the Progressive Period [4]. Bonner
tells us, too, that midwestern physicians tended to be nationalistic, an attitude
not restricted to the Midwest. A medical professor at Jefferson Medical College
in Philadelphia informed his students in 1847 that American physicians had
no need for the "conservative wisdom of the old world". "Ours is a land of
progress," he continued, and the "slow movement of European systems
suits us not"[36].

On most issues, physicians could be counted on to lend medical support
to prevailing beliefs. Southern physicians, who firmly believed in the health-
fulness of their climate, invariably ascribed the enormous death tolls during
yellow fever epidemics to the intemperance of foreigners and newcomers. The
temperance movement itself found physicians on both sides of the question,
since alcohol was a leading therapeutic. While a few advocated prohibition,
most were content to advocate moderation in the use of alcohol. When prohibition became a major issue the AMA sharply divided. Subsequent to the
passage of the prohibition act, a poll showed most members were inclined to
prescribe medicinal liquors. In consequence the Association changed its policy
from opposition to alcohol, and whiskey and brandy rejoined the United
States Pharmacopeia [33].

On virtually all questions relating to females, the doctors could be found
using medical arguments to bolster popular beliefs. In an age when the word
delicacy was virtually synonymous with prudery, the profession prided itself
on its delicate sensitivity. According to one of his students, in 1817 Dr
Thomas C. James, Professor of Midwifery at the University of Pennsylvania,
"had such a sense of delicacy that he could not bring himself to lecture on
the female organs of generation", but entrusted this part of his course to one
of his colleagues ([1], p.13). In 1850, a Professor of Midwifery and Obstetrics
at the Buffalo Medical College used a parturient patient for demonstration
purposes and precipitated outraged cries from both newspapers and medical
journals. One medical journal asserted that indelicate exposure was never
necessary. "Catheterism, vaginal exploration, manipulations ... whether
manual or instrumental; delivery by forceps, and embryotomy itself, can all

be performed by a competent man as well without the eye as with it." The whole art of the accoucheur, the editor asserted, could easily be acquired "under the ordinary covering" [25].

As knowledge of obstetrics and gynecology expanded and physicians began replacing midwives, the profession slowly moved away from false modesty. The introduction of the vaginal speculum around the mid-century was a major factor in undermining the secrecy attached to female genital organs. A Texas physician in 1860 made some shrewd observations about the use and abuse of this instrument. After noting that the medical profession was prone to fads, he declared that while hitherto the liver had been blamed for most ailments in the South, in females the womb was now held responsible for virtually all sicknesses. "Ulceration of the os uteri and also of the cervix of this organ seems to have sprung into existence, as if by magic," he declared, adding with a tinge of bitterness: "Indeed, I have known some places where you could scarcely find a woman whose uteri was not as well known to the eye of the medical man of the neighborhood as her face" [14]. Granting a touch of hyperbole, it is clear that in this area the medical profession was moving towards a more rational position. In so doing it encountered considerable public opposition. As late as the 1870's, Dr Thaddeus N. Ramy, a Cincinnati physician who permitted his students to observe labor and delivery, was sharply criticized, and it was 1890 before the University of Michigan required its medical students to attend deliveries [35].

While professional developments in medicine compelled physicians to oppose the secrecy associated with female sex organs, they can claim little credit for promoting a more rational attitude in other areas relating to females. The vast majority of them were convinced that women, like Blacks, differed from males anatomically, physiologically, emotionally, and mentally. In supporting these views, physicians were merely concurring with most contemporary leaders in religion, philosophy, and science. Medical practitioners, however, with their more detailed knowledge of anatomy – and presumably physiology – provided a good part of the evidence to justify the inferior position of women in society. They pointed to the fact that women were much more frail than men, that they were subject to periodic bouts of sickness (menstruation), and that above all they were highly sensitive creatures. Because their nerves were smaller and more delicate, they were much more susceptible to stress and hence were prone to a wide variety of nervous complaints.

As obstetrics and gynecology gradually became a medical specialty, a major emphasis was placed upon the role of the uterus in determining women's physical and mental state. Probably the best known statement of this thesis is the classic one by the prominent Philadelphia gynecologist Dr Charles D. Meigs, who proclaimed in 1847 that a woman is "a moral, a sexual, a germiferous, gestative and parturient creature". A few years later another physician expressed it even more succinctly when he said it was "as if the Almighty, in creating the female sex, had taken the uterus and built up a woman around it" ([40], p. 335). Part of the difficulty at this time lay in the mystery connected with the female biological cycle. For example, the argument as to whether the menstrual flow was stimulated by the ovaries, the uterus, or the Fallopian tubes continued almost to the end of the century. As late as 1875 an article in the *American Journal of Obstetrics* stated that since menstrual blood was the source of male gonorrhea, it was obviously an unnatural condition. Small wonder menstruation was often referred to as the "periodic ordeal" [6] !

Industry, technology, and urbanism were reshaping society in the 19th century, and among the changes they brought was a redefining of the female role. While working-class women could move from household industries and the fields into factories, there was no comparable occupation for the middle- and upper-class females. The new-found leisure gave the latter time for the fine arts and education, but education inevitably led them to compete with men. Recognizing this danger, consciously or not, the dominant males began a campaign to convince both themselves and women that intellectual endeavors were strictly in the male domain. Well before this time fears had been expressed that overstimulating the brain could bring on mental breakdowns and physical ailments, and with the rise of public education in the 19th century these dangers became a constant theme in medical and lay literature. The immature minds of children especially were thought to be in great danger from excessive study. Dr George Chandler wrote in the *Annual Report* of the Worcester State Hospital in 1849 that much of the prevailing insanity was the result of overcultivation of bookish or intellectual qualities – and he particularly blamed it on long confinement in schools. If this were true for children, and particularly for young girls, it must also apply to women with their limited brain capacity and much greater nervous sensibilities. The medical profession may not have originated this thesis, but it supplied most of the ammunition [43].

As early as 1853 the editor of the *Boston Medical and Surgical Journal* warned that the educational system was a threat to female health, declaring: "Every effort in the school room is to cultivate their minds at the expense of their bodies" [16]. Twenty-one years later, Dr Nathan Allen proclaimed that the Almighty had set limitations upon women. The uterus, with its "extreme sensitivity", "physiological importance", and "peculiar irritability", was the distinctive organ in females, a fact which, he said, educators must take into consideration [13]. It was clear to many physicians that the brain and ovary could not develop simultaneously, and that mental strain in young girls could have only a disastrous impact upon the health of women and in consequence upon that of future generations. A Harvard medical professor in 1873 wrote that females between the ages of 12 and 20 must concentrate upon developing their reproductive systems — hence brain work must be avoided. In 1900 the president of the American Gynecological Society warned teachers of schools for females to be aware of the "instability and susceptibility of the girl during the functional waves which permeate her entire being" and to provide rest during the menstrual periods. He also concurred with many of his colleagues in the view that higher education was beyond the physical capacity of females [6]. In 1950, Dr A. Lapthorn Smith, in arguing that the duties of motherhood were the direct rivals of brain work, unwittingly revealed the subconscious motive underlying the denigration of women's ability. The pursuit of learning, he stated, encouraged "an aggressive, self-assertive, independent character", which by making the male feel inferior made love impossible [32].

In their role as moral guardians, physicians also recognized that the frailer sex was beset by many other stresses and temptations. They warned of the danger from highly spiced foods or high-protein diets, both of which increased the sexual appetite and were liable to create unhealthy desires in young females. While most doctors recognized the value of mild exercise, occasional physicians joined in condemning the immorality of dancing. More typical of the profession, however, was an article in 1914 by Dr A. A. Brill which conceded that while the turkey trot appeared to be a "wild and emotional" dance, in reality it did not produce greater sexual excitement than the more conventional waltzing [5].

On the question of women's clothing the physicians generally were on the side of the gods. Medical journals repeatedly deplored rigid corsets and the mounds of clothing worn by upper-class women. Tight lacing was blamed, with considerable truth, for displacing the organs, limiting the function of the lungs, restricting the size of the pelvis, and interfering with uterine development. Using a spirometer one clinician demonstrated that tight corsets could reduce the lung capacity by 20 percent. Another used a manometer to test 50 women and found that the average corset exerted a pressure of 21 pounds, and that in one instance the pressure amounted to 88 pounds [32]. In criticizing the irrational clothing styles of middle- and upper-class women, physicians were merely supporting one of the aims of the health reformers of the 1830's and 1840's, and they had little more success than Amelia Bloomer and her cohorts. Dress reform awaited a complete change in the social and moral climate.

With respect to female medical education physicians displayed some ambivalence, although most orthodox practitioners opposed the entrance of women into medicine. In general they were appalled at the thought of young women being exposed to naked males, foreseeing a disastrous impact upon the morals and emotions of both female physicians and their male patients. Even those doctors who supported the principle of women practitioners based their support on the assumption that they would treat only female patients. John S. Wilson, an Atlanta physician, argued in the mid-century that women physicians were essential to "the safety and happiness of a large portion, of the most refined and lovely women...". He claimed that practitioners constantly encountered gynecological cases which had become incurable as a result "of the reluctance of females to submit to the use of the speculum". Many female diseases, he declared, could not be cured because of "the almost insuperable objections of the fair sufferers, to the inevitable exposure of their sexual secrets to a male physician" ([34], p. 397). In 1870, the editor of the *New Orleans Medical and Surgical Journal* urged giving women a fair chance at medical education provided that schools did not have mixed classes. He predicted that women physicians would "do little more than treat diseases of women and children", and in any case he was convinced that female doctors would "hardly last beyond the present generation" [21].

Far more physicians, however, reacted in complete outrage or derisive disbelief. The *New York Medical Journal*, in writing about a proposed female medical college in Philadelphia, expressed pity for the infatuated medical students. The male faculty members, he continued, should be "heartily ashamed of their imbecility and folly". "We saw in their museum," he concluded, "objects upon which no modest woman can look without a blush, in the presence of the other sex; nor any virtuous maiden study under the teaching of men, without mental impurity and moral deterioration" [18]. A Brooklyn doctor after discoursing on the degrading impact of medical education upon females, declared that not a decent family in the land would allow a woman doctor to enter its home [17]. A Philadelphia medical journal conceded that "in some degenerate age of the world women may be received into favor as practitioners of medicine", but expressed the view that they would inevitably fail as doctors in the present age [29].

Fortunately for women, the divisions within the medical profession worked to their advantage. In addition to the support from a few liberal physicians, irregular medical sects such as homeopaths and eclectics, which were fighting to survive, generally accepted females. Furthermore, nearly all medical schools were proprietary institutions competing for students, another circumstance which favored the women's cause. Nonetheless, by the 20th century, medical orthodoxy carried the day, with the result that subtle and overt discrimination gradually reduced the number of female medical students, a situation that remained unchanged until World War II.

Prior to the 20th century, venereal diseases were considered more of a moral problem than a medical one, and the refusal of many orthodox physicians to treat these disorders led to a flood of proprietary remedies and a host of so-called "Clap doctors" and other quacks, most of whom promised confidential, easy, and certain cures. Frighteningly, many of the advertisements for cures of "secret" or "confidential" diseases assured the patient that he could continue normal marital relations while undergoing the cure! While the profession collectively was not too concerned with venereal disease, individual physicians did recognize the need to deal with the problem. The first American medical journal, the *Medical Repository*, discussed a report on prostitution in New York City which placed the number of "Common prostitutes" at 1050 and the "Common bawdy and dancing-houses" at 160. The journal estimated the true number of prostitutes at 2100, but took consolation in the thought that New York had fewer "strumpets" than London. The editor deplored the lack of control over prostitution and asserted that this situation led to venereal diseases being "constantly in action, and diffused far and wide ... " [28].

Aside from occasional articles, venereal disease did not become a significant issue in medical journals until 1870 when the St Louis Board of Health passed the so-called "Social Evil Ordinance" which provided for the licensing and medical inspection of prostitutes. The local medical society was somewhat ambivalent about the measure, but in 1871 it did give tentative support. Whatever the reaction of the local physicians, the St Louis ordinance led to a national discussion as to the advisability of inspecting prostitutes. A good many prominent physicians, including Samuel D. Gross and J. Marion Sims, favored the idea. In his presidential address to the AMA in 1876, Sims declared that syphilis was no longer a purely medical problem for the therapist but one of concern to "the sanitarian, the philanthropist, the legislator, [and] the statesman ... " [7]. Both Gross and Sims decried the public ignorance and neglect of these horrible disorders.

John Burnham has pointed out that the medical profession reacted in three ways to the St Louis program and the whole question of venereal disease control. A good many physicians favored all possible regulations to curb venereal diseases; another group was dubious of inspecting prostitutes but favored other health measures; while still a third expressed complete outrage at the idea of legalizing vice. As the century advanced, two developments encouraged physicians to take a more determined stance on venereal disease. First, the growing recognition that many wives, children, and wet-nurses innocently contracted venereal diseases gradually undermined the concept that these disorders were literally the wages of sin. Second, as bacteriology advanced it became apparent that the medical complications of venereal diseases were far more serious than had been thought. Spurred on by these developments, intelligent physicians began urging their colleagues and the authorities to publicize the danger of venereal diseases and take measures against them.

Despite these developments, as far as laymen were concerned, sex and venereal disease continued to remain taboo subjects, and enough physicians shared the popular view to prevent medical associations from taking a firm position. In 1882 one of its committees recommended to the American Public Health Association that it advocate making venereal diseases subject to compulsory reporting and treatment. The proposal was turned down largely on the grounds that raising such an issue would bring public disapprobation on the Association and limit its effectiveness. A discussion in the New York Academy of Medicine some ten years later illustrates this same reluctance to question societal taboos. Two papers were presented before Academy members in May of 1892 urging, among other things, that syphilis be a reportable disease and that the newspapers be enlisted in the battle against it. Predictably, many opposing arguments were set forth, including a denial that syphilis was a serious disorder. The most telling one was first made by Dr E. L. Keyes when he declared that "such subjects cannot be voiced about publicly without deteriorating both ourselves and the public". Another physician ridiculed the idea of publicizing information on sex and venereal disease: " ... fancy how the reportorial imagination would run riot with interviews with prominent specialists." He concluded by warning his colleagues that "to attempt legislation is to stir up a hornet's nest about your ears" [7], p. 213, [8]. Although it is clear from the applause indicated in the minutes, that most of the members sympathized with the views expressed in the two original papers, the Academy nevertheless adjourned without taking any action.

By the early 1900's the ravages of venereal disease had become so apparent to physicians that Dr Prince A. Morrow, a prominent New York venereal specialist, and other leading medical men spearheaded a movement to bring the subject out into the open. Shortly thereafter he and his followers joined with the purity forces to organize the social hygiene movement. In response to these developments, medical journals throughout the country began publishing articles on the subject, sex education courses were introduced, and public health agencies launched educational campaigns. The drive against venereal disease peaked during World War I, and then lost momentum in the general political and social reaction of the 1920's. In 1920 the *New Orleans Medical and Surgical Journal* expressed the prevailing view when, after discoursing on a federal investigation of venereal disease in New Orleans, the editor concluded that neither investigation nor legislation would solve the problem – the only hope lay in the parent [23]. Sex and related topics once again became taboo until Dr Thomas Parran finally broke the conspiracy of silence in the 1930's. While individual physicians deserve a great deal of credit for breaking the taboo on the subject of sex and for turning a moral issue into a medical and public health one, the majority of medical practitioners gave only timid and cautious support.

If physicians can be credited with helping to change venereal disease from a moral issue to a medical one, they can also be charged with turning the moral question of masturbation into a medical problem. From earliest times semen was considered the essence of the human body, and any unnatural losses of it were assumed to bring dire consequences. While excessive sexual indulgence has always been thought debilitating, it was placed in a separate class from masturbation, a practice considered unnatural and hence more deleterious [15]. For most of Western history, masturbation received little attention except as a moral problem, but in the 18th and 19th centuries the medical profession began transforming it into a disease. The idea was first sounded early in the 18th century, and, while a good many physicians dismissed it as nonsense – John Hunter is reputed to have said that if masturbation caused insanity few of us would be sane – the concept of masturbation as a disease gained credence and was elaborated in the following century. By the second half of the century virtually every conceivable complaint, male or female, was ascribed to masturbation.

Equating loss of semen with diminution of the brain is another old thesis, but it appeared to be validated when the superintendent of the lunatic asylum at Worcester reported to the Massachusetts legislature in 1848 that 32 percent of the admissions were due to self-pollution (masturbation) [32]. By this date medical journals were beginning to devote more attention to the so-called sexual abuses. At first a good many American and British medical writers decried the thesis that masturbation *per se* was physically damaging, but by the second half of the 19th century it was clear that the pendulum was swinging away from this rational view. In the 1850's and 1860's American medical journals contented themselves largely with reprinting European articles on the dangers of masturbation or onanism, but as the century advanced they began supporting this position.

Dr Joseph Jones, a leading Louisiana medical professor and former president of the state's board of health, declared in 1889 that the "excitement incident to the habitual and frequent indulgence of the unnatural practice of Masturbation leads to the most serious constitutional effects and in some cases to . . . hopeless insanity." Among its many effects were despondency, loss of memory, irritability, digestive complaints, heart irregularity, prostration, headache, and neuralgic complaints. Even more grave was the prospect that the child of a masturbator was liable to hereditary insanity [12]. The records of the New Orleans Charity Hospital show that beginning in 1848 a good many patients were admitted for masturbation or onanism and that at least two deaths were attributed to this "disease".

Despite the obvious fact that the anatomy of males made them more likely to masturbate than females, the medical journals appear to have been far more concerned with its incidence among the "weaker sex". Precisely why this should have been the case is not clear, although I suspect prurience may have played some part. Probably more significant was the fear that female masturbation struck at the prevailing male assumption about the lack of sexual feelings among decent women. In light of this view, female masturbation had to be unnatural and hence pathological. In 1894 one physician referred to it as a "moral leprosy". In their desperate attempts to cure this dangerous condition, gynecologists resorted to surgical removal of the clitoris and the ovaries [3].

While the beginning of the 20th century saw the medical profession deemphasizing the physical effects of masturbation, well-established views die hard, and in the 1930's and 1940's many physicians were still warning the young man that each masturbation caused a little bit of his brain to die.

Probably the one area in which the American medical profession proved most effective in literally creating a moral issue was abortion. In an excellent study, James C. Mohr clearly demonstrates that physicians led the movement to enact and enforce anti-abortion laws in the latter part of the 19th century [37]. As of 1800, at least in the early stages of pregnancy, abortion was scarcely considered a legal question. Since America had no formal laws on the subject, the courts generally followed the English common law which did not recognize the existence of a fetus until it had quickened. While the nature of abortion is such that it does not lend itself to documentation, abortifacients were advertised in journals and newspapers, medical do-it-yourself books described how to "unblock menses", and letters and diaries reveal that the practice was fairly common. In the early part of the century, abortion received little attention, and when occasional individuals were charged with performing abortions, the courts usually dismissed the charges on the grounds that it was virtually impossible to determine intent. Early pregnancy could not be ascertained with any degree of certainty, and the accused could always claim they were simply treating obstructed menses or some other female complaint.

By the mid-century changes in society were responsible for a sharp rise in the incidence of abortion, particularly among middle- and upper-class Protestant women. This rise coincided with the mass immigration of impoverished Irish Catholics and raised the spectre that this latter, and presumably inferior, group would literally outnumber the Protestant majority. Moreover, the emergence of low cost mass-produced newspapers and magazines led to a flood of advertising by abortionists and the manufactures of abortifacients. Whereas abortion had been more or less a private matter, it was now becoming big business, with all the implied commercialism. These two developments provided an ideal environment for the medical profession to push for anti-abortion laws.

As indicated earlier, 19th-century physicians had little standing in American society. Unable to prevent or cure the major infectious diseases and scarcely much better off with respect to metabolic or degenerative disorders, they had little to offer patients save their moral support. To add to their woes, irregular practitioners, empirics, and quacks flourished as the public rejected the harsh and unsuccessful therapy of the regulars. For various reasons, but certainly as a means of asserting their moral leadership, the regular physicians led the fight for laws against abortion.

Ironically, while the early women's rights movement was accused of advocating abortion — and some of its leaders did — most of them assumed that equal rights for women would automatically solve the problem. Accepting the prevailing view that women had no interest in sex, feminists assumed that women wishing to restrict their families would simply abstain from sex. What is even more surprising is the failure of the churches to participate in the drive for anti-abortion laws. A few individual clergymen spoke out against abortion, but the majority, Catholic and Protestant alike, remained silent. In 1868, a speaker before the Missouri State Medical Association

complained bitterly that "our clergy, with some very few exceptions, have
thus far hesitated to enter an open crusade against [abortion]". This same
complaint was voiced by physicians in Michigan, Illinois, Kansas, and other
states, all of whom joined in decrying the reluctance of ministers to support
their moral crusade [37].

Largely as a result of pressure from local and state medical societies, by
1860 some 20 of the 33 states had passed abortion laws. Few of them, however, were effective, and even well-written laws were virtually nullified by
the attitude of the courts which still followed the quickening principle.
Nonetheless, the increasing visibility of abortion as a result of commercializa-
tion plus the educational campaign by physicians was gradually changing
public opinion. In the next 20 years, led to a considerable degree by the
AMA and its state and local societies, the anti-abortion movement made
rapid strides, and a flood of anti-abortion measures were passed by state
and territorial legislatures. More importantly, most of them specifically
denied the quickening concept, thus making the interruption of gestation
at any period a crime.

James C. Mohr postulates that organized medicine led the movement for
both professional and personal reasons. By fighting abortion, the doctors
were attempting to separate themselves from the irregulars and indirectly
seeking to promote the cause of medical licensure. He claims, too, that
abortion laws would bring the power of the state to help enforce the AMA's
own code of ethics, a serious problem in the late 19th century. A third
reason, and by no means last, was that by fighting for fetal life physicians
hoped to regain the moral leadership which they believed had formerly been
theirs. In addition to professional motives, many physicians joined the
crusade from strong personal feelings – moral objections to abortion, a
recognition that quickening had little significance in terms of fetal life,
the fear that abortion was a threat to white, upper-class Protestant domination, and, correctly or not, because they associated it with women's rights
[3].

Whatever the case, by 1900 public opinion had turned against abortion,
and it was considered morally and legally wrong. By this time, however, the
professionalization of medicine, as with other fields, was on its way to successful completion, and in consequence organized medicine lost interest in the
abortion issue. The 20th century saw the gradual elimination of midwives,
the physician's chief competitor, and the development of better abortion
techniques. Hence, abortion passed into the hands of the medical profession.
Not surprisingly, organized medicine today is playing no role in the fight

against abortion, and of those physicians who do speak out, far more favor legalized abortion.

As already indicated, the nature of the physician's work tends to make him conservative, and this conservatism generally carries over into social and moral questions. When the South began to close ranks on the question of slavery in the antebellum years, southern physicians argued that diseases in the South were distinct from those in the North, and that Blacks were physiologically and anatomically distinct from Whites and required a different form of medical treatment. When Dr E. D. Fenner started publishing his *Southern Medical Reports* in 1849 he asked his contributors to give "special attention to the diseases of *Negroes* ... ", and shortly thereafter the Medical Association of Louisiana appointed Dr Samuel A. Cartwright as chairman of a committee on the "Disease and Physical Peculiarities of the Negro Race". Within a short time Cartwright established — to his own satisfaction at least — that Blacks used 20 percent less air than Whites, had brains 10 percent smaller, and "that the same medical treatment which would benefit or cure a white man, would often injure or kill a Negro ... ". Another southern physician writing in the *Memphis Medical Recorder* stated that although the Black brain was only slightly smaller than that of Whites, it showed "a large preponderance of the animal over the intellectual functions". Other physicians agreed that "freedom to the negro, in the midst of civilization of the 19th century, is a curse, for it entails upon him insanity as its consequence ... " ([11], p. 270).

In the immediate postwar years, Southern medical journals generally downplayed the differences between the two races, but with the rise of Jim Crow later in the century, they were once again in full cry against Blacks. A Kentucky practitioner declared in 1895 that fear of the "negro-rape-fiend" was general throughout the South and that lynching was the only way to prevent rape. An Alabama doctor suggested in 1900 that the only solution to the race problem was to transport all Blacks, since freedom had turned them from harmless slavery into "a most vicious and dangerous element to our safety and civilization". In the meantime, he was content merely to castrate all Black criminals [2], [42]. In 1906, the *Atlanta Journal-Record of Medicine* editorialized that, after the Ku Klux Klan had provided an orderly trial, a doctor should castrate and brand Black rapists [15]. Southern practitioners were not the only ones preoccupied with Black sexual abilities; the *New York Medical Journal* in 1911, in discussing the race problem, spoke of the Black's "natural sexual propensities" [27]. Not to be outdone, the *New Orleans Medical and Surgical Journal* declared solemnly in 1909 that "the white man's brain is capable of more development because his skull does not harden or ossify as early as the black man's" [22]. As the 20th century advanced, medical journals dropped the subject, probably reflecting changing societal attitudes and the tendency for medical journals to become more scientific and technical.

One area in which the medical profession could justifiably assume leadership was public health. The profession had sought this early in the 19th century, but divisions within the ranks limited its efforts. By the latter quarter of the century the biological sciences were providing medicine with a fund of specialized knowledge. Since public health is the broadscale application of prevailing medical knowledge, physicians could claim with considerable truth that the field belonged to them. Here again, however, in asserting this claim, physicians were staking out an area of authority and seeking a special status in the community comparable to that of lawyers, engineers, and so forth. Public health is inextricably entwined with social and economic considerations and human behavior; hence it lends itself to moralizing. The moral overtones which characterized much of medical writings ring out even more clearly in the pronouncements against disease and other urban ills. Dr Andrew H. Smith, in giving the Anniversary Discourse before the New York Academy of Medicine in 1890, declared that unsanitary working conditions, excessive drinking, and the other maladies of society would grow unless their "natural protectors", the medical profession, assumed leadership [39]. The *Journal of the American Medical Association*, in 1897, called for the establishment of committees to bring the power of the medical profession to bear upon elected officials in support of reform and social education [20]. A professor of surgical pathology urged before a medical class graduating in 1899 that each doctor "should go into local politics with the same antiseptic methods which he uses in his purulent surgical cases, and bring them back to a state of cleanliness and sweetness . . . " [41].

For much of Western history physicians performed a good measure of charitable work. The motives for doing so were many: charity justified charging larger fees to those who could pay; it provided clinical experience for apprentices and medical students; and experimenting on the poor gave the early specialists an opportunity to improve techniques and methodology. In addition, many physicians were sincere, dedicated individuals, but this sincerity and dedication gradually became a mantle worn by the entire profession. Physicians have been fortunate, too, in that their economic interests in the 20th century coincided to a considerable degree with the common good. Who could question raising the standards of medical education and eliminating quacks and charlatans through licensure requirements? Yet a not-so-incidental effect of these steps was to restrict medicine to the middle and upper classes and reduce the number of medical schools by half. By its control of medical schools and licensing agencies, the profession drastically reduced the number of practitioners at a time when medical advances and a higher standard of living was creating a vastly increasing demand for services. The net effect of all this has been a sharp improvement in the economic and social status of physicians. Since economic success and "virtue" have traditionally gone hand in hand in America, it would appear their moral leadership has been confirmed.

University of Maryland
College Park, Maryland

BIBLIOGRAPHY

1. Atlee, J.: 1883, 'Annual Address of President', *Journal of the American Medical Association* 1, 12–17.
2. Bankston, R. C.: 1900, 'Some Views on the Race Problem', *Alabama Medical Journal* 12, 646–648.
3. Bloch, A. J.: 1894–1895, 'Sexual Perversion in the Female', *New Orleans Medical and Surgical Journal* (new series) 22, 1–7.
4. Bonner, T.: 1953, 'The Social and Political Attitudes of Midwestern Physicians, 1840–1940: Chicago as a Case History', *Journal of the History of Medicine and Allied Sciences* 8, 133–164.
5. Brill, A. A.: 1914, 'The Psychopathology of the New Dances', *New York Medical Journal* 99, 834–837.
6. Bullough, V. and Voght, M.: 1973, 'Women, Menstruation and Nineteenth-Century Medicine', *Bulletin of the History of Medicine* 47, 67–80.
7. Burnham, J. C.: 1971, 'Medical Inspection of Prostitutes in America in the Nineteenth-Century: The St Louis Experiment and Its Sequel', *Bulletin of the History of Medicine* 45, 203–218.
8. Minutes of the Section on Public Health; May 17, 1892, New York Academy of Medicine.
9. City Inspector of New York: 1861, *Annual Report* Jan. 13, 1862 Document No. 4, Board of Aldermen, New York, pp. 54–55.
10. Davis, M. L.: 1805, *A Brief Account of the Fever Which Lately Prevailed in the City of New York*, pamphlet, New York.
11. Duffy, J.: 1968, 'A Note on Ante-Bellum Southern Nationalism and Medical Practice', *Journal of Southern History* 34, 266–276.
12. Duffy, J.: 1963, 'Masturbation and Clitoridectomy: A Nineteenth-Century View', *Journal of the American Medical Association* 186, 246–248.

13. Duffy, J.: 1968, 'Mental Strain and "Overpressure" in the Schools: A Nineteenth-Century Viewpoint', *Journal of the History of Medicine and the Allied Sciences* 23, 63–79.
14. Duffy, J.: 1958–62, *The Rudolph Matas History of Medicine in Louisiana II*, Louisiana State University Press, Baton Rouge.
15. Editorial: 1906, *Atlanta Journal Record of Medicine* 8, 456–468.
16. Editorial: 1853, *Boston Medical and Surgical Journal* 49, 187–188.
17. Editorial: 1867, *Boston Medical and Surgical Journal* 76, 503.
18. Editorial: 1850, 'Female Medical College', *New York Medical Gazette and Journal of Health* 1, 247.
19. Editorial: 1897, *Journal of the American Medical Association* 29, 389–390.
20. Editorial: 1894, 'Medical Politics', *Cincinnati Lancet-Clinic* 72, 308–309.
21. Editorial: 1870. *New Orleans Medical and Surgical Journal* 23, 394–395.
22. Editorial: 1909–1910, *New Orleans Medical and Surgical Journal* 61, 642–643.
23. Editorial: 1920, *New Orleans Medical and Surgical Journal* 72, 101–104.
24. Editorial: 1845, *New York Journal of Medical and Collateral Sciences* 4, 87–89.
25. Editorial: 1850, *New York Medical Gazette and Journal of Health* 1, 106–107.
26. Editorial: 1881, *The New York Times*, April 14.
27. Editorial: 1911, 'Race Question in South Africa', *New York Medical Journal* 93, 281.
28. Editorial: 1804, *The Medical Repository*, Second Hexade 1, 90–91.
29. Editorial: 1859, 'Woman Doctor', *Medical and Surgical Reporter* 2, 275–276.
30. Engelhardt, H. T., Jr.: 1974, 'The Disease of Masturbation: Values and Concepts of Disease', *Bulletin of the History of Medicine* 47, 234–238.
31. Grob, G.: 1977, 'The Sexual History of Medicine and Disease in America: Problems and Possibilities', *Journal of Social History* 10, 391–409.
32. Haller, J. S. and Haller, R. M.: 1974, *The Physician and Sexuality in Victorian America*, University of Illinois Press, Urbana.
33. Jones, B. C.: 1963, 'A Prohibition Problem: Liquor as Medicine 1920–1923', *Journal of the History of Medicine and Allied Sciences* 18, 353–369.
34. Kaufman, M.: 1973, 'John Stainback Wilson and Female Medical Education', *Journal of the History of Medicine and Allied Sciences* 28, 395–399.
35. King, A. G.: 1975, 'Obstetrics and Gynecology in Cincinnati', *Cincinnati Journal of Medicine* 56, 265–268.
36. Miller, G.: 1959, 'Dr. John Delameter, "True Physician" ', *The Journal of Medical Education* 34, 24–31.
37. Mohr, J. C.: 1978, *Abortion in America: The Origins and Evolution of National Policy*. Oxford University Press, New York.
38. Runes, D. D.: 1947, *The Selected Writings of Benjamin Rush*, Philosophical Library, Inc., New York.
39. Smith, A. H.: 1890, 'The Family Physician of the Future', Anniversary Discourse, *Transactions* IV (2nd series), New York Academy of Medicine, 49–50.
40. Smith-Rosenberg, C. and Rosenberg, C.: 1973, 'The Female Animal: Medical and Biological Views of Woman and Her Role in Nineteenth-Century America', *Journal of American History* 60, 332–356.

41. Southgate, L.: 1899, 'The Physician as a Citizen', *Cincinnati-Lancet-Clinic* 81, 478–481.
42. Weir, J.: 1895, 'The Sexual Criminal', *Medical Record* 47, 581–583.
43. Worcester State Hospital: 1849, *Annual Report* 17, 45–52.

SAMUEL GOROVITZ

THE PHYSICIAN AS MORAL ARBITER

When asked to comment about the physician as moral arbiter, I thought it useful to begin by considering just what a moral arbiter would be. To speak of someone as a moral arbiter, or to speak of some group as functioning in that role, is to say that there is arbitration and that it concerns moral matters.

Let us first clarify the scope of arbitration in question; that is, just what moral matters are. As I understand the term, morality does not refer to questions of law, economics, psychology, sociology, prevailing public policy, history, or religion. All of these areas may have some bearing on questions of morality; I am sure that at least most of them do. But they are not the same as morality. The law may specify clearly what is legally required in a given situation, but it is easy enough to find examples where we are compelled to ask whether, on moral grounds, the law should be broken or challenged by civil disobedience. Many would argue, for example, that in a state which outlaws abortion, a physician still has a moral problem when asked to abort a pregnancy in the 13-year-old victim of rape by an escapee from a state institution for the criminally insane who has serious heritable diseases. Notice I have said only that the physician is faced with a moral dilemma; I have not indicated what the physician should do. I claim only that it is meaningful to ask what the physician ought to do. But there is no question about what the law requires in this example; thus the question of what the law requires and the question of what morality requires cannot be the same. Morality, therefore, is not the same as law, even though the relevant legal facts may have substantial bearing in our moral deliberations.

Economics also considers questions closely related to moral issues. Production, supply, demand, price, and distribution are factors closely related to questions of social justice, equity and the satisfaction of human values. But the economic aspects of a case do not alone entail any moral conclusion. The question of life-extending treatment − of "pulling the plug", to use that fashionable and deplorable colloquialism − is easily resolved on economic grounds. It is almost always cheaper, more efficient, to "pull the plug" when a patient's prospects for significant recovery are very slight. But we can ask meaningfully whether doing so is right. And no matter what the answer, that the question is meaningful indicates that rightness is something

23

William B. Bondeson, H. Tristram Engelhardt, Jr., Stuart F. Spicker and Joseph M. White, Jr. (eds.), New Knowledge in the Biomedical Sciences, 23–31.

other than economic efficiency alone. So moral judgments are not economic judgments.

Similarly, we can show that what is psychologically most comfortable or most ennobling, what is sociologically most usual, what accords with prevailing public policy, what is most in keeping with historical precedent or tradition, and what conforms to the strictures of whatever religious viewpoint, if any, one favors, can all be questioned on moral grounds. Therefore the question of moral judgment cannot be precisely the same as questions addressed in these other areas.

When I refer to moral judgments, I refer to judgments about that elusive, complex, yet centrally important cluster of concepts that we speak of in terms of justice, human dignity, rights, the resolution of conflicts among rights, and integrity. It is not easy to clarify what is meant by all that language, and I will not try to do so here. I just want it to be clear at the outset that those are the sorts of issues that are involved in making moral judgments.

Now what about arbitration? It is important to recognize that an arbiter is one who judges, who has absolute control or authority – the *Oxford English Dictionary* uses the expression "supreme ruler". So in speaking about moral arbiters, we are not talking about mediators, advocates, or lobbyists. And, at least for the moment, we are not even talking about moral leadership, such as might be provided by the example of a saintly life or by unusual statesmanship. Our topic, then, concerns the notion of the physician functioning with real – indeed, decisive – authority in regard to moral issues.

There is still an ambiguity in the topic. For the phrase "the physician" can be taken to refer either to individual physicians practicing their art in all their diversity, or it can be taken as referring to the collective behavior of the community of physicians. Professor Duffy, in his overview of the physician as moral arbiter in American history, has focused mainly on the attitudes and behavior of physicians as a profession and, earlier, as a collectivity of individuals striving toward professional status [1]. My emphasis will be more specifically on the conduct of physicians as individuals.

There are, of course, important connections between what one can say about a group and what one can say about the individual members of that group. The possibilities of individual behavior are dependent in various ways on the status of the group. For example, individual physicians could not legally administer narcotic injections or perform surgery unless the profession in general, or at least the relevant subset of the profession, had the privilege of engaging in such practices. But there are important differences between the behavior of a group as a profession and the behavior of individual members of that group, and these differences are crucial for our present concerns.

Professor Duffy has given us a rich, careful and enjoyable account of the relationship between the medical profession and various morally charged questions of social policy. He has primarily shown that physicians as a profession have not functioned as moral arbiters to any significant extent. Along the way, he has shown quite effectively that they have not functioned as moral leaders either, but rather have behaved essentially as moral followers, sometimes reflecting whatever the current foolishness of the time happened to be. Indeed, it is only with respect to one example that Professor Duffy argues that physicians as a class played a major role of moral leadership − this is in regard to casting the question of the justifiability of abortion in moral terms in the public debate. But even here, I think, one can question whether it was physicians who made abortion a moral issue. Surely it was considered a morally significant problem long before the events described in Professor Duffy's essay, and surely many writers, including philosophers and theologians of earlier ages, discussed abortion not just as a question of public policy, but as a morally significant issue [4]. Of course, this minor point of dissent is no quarrel with Professor Duffy's account of events in American history. It is only to observe that there was a prior awareness of the moral character of debate about abortion, to which Americans in their early history were insensitive. But that is hardly implausible, given the prominence of moral insensitivity as a foundation of our Nation's development.

Professor Duffy's conclusions are important ones to understand. The social role of physicians, about which I will say more, is such that it would be not merely a mistake, but a dangerous mistake, to view physicians as having historically been moral arbiters or even moral leaders. It is therefore useful to have a carefully documented account before us supporting the proposition that in regard to moral leadership, physicians have essentially just been folks like the rest of us. That they have not been moral arbiters, historically or presently, is wholly appropriate because there is nothing in the training or expertise of the physician which would justify any particular claim to moral authority or even moral insight.

When we turn to the behavior of individual physicians, the situation looks dramatically different. Illustrations are legion that show how physicians in individual cases have made and implemented decisions, on essentially moral grounds, that have had resounding impact on the lives of the people whom they influence. Surely the reader need not be convinced of the point, but in order to be quite explicit I will cite some examples. The newly pregnant woman who raises the question of abortion with her physician, only to be told that abortion is murder, wrongful taking of human life, medically inappropriate, and out of the question, has, when circumstances prevent her from turning elsewhere, been subjected to moral arbitration by her physician. And we have a similar phenomenon in the less dramatic case of the physician who makes a decision about the administration of analgesic medication largely, even if unwittingly, on the basis of his own views about the relative importance of relief from suffering and the maintenance of alertness, or his own capacity to tolerate pain, or his own opinions about whether a little suffering is good for the character or bad for patient morale [5].

Individual physicians find themselves in positions of enormous power, and it should be no mystery why. Professor Duffy speaks of the public recognition of a highly specialized knowledge on the part of the profession, and I would add to that public recognition a large dose of fear mixed with hope — in both regards sometimes rational and sometimes not. Our awareness of the fragility of life and health, and our recognition that it is life and health with respect to which the physician presumably has special skills and expertise, makes the physician not only a source of hope, comfort, and cure, but a vital force whom we dare not alienate, offend, or defy. This accounts largely for some quite remarkable characteristics of the social role of physicians. And that role really is bizarre, if we step out of our familiarity with it to perceive it as if we were visitors from another planet on which there was no illness or injury, and hence no medicine or understanding of medicine.

Just think of the things they do to one! They go up to people whom they hardly know and say "Take off your clothes". They then invade the privacy of the person in the most intimate ways, poking things into all orifices, and sometimes making new ones, causing people to eat toxic chemicals, cutting them open and discarding unwanted parts, and leaving behind them a wake of illness and injury — their word for it is morbidity — in the light of which it is a very risky thing to have anything to do with them. That sort of behavior is felonious assault, plain and simple, and it would land the average person straight in jail. Yet we not only tolerate this from, but expect it of, physicians.

In a land purportedly without a titled aristocracy, we see physicians jealously protecting the pretension that the degrees they have earned make them titled aristocrats. Call a professor "Mr" rather than "Professor" or "Doctor", and, at least at any decent university, he won't even notice. Call a clergyman "Mr" instead of "Reverend", and he will notice, but forgive.

Call a physician "Mr", and you have committed a social offense of the most extreme sort. You will be set right in short order, if not by the physician himself, then by his zealous palace guard. Some physicians even come to believe that, on the occasion of the awarding of that degree, the "M.D." designation becomes a part of their names, as if some fundamental transformation in state of being had occurred. (It is possible to demonstrate this phenomenon by asking a group of physicians to write their names – just their names – on slips of paper. Some of them will actually show that they think the "M.D." is part of it, as if one's educational history is inseparable from who one is in the most essential way.)

I do not want you to misunderstand; this is not an antimedical diatribe. Although iatrogenic illness *is* a major feature of medical practice, Ivan Illich is wrong, all things considered, when he argues that medical practice is primarily an enemy of health; I for one am glad to know that, in spite of its dramatic limitations and glaring weaknesses, medical help is available if I need it [2]. My point is this: medical behavior is bizarre; it violates many different strictures about what counts as acceptable interpersonal behavior. It therefore stands in need of explanation and, particularly, of justification. It can be explained, and often justified, but those tasks are not trivial or easy. And they cannot be performed once and for all, by the profession or by any one of its individual members.

The explanation of why we tolerate the assaultive aspects of medical behavior lies in part in the fact that, in spite of the harm that they do, physicians also help, and much of the harm is a price that must be paid in order to gain help. Another part of the explanation is that we regress to some extent when illnesses befall us. We become more dependent and, in ways that we are beginning to learn how to identify and document, less effective in some of our cognitive capacities. We look to physicians with fear and, often, unreasonable hopes. But in the final analysis, physicians do most of what they do because we allow and encourage it, which we do in large measure because we see it as being in our interest.

We should be aware of this fact, but this should never obscure from us the additional fact that this intrusive behavior needs to be justified not only as a general phenomenon, but case by case, instance by instance. It is this point basically that underlies the doctrine of informed consent, according to which, with rare exceptions, it is a battery to impose medical treatment on someone without that someone first having granted uncoerced and informed permission for the treatment. We accept as a basic value the proposition that one must leave others alone unless one can bear the burden of justifying not doing so. Physicians typically can justify what they do to others, and therein lies enormous danger. For physicians, drawing on the power and authority that is theirs, often lose sight of the fact that each application of that power must be separately justified. They then override the interests, autonomy, rights, and dignity of the persons who are their patients.

They do this whenever they arrogate to themselves the authority to settle any non-medical aspect of a question involving the lives, interests, and values of their patients. And, in particular, they do this whenever they make what is essentially a moral decision regarding options available to their patients. Such behavior is always an unwarranted arrogation of authority, since with respect to moral matters, physicians have no particular authority and no particular expertise. In some ways, in fact, as a result of their involvement in familiar conventions of practice, they are less insightful and sensitive morally than many of the others around them.

It is therefore particularly important to circumscribe the authority of the physician, lest the substantial power and authority that are woven into the fabric of the practice of medicine overreach their proper bounds. Whereas physicians as a professional class do not function as moral arbiters, individual physicians sometimes do, and when they do, an abuse has occurred — precisely because that arbitration has no justification.

It is worth noting that it is not just physicians who are in a position to function unjustifiably as moral arbiters. Anyone who is in a position of real power and authority can do so. Tomas de Torquemada was not a physician. Sheriffs, faculty members, school superintendents, and corporate executives, among others, are all in a position to act as moral arbiters, making decisions on moral grounds and imposing these decisions on others who do not or perhaps cannot resist or challenge their authority. In all of these cases, moral arbitration seems to me an imposition of authority that has no justification. It is not just when physicians function as moral arbiters that an abuse has occurred; I am suggesting that moral arbitration is, in general, abusive.

This has not been the case always and everywhere. There have been times and circumstances under which moral arbitration seemed welcome and appropriate. For example, one of the traditional functions of the village rabbi was precisely as a judge in regard to moral matters, and individuals in dilemma as well as parties in dispute would come to the rabbi in search of a resolution of the quandary or dispute. Here, a common allegiance to mutually accepted values provided the conceptual background for the arbitration. Similar phenomena occur in other closely knit communities with a shared

perspective both on basic values and on the methods and principles for resolving particular questions of value in terms of those basic values. But it
is characteristic of our time and circumstance that no such comprehensive
uniformity of viewpoint about values exists.

Some people have seen this circumstance as an indication of moral decay
or of moral chaos, lamenting the loss of a unified moral outlook precisely
because it is such an outlook that makes moral arbitration possible and
legitimate [3]. It is possible, however, to view the diversity of values that
exist in a pluralistic society as a mark of moral progress rather than of moral
decay — and to do so without embracing moral relativism or subjectivism.

The various moral theories that have currency, as well as those which
enjoy historical prominence, differ substantially in many ways. They differ
in the moral weight they assign to the consequences of actions and in the
moral weight they assign to motives. They differ in the relative priority they
assign to rightness as opposed to goodness. And they differ in other respects
as well. Each of them, however, insofar as it is credible, reflects some feature
of the values we do have — but for this correspondence of a moral theory
with some signficant aspect of our moral outlook, that theory would gain
no substantial hearing. Collectively, they provide an overview of moral value,
and the features they share constitute a base line for moral judgments. That
base line includes the acknowledgement that moral judgments are univer-
salizable — that is, moral requirements, such as they are, exempt no one and
favor no one. Also included is a concern with personal liberty and with social
good, although that concern is manifested in very different ways. Other
moral criteria, too, are ingredients in a moral common denominator which
provides a basis for limited, but fundamental, agreement among proponents
of quite different moral positions. One should not be distracted by the
differences to the point of losing sight of the commonality. To agree on the
basic moral significance of a respect for fairness, for personal autonomy, for
human dignity, for equality in the moral significance of all persons, and
for personal liberty, is to agree on a great deal of moral substance. It is
to separate oneself from the defender of a perfectionist ethic or of the view
that puts state before citizen; it is to take a substantive stand. These are
widely shared values that transcend most of the differences that divide what
is described as being our pluralistic culture.

To embrace these values is, nevertheless, to leave a large number of moral
questions open. It is to leave open such questions as how much personal
liberty should be sacrificed in pursuit of social equity, and how much adherence to principle is worth when it conflicts with human happiness. How

one makes the inevitably necessary tradeoffs among conflicting values, inter-personally and intrapersonally, is very much a function of the details of one's individual moral outlook. Further, I would argue, how one resolves or deals with such questions of value is an important ingredient in one's character and personality. To respect individual persons is to respect such distinctive ingredients of character and personality. It is, therefore, a consequence of a certain moral position — one including respect for persons — that within the broad outlines of the moral outlook I have briefly described, one must respect the pluralism of moral interpretation that exists within a community of distinctive, albeit interdependent people.

Moral arbitration then becomes a process we have outgrown. That is not to say that we should throw our hands up in the face of moral conflict, either accepting it as innocuous or lamenting it as intractable. It is only to say that it is no proper way to resolve all such conflict to have an ostensible moral authority pass down judgments in the mode of arbitration. Admittedly, there is a loss of efficiency in moving from moral arbitration to other modes such as negotiation and mediation for the resolution of disputes, but ef-ficiency, after all, is only one of the values we respect, and it should therefore come as no surprise that we honor it only to a degree.

It is time to return again to the medical profession. If, as Professor Duffy has persuasively argued, physicians as a class have not functioned as moral arbiters or even as moral leaders, and if, as I have further claimed, individual physicians function only inappropriately as moral arbiters and have no particular claim to moral leadership, what is there left to say about physicians and moral judgment? What is left, I believe, is most important of all. For phy-sicians — not uniquely, but very significantly — are in positions of substantial influence both in regard to the effect they have as clinical practitioners on their own individual patients and in regard to the effect they have as members of professional organizations and as citizens on a broader population. And physicians, like the rest of us, are moral agents; that is, they are persons who can act and who have responsibility for acting with conscientiousness, respect for other persons, and a regard for the basic values that are widely shared in our pluralistic society.

Physicians have no particular moral authority and no particular claim to moral leadership. But as moral agents they, like the rest of us, can do well or badly. Since what they do, given their particularly influential social role, has crucial effect on large numbers of individual people, our concern with physicians and morality should lead us to ask how we can diminish the extent to which physicians do function as illegitimate moral arbiters, and increase the extent to which they are likely to act with moral sensitivity and integrity. Acting with moral sensitivity and integrity is no easy task for anyone — at least if one aspires to meet high standards. For physicians in particular it is especially difficult, given the pressures and demands they face. Far from being moral authorities, they need and deserve all the help they can get, and the day still seems sadly far away when adequate attention is paid to these matters in their basic and continuing medical education.

University of Maryland
College Park, Maryland

BIBLIOGRAPHY

1. Duffy, J.: 1982, 'The Physician as Moral Arbiter in American History', in this volume, pp. 3–21.
2. Illich, I.: 1976, *Medical Nemesis*, Pantheon, New York.
3. MacIntyre, A.: 1975, 'How Virtues Become Vices: Values, Medicine and Social Context', pp. 97–111, and Gorovitz, S.: 'Moral Philosophy and Medical Perplexity', pp. 113–121, in H. T. Engelhardt, Jr. and S. F. Spicker (eds.), *Evaluation and Explanation in the Biomedical Sciences*, D. Reidel, Dordrecht, Holland.
4. Noonan, J. T., Jr.: 1970, 'An Almost Absolute Value in History', in J. T. Noonan, Jr. (ed.), *The Morality of Abortion*, Harvard University Press, Cambridge, Mass., pp. 1–59.
5. Veatch, R. M.: 1977, 'The Case of the Broken Leg', in *Case Studies in Medical Ethics*, Harvard University Press, Cambridge, Mass., pp. 17–21.

SECTION II

THE COSTS OF NEW KNOWLEDGE

NICHOLAS RESCHER

MORAL ISSUES RELATING TO THE ECONOMICS OF NEW KNOWLEDGE IN THE BIOMEDICAL SCIENCES

1. PLANCK'S PRINCIPLE OF INCREASING EFFORT

Over the past few generations there has been an exponentially increasing investment of human and material resources in scientific inquiry, particularly medical research. Nevertheless, there remains the economists' uncompromising question regarding the actual structure of the relationship between resource investment and product output. In particular, the problem arises of whether, as science progresses, a fixed amount of effort continues to yield uniformly significant results, or whether a process of declining yields is operative in this respect. Even greatly increasing resource investments will fail to generate a corresponding increase in output if the unit cost of production is rising.

A great deal of impressionistic and anecdotal evidence certainly points towards the increasing costs of high-level science. Scientists frequently complain that "all the easy researches have been done".[1] The need for increasing specialization and division of labor is but one indication of this. A devotee of scientific biography can easily note the disparity between the immense output and diversified fertility in the productive careers of the scientific collosi of earlier days and the more modest scope of the achievements of their latter-day successors.

It is clearly implausible to interpret this shrinkage as indicating that the days of greatness are over and that our contemporaries are men endowed with less brain power or with diminished capacity for hard work. Rather, one is drawn towards the very different conclusion that the work is simply getting harder. This poses the prospect that a stonier soil is being farmed — one where comparable effort simply can no longer yield comparable returns.[2] The successive victories of science, like the battles of Marlborough, are won only at an ever-mounting cost.

There are, it would seem, substantial grounds for agreement with Max Planck's appraisal of the situation:

To be sure, *with every advance [in science] the difficulty of the task is increased; ever larger demands are made on the achievements of researchers*, and the need for a suitable division of labor becomes more pressing ([11], p. 376).

35

William B. Bondeson, H. Tristram Engelhardt, Jr., Stuart F. Spicker and Joseph M. White, Jr. (eds.), New Knowledge in the Biomedical Sciences, 35–45.

The underlined thesis of this quotation will here be characterized as *Planck's Principle of Increasing Effort*. We shall interpret this as asserting that successive substantial discoveries become more and more expensive over the course of time in terms of the investment of talent, manpower, and material resources — that scientific work is subject to an escalation of costs. Accordingly, we construe this principle of increasing effort in specifically the following sense: As science progresses within any of its established branches, there is a marked increase in the over-all resource cost of realizing scientific findings of a given level of intrinsic significance (by essentially absolutist standards of importance).

The medical field affords a particularly vivid illustration of the extent to which latter-day problems tend to be more intractable than earlier ones and demand for their solution a vastly greater resource investment. The historical record of the success of modern medicine is doubtlessly impressive: more than half of the big killer-diseases of 1900 have virtually been eliminated as serious threats. But what is significant from our angle is the greater intractability of the problems that remain [7]. Finding a cure for tuberculosis, gastritis, or diphtheria was simple compared to finding a cure for today's catastropic diseases [10]. But the remarkable aspect of this phenomenon is its indication of the *extent* to which the later problems become more difficult and demand ever increasing levels of effort for their resolution — in the biomedical field as in natural science. The operation of a principle of cost-escalation has become strikingly manifest in the contemporary medical research [1, 6, 7].

2. FIRST THINGS FIRST: TECHNOLOGICAL ESCALATION

Nature inexorably exacts a *dramatically increasing effort* in terms of enhanced sophistication in data-deployment for revealing her 'secrets' and accordingly becomes less and less yielding to the efforts of our inquiry at given fixed levels of information-gathering technique ([11], p. 9). This accounts for the continual introduction of more and more sophisticated technology into inquiry in natural science and the subsequent increasingly extensive reliance upon it.

In natural science we do the easy things first. The very structure of scientific inquiry forces us into the situation reminiscent of an arms race: technological escalation where the frontier-equipment of today's research becomes the museum-piece of tomorrow under the relentless grip of technical obsolescence. It would thus be as futile to follow the authors into hankering after the days of "string and sealing-wax" apparatus as it would be to join Talleyrand in lamenting the lost *douceur de la vie* of the old regime. There is no point in blaming human foibles or administrative arrangements for a circumstance that is built into the very structure of investigation in natural science (realizing, to be sure, that the facts that make bigness a necessary condition of significant progress do not establish it as sufficient). The enormous power or sensitivity or complexity deployed in present-day experimental science has not been sought for its own sake, but rather because the research frontier has moved on into an area where this sophistication is the indispensable requisite of on-going progress.

A homely fishing analogy of Sir Arthur Eddington's is useful here [4]. He saw the experimentalist as a "trawler" — that is, as one who trawls nature with the "net" of his equipment for detection and observation. Now suppose (says Eddington) that fishermen trawl the seas using a fish-net of two-inch mesh. Then fish of a smaller size will simply go uncaught. And the theorists who analyze the experimentalists' catch will have an incomplete and distorted view of aquatic life. Only by improving our observational means for "trawling" nature can the existing limitations be mitigated. Technological escalation is an imperative of scientific progress. The range of phenomena to which the old data-technology gives access is soon exhausted. And the same is generally true with respect to the range of theory testing and confirmation that the old phenomena can underwrite [3, 8, 9].

Once all the findings accessible at a given state-of-the-art level of investigative technology have been realized, one must continually move on to a more expensive level. An on-going enhancement in the quality and quantity of the data-input requires more accurate measurements, more extreme temperatures, higher voltages, more intricate combinations, etc. On such a view, the phenomenon of cost-escalation is explained through a combination of the finitude of the body of first-rate results realizable *within a given level* of investigative technology, together with a continual (geometric) increase in the resource-costs of pushing from one level to the next.

This fundamental phenomenon of technological escalation, operative throughout the natural sciences and certainly in the medical field, serves to account for the recent rise of high-technology medicine that is a characteristic feature of present-day frontiers of research and therapy.

3. COST-ESCALATION IN RESEARCH

The issue I primarily want to pose in this context comes in the more comfortable form of a resource-allocation question. Specifically, it is the problem of cost-benefits in medical research.

Historically, this was not an issue. Even a single generation ago, the amount of money and talent invested in medical research was a trivial factor in the wider economic scheme of things. For example, less money was spent on polio research in the entire prewar generation 1915–1945 than in the years during the decade after 1948. And throughout the early 1960's substantially more was spent on medical research than on nursing home care throughout the U.S. In the early 1970's we spent annually on medical research and development an amount standing at some 6 percent of the total costs of hospital care and at more than 12 percent of the sum-total of physicians' services.

In recent years, the growth of medical research and development expenditures has been particularly dramatic, to the point where these costs are a substantial share of the over-all pie of total health costs. Medical research and development outlays have increased from a 3 percent slice of a $26 billion pie in 1960 to a 4 percent slice of a $94 billion pie in 1973 – an impressive quadrupling from $.85 billion in 1960 to $3.5 billion in 1973 [1]. An overview is given in Table I:

TABLE I

	(1) Total Health Expenditures (in 10^9)	(2) (1) as % of GNP	(3) Medical Research Expenditures (in 10^6)
1950	12.0	4.5	73
1955	17.3	4.5	139
1960	26.9	5.2	471
1965	43.0	6.2	1282
1970	74.7	7.6	1637
1975	131.5	8.6	2920
1977	170.0	9.0	3438
1978*	192.4	9.1	3991

*Preliminary data.
Source: Statistical Abstracts of the U.S., 1979 (p. 100, display Nos. 143 and 144).

A very general and fundamental point about the development of science is forceably illustrated by biomedical research rather than violated by it. In the course of scientific progress one solves the relatively easy and straightforward problems first and delays the relatively more complex and intractable ones. As time goes on, problems become more difficult and expensive to resolve.

In the final analysis, there is nothing unique to natural sciences as regards the basic principles operative here. For we are concerned with an endeavor to push a technology to the limits of its capacity, and one knows from innumerable cases there is an analogous cost-increase in any situation where technology is used to press towards *any* natural limit, even in situations quite outside the strictly scientific context. (See Figure 1 for a vivid illustration.) The cost of increasing effectiveness grows dramatically in all such contexts.

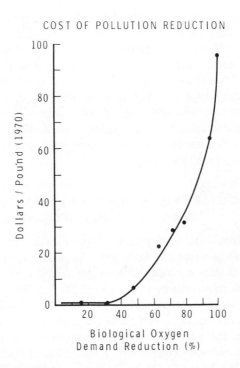

COST OF POLLUTION REDUCTION

Fig. 1. Cost of pollution reduction. Note: Incremental cost of reducing organic wastes from a 2700 ton-a-day beet sugar plant rises steeply as emission standards approach complete purity. Reduction of biological oxygen demand (a measure of the oxygen required to decompose wastes) cost less than $1 a pound up to 30 percent reduction. Reduction beyond 65 percent requires more than $20 for each additional pound removed, and at 95 percent reduction, each pound removed costs $60. From *Second Annual Report of the Council on Environmental Quality* (Washington, D.C.: Government Printing Office, 1971).

The record of recent success in medical research is without doubt impressive: more than half of the catastrophic diseases of 1900 have virtually been eliminated as serious threats. Yet a significant number of these remain, and the cost of eliminating them is great. In 1962, a total of 1032×10^6 was spent on medical research in the U.S., distributed as follows [2].

117×10^6 Cardiovascular Disease
128×10^6 Cancer
787×10^6 Other

The U.S. was spending more money (and effort) on cancer research in 1962 than it was spending on *all* of medical research in 1950 — more than had been spent on all of medical research in the history of mankind until 1940. Phenomenally, this massive expenditure has more than doubled to 2277×10^6, an amount that is more than 4 percent of what private consumers are spending on medical care [2]. The scale of this research effort is truly impressive. It is sobering to contemplate the vast efforts and expenditures of present-day drug research when one considers that the basic research that led to the discovery of penicillin was a shoe-string operation whose whole cost did not come to more than $20 000.

4. THE SPILL-OVER FROM RESEARCH TO THERAPY: THE RISE OF HIGH-TECHNOLOGY MEDICINE

The movement from inquiry to application, from medical research to medical treatment, represents a sure and fairly swift transition. Technological escalation of research is thus accompanied by technological escalation of therapy. The development of scientific medicine over the last 100 years has moved *pari passu* with technological revolution of breath-taking rapidity and scope. The devices used in contemporary medical treatment and the instrumentalities used to produce the *materia medica* of contemporary therapy are clearly among the most elaborate creations of a technological civilization. Increasingly, and dramatically, medicine has become a high-technology enterprise.

And, of course, sophisticated technology is *expensive* technology, both as regards the processes of its production and the *quality* of the manpower inputs for its effective utilization. The scientific implications of the procedures of modern medical research have run parallel with the skill-utilizing sophistication of the delivery system through which the products of modern medicine reach their consumers.

The consequences of this situation are all too well known. The costliness of modern high technology medicine is an important issue of social concern and political controversy. We are deluged day by day with such statistics as that the cost of a room at Massachusetts General Hospital now averages over $300 a day, including ancillary facilities (such as operating rooms), a figure roughly five times as large as that for 1966 [12].

And once the issue of costs rises to such prominence, that of cost-effectiveness is not far behind.

Many observers have commented on the ironic fact that, as one acute British writer recently put it:

It is precisely during the last two decades — when scientific medicine is alleged to have blossomed and when the quality of resources allocated to medical care has rapidly increased — that the decline in mortality that has been associated with industrialization has tapered off to virtual zero ([10], p. 2).

Indeed some observers see the situation not in terms of a slow-down but in terms of a stoppage. The eminent Australian immunologist Sir MacFarlane Burnett (Nobel Laureate in Medicine, 1960) after surveying work in the biological sciences concludes:

None of my juniors seems to be as worried as I am, that the contribution of laboratory science to medicine has virtually come to an end. The biomedical sciences all continue to provide fascinating employment for those active in research, and sometimes enthralling reading for those like me who are no longer at the bench but can still appreciate a fine piece of work. But the detail of an RNA phage's chemical structure, the place of cyclostomes in the evolution of immunity or the production of antibody in test tubes are typical of today's topics in biological research. Almost none of modern basic research in the medical sciences has any direct or indirect bearing on the prevention of disease or on the improvement of medical care [1].

It has become questionable whether massive effort and expenditure in research and technologically sophisticated therapy is able to yield a statistically significant result in terms of life-prolongation.

The interesting question of costs and returns thus comes to assume a particularly problematic and embarrassing form.

5. THE MORAL DIMENSION

The title of my essay spoke of not only the "economics" of new knowledge in the biomedical area but of the "moral issues" that arise in this connection. So far I have addressed myself primarily to the former topic. It is time now to turn to the latter.

The issue gains its moral dimension through the inevitable fact of the finitude of our resources. In the past, the biomedical sciences have flourished at a logarithmic growth-rate whose ever-accelerating increases cannot be projected into the future. Take the cost of delivering medical services in the U.S.A., for example. If these costs continue to rise at today's rate, by the year 2020 A.D. they would amount to the whole of our gross national product.

We are entering an era of zero growth — which means an era of effective scarcity in many regards. (For conditions of scarcity exist whenever one's resources, however ample, are inadequate to do *everything* that one would like to do.) At this stage forced choices come upon us and we must select priorities. Issues of a fundamentally ethical and moral character now come to be confronted.

And here I reach the core thesis of my discussion: the fact that the very economics of modern high-technology medicine itself poses moral problems of the most acute and difficult variety. It is, of course, easy to say "all these are merely *economic* questions — questions of the allocation of resources". But it is clear that these economic issues are fraught with moral and ethical ramifications. The crucial issue throughout is not one of efficient means to agreed ends, but of the very ends and objectives of the enterprise. Let us consider some aspects of this question of ends.

Throughout recent times American medicine has been governed by a simple precept: "The patient deserves the best" — where the medical needs of people are concerned nothing less than the very best is viewed as minimally acceptable.

This reflects an attitude which I find admirable and which I largely share. But its application is nevertheless highly problematic.

The situation in contemporary medicine is reminiscent of the late Roman empire — strength at the outer frontiers and a great multitude of weaknesses and problems in the less exotic regions closer to home.

The economics of the situation puts some very difficult and uncomfortable questions on the agenda:

(1)   Considering the great expense in manpower and resources involved, should there be a major redeployment from research to therapy?

(2)   Should we redeploy resources from complex and expensive high-technology intervention to lower-technology therapy and, above all, to preventive medicine?

(3)   Should be abandon the idea that "only the very best is good enough"?

And at just what stage are we towards an optimizing rationale in the delivery of health care?

The economics of the evolution of new knowledge in the biomedical sciences has put before us some very difficult and painful choices — choices fraught with far-reaching moral ramifications.

How are such choices to be resolved? What rationale can be developed for making them one way rather than another? The appropriate standard is perhaps relatively clear. It is the minimization of human suffering, on balance and across the whole spectrum, over the forseeable future. It is a matter of augmenting the range of human life to the greatest extent compatible with a minimal quality — roughly the standard of utilitarianism. And when (as with the question of research expenditures) this standard dictates the payment of a greater cost now for the sake of a greater benefit in the future, we must not shrink from a willingness to pay it.

To be sure, all these questions of social ethics and public policy are highly controversial.

It is none too soon to begin to debate the issues at the level of general theory before they bewilder us at the level of detailed practice. It is well to clarify the theoretical issues before the push and shove of political controversy blocks any prospect of calm and informative debate. The questions of public policy that arise in this area are not minor epiphenomena but cut through to the very heart of things. The traditional stance of political liberalism has always been oriented towards the rights and claims of the individual. Its line is that the individual is supreme, and that his interests are the ultimate arbiter of public policy which no purported wider public needs and interests can properly overrule. Opposed to this individualistic liberalism stands the tradition of holistic concern for "the good of the whole" so prominent in Hegel and the political philosophies that represent the evolution of the tradition he set afoot. At this level, it seems, we are going to have to face some very far-reaching issues of distributive justice in the delivery of health care services. These questions relate to the third point above, that the claims of the individual are absolute and that only the best is acceptable in our treatment of individuals. For we are rapidly entering an era where the best is only attainable for some at the expense of failure to realize a system that serves the best interests of the wider community.

In closing I would like to say something about the political ramifications of the cost-effectiveness considerations adduced above. In that fascinating government publication *Science Indicators* [13] we find the question

"Do you feel that science and technology change things too fast, too slowly, or just about right?"

Some 53 percent of the respondents answered this question *too slowly*. On the other hand, there was also the question:

"In which of the areas listed (below) would you most like (and least like) to have your taxes spent for science and technology?"

Topping the list with 69 percent here was "improving health care". People seem to feel that improvements in the health care area are needed, are worth paying taxes for, but are forthcoming at too slow a rate.

Now where will we stand when it becomes clear that ever more massive expenditures yield ever lessening returns in actual improvement? I myself sense a real potential danger here − the danger of the demagogy of unmet expectations and scapegoatism − a revulsion not just against science and technology, but against reason and the life of the mind. It is none too soon to start worrying about what will happen when people come to realize increasingly − and with growing disillusionment − that spend though we will and must on research in science and medicine, the age of swift and massive returns is coming to an end.

University of Pittsburgh
Pittsburgh, Pennsylvania

NOTES

[1] The sentiment is not new. George Gore vainly lambasted it 100 years ago: "Nothing can be more puerile than the complaints sometimes made by certain cultivators of a science, that it is very difficult to make discoveries now that the soil has been exhausted, whereas they were so easily made when the ground was first broken . . . " *The Art of Scientific Discovery* (London, 1878), p. 21.
[2] This prospect seems borne out also by a phenomenon whose reality, though it is difficult to substantiate, is nevertheless unquestionable − namely, that there are nowadays not a few authentic scientific geniuses of the first order who never managed to produce first-magnitude results. (For obvious reasons, one is hesitant to cite examples.)

BIBLIOGRAPHY

1.   Burnet, Sir M.: 1971, *Genes, Dreams, and Realities*, Basic Books, New York.

2. Cooper, B. C., Worthington, N. L., and Piro, P. A.: 1974, 'National Health Expenditures: 1929–1973', *Social Security Bulletin* 37, 2.
3. Duhem, P.: 1969, *To Save the Phenomena*, trans. E. Doland and C. Maschler, University of Chicago Press, Chicago.
4. Eddington, A. S.: 1978 (Reprint of the 1928 edn.), *The Nature of the Physical World*, AMS Press, New York.
5. George, W.: 1975 (Reprint of the 1936 edn.), *The Scientist in Action*, Arno Press, New York.
6. Hodgins, E.: 1956, 'The Strange State of American Research', in the Editors of *Fortune* (eds.), *The Mighty Force of Research*, McGraw-Hill, New York, pp. 1–20.
7. Illich, I.: 1977, *Limits to Medicine*, Penguin Books, New York.
8. Mittelstrass, J.: 1962, *Die Rettung der Phänomene*, de Gruyter, Berlin.
9. Newton, I.: 1936, *Philosophiae Naturalis Principia Mathematica*, F. Cajori (ed.), University of California Press, Berkeley.
10. Pawles, J.: 1973, 'On the Limitations of Modern Medicine', *Science, Medicine and Man* 1, 1–30.
11. Planck, M.: 1949, *Vorträge und Erinnerungen*, S. Hirzel Verlag, Stuttgart.
12. Shabecoff, P.: 1978, 'Runaway Medical Costs', *New York Times*, May 12, 1978, p. A–18.
13. U.S. Government Printing Office.: 1975, *Science Indicators – 1974*, publication No. 038–000–00253–8, Washington, D.C.
14. Werheimer, P., *et al.*: 1965, *Chemistry: Opportunities and Needs*, National Academy of Sciences, National Research Council, Washington, D.C.

RICHARD M. ZANER

ONLY THE BEST IS GOOD ENOUGH?

Nicholas Rescher's argument is wonderfully direct and important. Moreover, he raises exceedingly grave moral questions, questions which are simply "ungetaroundable", to use C. I. Lewis's plain term for what is insistently present.

Built into "the very structure of scientific inquiry", as Rescher emphasizes, are a number of difficult moral issues ([3], p. 36). Planck's "Principle of Increasing Effort", as Rescher terms it, has a necessary correlate in what I might call *Rescher's Principle of Necessary Escalation*. Most tersely expressed: "Technological progress is an imperative of scientific progress" ([3], p. 37). Scientific progress brings increasingly more difficult problems, requiring more sophisticated and thus more expensive technology. From that follows the further escalation: by a "sure and fairly swift transition" ([3], p. 40), the high-technology of research spills over into a high-technology deployment in therapeutic practice. Thus, scientific progress, and everything tied in with it, is subject to a necessary escalation of technological sophistication and economic expense – both exhibiting geometric curves.

As Rescher insists, too, the inner structure of science has an almost fatefully lock-step movement – "Nature inexorably exacts a *dramatically increasing*" and *expensive* "effort" ([3], p. 36). Yet, as I understand Rescher's argument here, the "spill-over" into therapy *can and possibly must be stemmed*. The breach in this "inexorable" movement is formed, I take it, by the necessary if embarrassing wedge of the moral dimension. The escalation of research technology ineluctably meets up with the impressively "greater intractability of the problems that remain" ([3], p. 37), requiring a geometric increase in the resource-costs of research ([3], p. 37). Along with the inevitable finitude of resources, with equal fatefulness are raised the moral problems of *scarcity*, hence of priorities as to what and whose ends are to be realized. The fact that we may be entering an "era of zero growth" underscores the moral dimension of scientific medical progress all the more. Put all these together with the very real questions raised by John Rawls and MacFarlane Burnett, whom Rescher cites ([3], p. 41), about the decline and possibly even the stoppage in therapeutic benefit from basic research these days, and we have a veritable nest of angry, buzzing moral issues!

47

William B. Bondeson, H. Tristram Engelhardt, Jr., Stuart F. Spicker and Joseph M. White, Jr. (eds.), New Knowledge in the Biomedical Sciences, 47–52.

Rescher's further and rather painful point makes even more evident just how double-edged are our dragon-slaying swords in biomedicine. Our vulnerable and fully admirable tradition has its basic precept: "The patient deserves the best" ([3], p. 42). A powerful point which not only serves the patient, but the medical community's own interests when it serves to justify its research, its technology, and its facilities. But the patient and his immediacy of affliction lie close to hand, mundane perhaps, and all too familiar. The thrust of escalating scientific research lies elsewhere, at the frontiers wherein the exotic and the eerie hold sway. And, Rescher reminds us, the logic at work in scientific research inevitably results in "strength at the outer frontiers" but "a great multitude of weaknesses and problems in the less exotic regions closer to home" ([3], p. 42).

Thus do his three, exceedingly "uncomfortable" clusters of moral questions arise with striking necessity: (1) Given the economics of research, *should there be* a "major redeployment from research to therapy"? (2) *Should* we redeploy resources from those expensive frontiers to a lower technology therapy and "above all" to preventive medicine? (3) *Should* we abandon the prevailing moral precept that only the very best is good enough? And just what can "good enough", i.e., the "optimal", mean for health care in these times of scarcity?

Thus, Rescher's concluding appeal: before we become bewildered by the intricacies and plain intransigence of detailed practice in the context of dizzyingly complex therapeutic technologies; before we become inextricably caught up in the escalational spiral of research to the point of no return; before we become enmeshed in the literal push and shove of political controversy, "calm and informative debate" over the "very difficult and painful choices" is utterly necessary ([3], p. 43).

No one point in particular strikes me as needing more pointed reflection. Working out the theoretical, practical, and even political details of that "simple precept governing American medicine in recent times" — that "the patient deserves the very best" or "Only the very best is good enough" become "highly problematic", as Rescher charges us to recognize. Why is this? He suggests one sort of reason, that the escalation "at the frontiers" of research seems inevitably to weaken the enterprise closer to home ([3], p. 42). "Home", presumably, is clinical practice, or as he says, "lower technology therapy" and involves "above all — preventive medicine" ([3], p. 42).

It is not merely that we are beset by difficult problems and faced with painful choices. It is also our misfortune, or our challenge, to be confronted with a foundational decision demanding our attention now, and which simply brooks neither carelessness nor inattention. *Even to ask whether such a basic precept*, so formative of medical thinking and practice, *might have to be abandoned*: that very question signals the depth of the dilemma — moral and medical — in which we currently find ourselves. Can we really think that *"less* is the very best" might possibly be "optimal"? What is it that Rescher is pointing to?

I want to keep attention riveted on that issue which clearly involves not merely making choices, but also questions the precept at the very foundation of medicine and its rationale, which not only shapes medicine's own most intimate moral attitudes, but also functions as a powerful justification for medical research and technology, within medicine itself and for medicine's public stance and posture (whether in the vaguer sense, or the more specific sense of governmental or other granting agencies). If medicine might no longer be able to say to the supporting public that it truly seeks to deliver only the "very best" to patients, then it also seems clear that medicine would lose its principal justification to that public.

Rescher squarely states that issue and suggests clearly just how it necessarily emerges from within the very structure of science itself, and this is one of the best reasons I find his presentation worthy of our careful attention.

As I see it, to formulate my own concerns here, Rescher's question is not merely an appeal for a "redeployment" of resources from complex and expensive technology intervention to more humdrum and lower-technology therapy. It is rather an appeal for an effort to breach the seemingly closed dynamism between theory/research and clinical/therapeutic practice. There is a continuous and dialectically interlocked circle whereby theory leads into large-scale changes in technical application, the latter becoming a source of theoretical insights not achieved in research by itself, as well as supplying new and more effective tools for laboratory research, which yield new increments of knowledge ([2], pp. 200–207). And, it is precisely that circle which Rescher's argument leads us to contemplate in a new way: just what is "an *optimizing*" rationale in the delivery of health care today? ([3], p. 43).

Hans Jonas contends that for modern science, "Theory itself has become a function of use as much as use a function of theory. Tasks for theory are set by the practical results of its preceding use, their solutions to be turned again to use, and so on. Thus, theory is thoroughly immersed in practice" ([2], p. 209). Practical use is thus no accident to theory, but is integral to it: "Science", Jonas asserts, "is technological by its nature" ([2], p. 198). And just this, I think, is what is suggested by Rescher's "principle of necessary escalation", as I have termed it.

Given these points, what needs to be recognized is that to the very extent that modern medicine has effectively allied itself with the physical and biological sciences, its understanding of what is "the very best" is necessarily derived from that same source. What is "best" for the patient is one or another form of what happens, in Rescher's phrase, "at the frontiers": What is "close to home", thus, is a therapeutic version of what lies in the "exotic" frontiers of research. As the research, i.e., the "genuinely scientific", frontiers become shaped in high-technology ways, so too does the "homefront" of therapy. Thus, when Rescher asks about possible "redeployment of resources", it is no answer to him to say that theory and research obviously spill over into clinical practice (new and complex life-sustaining technologies, computer-assisted diagnostic techniques, large urban medical centers, whole-body x-ray, etc.). It is no answer because to assert that is merely to reassert the principle of necessary escalation, and precisely the workings of that principle are what has led to the "weakening" of the home front, and the raising of doubt about the very meaning of "very best" for patients. "It has become a real question", Rescher reminds us, whether "massive effort and expenditure in research and technologically sophisticated therapy is able to yield a statistically significant result in terms of life-prolongation" ([3], p. 41), or, as might be said, in terms of improved health care or preventive medicine. The "cost-benefit" cycle, "historically ... not an issue" ([3], p. 38) is itself a consequence of the very logic of scientific progress which Rescher and Jonas have delineated, and leads just as inexorably to its own demise, it seems: the "costs" of research and resultant "costs" of therapy no longer yield "benefit" either for research or therapy. That is one reason for the "weakening on the home front". But there is another which might be mentioned.

Such technology harbors enormous power; beyond the more obvious senses of that power is one which may too easily escape our attention. Medical and other forms of modern technology function forcefully in the surrounding social milieu as a source for persons and institutions outside of medicine for powerful models, metaphors, images, by which to understand themselves and one another. In a word, the power of that technology is, in part, defined by its *authority* in the social milieu of its practice: we come to view ourselves and other people in the ways encouraged by medicine. A "complaint", for instance, can with astonishing swiftness come to be understood as an "illness", and then with equal speed as a "disease", which then, clearly and imperatively, is seen to stand in need of medical expertise to "cure" and "heal".

"The patient deserves the very best", and so far as the "best" is itself associated closely with, and even derived from, what Rescher calls "the frontiers", then, what is "close to home" gets viewed, pictured, understood in terms of and as in need of the extraordinarily high-powered technology operative at the frontiers: "science", in a word, is indeed taken as able to "save" us. Yet, by that very fact does the "home front" become "weakened", Rescher says; and this, I take it, means that "the patient", presumably the focus for all this high-powered technology, consequently stands to lose, or in many respects has already lost.

To be afflicted or impaired is to find oneself affected or disturbed in respect of what constitutes one's essential humanity: the ability and the effort it takes to choose one's momentary tasks or a longer-range plan of action; and with this, one's sense of autonomy, of being relatively independent of the services and attentions of other persons, comes to be weakened; and thereby, too, one's own integral sense of oneself, and one's own body, becomes affected and diminished. To find oneself as a medical patient is to find oneself, to one degree or another, in the hands of the anonymous others, unable at times even to feel, to think, to choose or act on one's own: one's dependency heightened and beyond one's immediate scope, one's sense of oneself as a spontaneous agent lessened.

And just here lies the double-edge of the issue; what passes for "the very best" in the phrase, "only the very best is good enough", often is precisely what enhances, complicates, and even adds to the sense of the patient's affliction. The highly technologized and bureaucratized settings of urban health centers (which also serve as models for most other places of medical care these days) may well heighten and complicate the alienation and disorientation already present in the very fact of one's weakened condition.

The sheer presence in a social nexus of acknowledged authority and power, then, invariably impacts that social nexus in clear and significant ways. In clearer terms, the members of the social milieu come to view themselves in ways implicitly and explicitly operative in medicine: ourselves, our bodies, no less than our complaints become "medicalized", and we come to understand "what's 'good' and 'bad' for us" in much the same way as we come to depend on medicine to tell us what is "life" and what is "death".

There are, obviously, numerous further implications of Rescher's questions, but this seems neither the place nor the time to explore them. Permit me only the chance to restate the major point. Rescher's argument shows that the moral questions he delineates (and more besides) are inherent in the very structure and progress of science and medicine. But those moral questions, I have suggested, all rest on a single and extremely difficult, double-edged blade: their clarification, much less their resolution, depend on the clarification of the sense of "very best", and reflection on this suggests that the tough economic issues depend upon the even more intractable moral problems. I am not at all sure whether we should "abandon" the formative precept of medicine; what I am certain of, however, is that the sense of "best" in much of current medicine is but a reassertion of the very condition which on the other hand makes the sense of "best" problematic.

What I would thus urge, fully harmonious, I believe, with Rescher's argument, is that by breaching the dialectical dynamism expressed by his principle of necessary escalation, what is in effect accomplished is the recovery of a very different sense of "very best" — one whose realization in concrete practice may or may not be "expensive" in terms of dollars, but is surely at once much needed, and its clarification requires a basic reassessment of the priorities and values intrinsic to research and practice in medicine. Without that clarification, whose time may well be already past, we might well find ourselves having no "prospect for calm and informative debate" ([3], p. 43), for the fateful necessity of high-powered technology is not only formidable in itself, but has generated equally formidable political and social contexts and core of support, complete with all the tools and images needed to silence many detractors; or failing that, to co-opt their arguments. As John Fowles trenchantly put the point: "the holy of holies in our times is not the temple but the shop", and things human, natural, arcane or artifactual have become "monetized" ([1], pp. 3, 173—175). Not only goods and services, but as is strikingly clear in medicine, even time has its price. Achieving "the very best" in a time shot through with powerful economic metaphors may well be little more than stuff for nostalgia.

Vanderbilt University
Nashville, Tennessee

BIBLIOGRAPHY

1. Fowles, J.: 1964, *The Aristos: A Self-Portrait in Ideas*, Little, Brown and Company, Boston.
2. Jonas, H.: 1966, *The Phenomenon of Life: Toward a Philosophical Biology*, Delta Books, New York.
3. Rescher, N.: 1982, 'Moral Issues Relating to the Economics of New Knowledge in the Biomedical Sciences', in this volume, pp. 35—45.

SECTION III

COSTS, BENEFITS, AND THE RESPONSIBILITIES
OF MEDICAL SCIENCE

TOM L. BEAUCHAMP

MORALITY AND THE SOCIAL CONTROL OF BIOMEDICAL TECHNOLOGY

As biomedical technology has expanded, the quantity of resources has increased, and scarce resources have become scarcer. Expensive equipment, medicine, artificial organs, blood for the treatment of hemophilia, donors for organ transplant operations, and research facilities are all in limited supply. Often when research presents us with a new technology, we find ourselves uncertain whether to fund its application and, if so, how extensively to produce it. One problem is economic: how are these resources to be most efficiently provided? How can more people be helped, and how can costs be reduced? Other problems are ethical: by what principles, procedures, and policies can justice in the production and distribution of resources best be ensured? There is thus both an economic dimension and an ethical dimension to these problems, which I shall refer to, in general, as problems of macroallocation.

There are two dimensions to planning how financial resources shall be exchanged for technological and medical resources. (1) How much in the way of our total available economic resources should be allotted to biomedical research and technology, to routine services, and to clinical practice? (2) Once amounts are allotted to biomedicine, how much should go to which specific projects? For example, how much should go to cancer research and how much to the production of technological equipment used for therapy? These macroallocation decisions have become increasingly important because of heavy federal and foundation involvement in research and treatment programs. Those who formulate such policies are understandably impatient with abstract philosophical arguments showing that some philosopher or philosophical system provides the correct theory of justice but failing to show the concrete commitments of the theory as a public policy instrument. The person who makes decisions about funding technology is confronted with an array of such concrete alternatives, each of which has its own nexus of positive and negative factors, and these alternatives are far from the abstract ones over which philosophers commonly contend.

An evaluative analytical framework for processing economic data, technology assessments, etc., is thus needed. That framework can then function as a public policy instrument so that questions of the control and application

55

William B. Bondeson, H. Tristram Engelhardt, Jr., Stuart F. Spicker and Joseph M. White, Jr. (eds.), New Knowledge in the Biomedical Sciences, 55–76.

of new knowledge can be handled in a principled rather than an arbitrary way. Eventually I argue for one such systematic analytical framework in this essay. I begin, however, with a series of arguments intended to show that some proposed approaches will not suffice as frameworks for resolving the fundamental problems of philosophy and technology that can correctly be classified as problems of public policy.

I

(1) It might be argued that philosophers ought not to engage in the evaluation of technology because such evaluation is a public policy matter best left to experts in policy. The problem with this contention, as a solution to the issues here under consideration, is that "public policy" has no unique method providing a framework for evaluation. This vacuum is illustrated in the case of the public policy device known as "technology assessment". The federal government's Office of Technology Assessment provides no unique *method* for constructing policy beyond an unusually thorough and comprehensive approach to decision-making. The very concept of technology assessment — as outlined by Joseph Coates, a former manager of the technology assessment program at the National Science Foundation — suggests as much:

Technology assessment is a class of policy studies which systematically examines the effects on society that may occur when a technology is introduced, extended, or modified with special emphasis on those consequences that are unintended, indirect, or delayed ([3], pp. 341–343).

Mr Coates further maintains that technology assessments have no distinct methodology and are more akin to art than to science. Those engaged in technology assessments thus may deserve commendation for their unusually thorough and comprehensive studies, but not for some unique methodology they have developed.

This thesis, I would argue, fits the expertise available in *all* federal regulatory agencies. As Dan Fenn has correctly observed about regulatory agencies:

To hear ourselves talk, one would think that there is some pristine and whole object called "good public policy" sitting out there that is constantly being . . . ruined by the attacks of "special interests". Actually, . . . public policy emerges as the end-product of a process in which a variety of interests take their whacks. It is more like a snowman created by a gang of kids building here and altering there until it satisfies . . . ([6], pp. 191–192).

As a description of available procedures for evaluating technological knowledge and its uses, Fenn's description is accurate. Nonetheless, the question remains as to how regulators *ought* to proceed, which is one issue under discussion in this paper. I should like to say at the outset that I am not as pessimistic as Fenn and others that federal regulatory agencies are incapable of rationally and systematically regulating industry, while protecting the public health and welfare. Certainly I do not subscribe to Louis Kohlmeier's view that "the flaws in the regulatory process are fatal and [they are not] trustworthy repositories of the public interest" ([8], p. 183). The primary problem, as I see it, is neither that these agencies are inherently political nor that they have been "captured" by industry. The problem is rather that they need but do not possess a methodology that frees them from capture by either political or industrial interests, while at the same time enabling them to carry out their assigned duties with efficiency. It is this need for a methodology that I shall be discussing.

(2) A second approach to the problem of how to control new technological knowledge is to employ a theory that recognizes *rights* to medical care, including rights to new technological breakthroughs in biomedicine. Despite the acceptance of this approach by a number of contemporary figures in politics, law, biomedical ethics, and federal regulatory agencies, it is unsuited for our purposes. If there were a *legal* right to health care, perhaps such rights claims might be readily endorsed, but since no established legal right exists at the present time — beyond medicare and medicaid — the claim must rest on an appeal to *moral* rights. Yet we do not agree as a society on the existence of any list of moral rights beyond (perhaps) very abstract rights to life, liberty, and personal property. Specific rights, such as the right to equal employment opportunities or to a new application of technology, are never forcefully assertable independent of a social and legal context within which those rights are granted and insured. Any right to new products of technology or even to health care would be a right of this sort.

Moreover, rights are analyzable in terms of negative and positive obligations: characterized respectively, as the obligation to refrain from some action and an obligation to actively provide some good. Positive rights, or the right to be provided with something, are generally more difficult to defend than are negative rights; yet in the arena of biomedical technology and its applications, positive rights are proposed. Even were it demonstrable, then, that we have such rights, the proof would rest on a showing that someone or some institution has an obligation to provide that to which we have such rights. A theory of obligations thus must precede a theory of individual rights. But now we have come full circle, for the question is whether we *should* allocate our resources so that individuals obtain such a right. We need a system of deciding on the acceptability of allocations prior to asserting rights to those specific allocations.

(3) A third approach taken to problems of macroallocation and regulation appeals to principles of distributive justice. It has been notoriously difficult to bring theories of justice to bear with decisiveness on practical problems such as those of public health. A part of the difficulty lies in the use of theories that are uselessly abstract, as I previously mentioned. Consequently philosophers have virtually never attempted to apply theories of justice in very concrete ways. However, in a recent and influential article, Dan E. Beauchamp has outlined a theory of distributive justice that he believes would directly and beneficially affect public health policy and technological advance. This theory and its weaknesses deserve examination. While I shall discuss *only* the weaknesses of this one theory, it is my belief that most available theories of justice either suffer similar deficiencies or fail in similar ways when applied to problems of technology and public policy.

Beauchamp argues as follows: Death and disability are more likely to be dramatically reduced through preventive programs rather than through advances in biomedical technology. We ought therefore to reorient our health allocations by severe cutbacks in technological research and its application. However, broad preventive measures are costly and will place a new burden on the dominant classes in society, who have resisted such allocations and will continue to do so. Their resistance is rooted in what Beauchamp calls the free market conception of justice, which emphasizes individual responsibility and effort — especially responsibility for one's own health. In opposition, Beauchamp argues for a theory of social justice that would restructure society by allocating massive expenditures for public health measures: ([1], pp. 42–48, [2], pp. 4–6).

The preponderance of our public policy for health continues to define health care as a consumption good to be allocated primarily by private decisions and markets, and only interferes . . . to subsidize, supplement or extend the market system when private decisions result in sufficient imperfections or inequities to be of public concern. Medicare and Medicaid are examples . . . .

Market justice is a pervasive ideology protecting the most powerful . . . . [But] public health should advocate a "counter-ethic" for protecting the public's health, one articulated in a different tradition of justice . . . .

Instead of "market justice", which essentially uses no principles for patterns of distribution (as, for example, in Robert Nozick's *Theory of Justice*), Beauchamp substitutes "social justice". "Social" is presumably to be contrasted to "market" because the emphasis is on society's responsibility rather than the individual's. Beauchamp believes the ethic he proposes is preferable, both because market justice does not work to reduce death and disability substantially and because his view would eventuate in "the protection of all human life". This ethic is said by Beauchamp to be "a radical counter-ethic", not because it entails a radical political theory, but rather because it demands a radically new system of allocation for preventive health measures. Beauchamp's program is also explicitly anti-technological, because biomedical technology is from his perspective a poor investment. His reason is that technology produces stop-gap techniques such as life-prolonging equipment, at large expense, but without substantially improving public health. His charge, then, is that the promotion of biomedical technology at the expense of preventive measures is an irresponsible use of public financial resources.

How are we to evaluate this anti-technological program advanced in the name of social justice? There are several reasons for doubting the merit of these proposals. First, Beauchamp complains that market justice is a "pervasive ideology" protecting the powerful. He does little, however, to argue that it is ideological, or to dispel the suspicion that his own position is no less ideological. Presumably, theories of market justice rest on a view of individual responsibility which assumes that autonomous persons are capable of protecting themselves, and therefore do not need the protection of others. Beauchamp's theory, by contrast, assumes that individuals are not responsible for most of these health problems, either because the problems are externally inflicted or are the result of the individuals' own substantially nonvoluntary behaviors. Yet he offers no proof that his own root premises are preferable to the premises of the market conception. This is not to say that ideologies and basic convictions cannot be argued for, but only to say that Beauchamp offers no such arguments. Yet it is all the more important in the present case that he present such an argument because of the now widely held conviction that government assistance *cannot* eradicate such problems.

Second, Beauchamp's theory presumably rests on some principle of distributive justice sufficient to support the resource reallocations he proposes. What at bottom is his principle? It seems to be one of need. Yet how are we to understand the notion of a need? This term is subject to different interpretations, and requires considerable refinement to become serviceable for public policy. Any such theoretical refinement must also explain why need is a more fundamental distributional principle than is, for example, ability to pay. If the principle of need is believed irrelevant for a given context (while contribution and merit, e.g., are argued to be the relevant principles), then one would be opposed in principle to the public policies outlined by Beauchamp. Many policy disputes about technology production and distribution are reducible to a debate over which principle of justice has primacy in a given context.

Third, Beauchamp's program is, by his own admission, based on "collective" action, and the most vital issue with which he is grappling, in my view, is that of how much to allocate to preventive health measures. His "counter-ethic" and apparent use of a principle of need lead him to the view that very substantial allocations for preventive programs would be justified. Thus, he proposes that we allocate funds to eradicate or at least reduce environmental pollution, automobile related injuries and deaths, tobacco use, alcohol use, drug induced deaths and disabilities, the ineffective distribution of medical care, and hazards of the workplace. These sweeping proposals for federal action quickly amount to the unrealistic, when placed in the framework of present financial resources. They would probably entail severe burdens for poor and rich alike, in a society which, I suggest, is not as a *collective* unit willing to bear such costs or anything like them. Beauchamp is certain to respond to this argument that his preventive measures will actually conserve financial resources in the long run by reducing outlays for patient care, but as we shall later see, this consideration is one strictly of costs and benefits and is not a special justice-regarding reason derivable from his theory.

The mistake made by Beauchamp in developing his views is one that many philosophers and their followers have made. Since Plato, it has been believed that general philosophical considerations can determine how to resolve dilemmatic social problems and policies. Yet, as I see the situation, it is impossible to apply abstract principles of justice to minute areas of social policy — such as whether to produce an artificial heart. The point could be put this way: just as policy-makers stand in danger of arbitrary judgments on grounds of their own moral and evaluative preferences, so do those committed in advance to some single inflexible conception of justice and social order (e.g., as in Beauchamp's vision that society should be egalitarian rather than libertarian). Philosophers interested in public policy would do well to start in the midst of policy problems, where financial exigencies and political realities already exist and cannot be swept behind a veil of ignorance. And until some account of justice begins in this climate, what is written about justice will play a negligible role in influencing policy decisions.

II

Two primary questions remain unanswered. First, how in general can resources and technological advances be equitably distributed so that a disproportionate share of resources is not rationed to the politically and economically powerful? Second, how in particular can public policies intended to regulate, fund, and supply biomedical technology be justified? I shall now offer a *utilitarian* ethical justification which, though strictly programmatic, is intended to provide a workable solution to these questions and an alternative program to those previously criticized. The particular utilitarian method I shall support is the device sometimes linked to technology assessment but generally known as cost/benefit analysis.

Among the uses of cost/benefit analysis is its clarification of the overt and covert tradeoffs often made in public policy decisions. These are tradeoffs, for example, between lives that will be lost and money expended on new technology that might save them, between environmental quality and factory productivity, and between the quality of gasoline and the quality of the health of those who produce it. The simple idea behind these often complicated procedures is that the cost/benefit analyst should measure or at least carefully describe costs and benefits by some acceptable device, at the same time identifying uncertainties and possible tradeoffs, in order to present policy makers with specific, relevant information on the basis of which a decision can be reached. Although such analysis usually proceeds by measuring different quantitative units – e.g., number of accidents, statistical deaths, dollars expended, and number of workers fired – cost/benefit analysis by its very methodology attempts in the end to convert and express these seemingly incommensurable units of measurement into a common one, usually monetary. Although this ultimate reduction frequently cannot be achieved, when it can be achieved the method takes on unusual power, because judgments about tradeoffs can be made on the basis of comparable quantities. Consider the case of the technologically feasible Totally Implantable Artificial Heart (TIAH) [4]. Because death for some persons will be a consequence of not producing it, we might attempt to assign a cost figure by a technique that measures our willingness to pay for such a reduction in the probability of death. We could then decrease, though not eliminate, the risk of cardiac death by paying at that level for the technique.

There are several reasons why cost/benefit analysis might be considered an inappropriate and even morally objectionable methodology for the formulation of public policies (though I, of course, do not share this overall view).

First, difficulties lie in the path of making commensurable all units it is desirable to compare. This problem can itself lead to arbitrary decision making, and cost/benefit methods have long proved difficult to implement concretely. Economists have primarily discussed how such analyses can be carried out in theory rather than in practice, and we have often been left without a means for reducing all tradeoff variables into acceptable quantitative units. Moreover, it can be argued that if consumer-relative evaluation methods are used, it is not likely that consumers can discerningly relate what it is worth to them to reduce risks, especially where percentages are small and stretched over large periods of time. And there also are unresolved problems concerning how to compute discount rates, psychological effects, and indirect effects of certain social interventions.

Nonetheless, despite these deficiencies and others still to be mentioned (cf. Section III), and despite the embryonic status of cost/benefit analysis — a method I acknowledge to be underdeveloped and imperfect — I believe that the cost/benefit approach holds out greater promise as a methodology for public policy control of biomedical technology than any alternative now on the horizon. Accordingly, I think we should devise the most comprehensive, discerning and impartial cost/benefit analyses possible, accepting the dictates of these analyses almost come what may. This proposal would be regarded in many circles as a radical one, and some specific examples of cost/benefit analyses should now be mentioned in order to make clearer how the methodology works and could be utilized for policy purposes. Here are two brief biomedically-related examples.

First, there is the study by Klarman of the benefits of eradicating syphilis in the United States [7]. Benefits in this case are the averted costs of, for example, medical care expenditures, economic deprivation from loss of employment, and pain and disablement during and after the disease. In this study the costs incurred in 1962 were measured at $117.5 million. The value of the disease's total eradication would be equivalent to this annual sum projected in perpetuity. By employing discount rates, Klarman argued that the present capital value of this eradication would be several billion dollars. Having arrived at these benefits (based on cost eradication), costs of necessary treatment programs could then be figured for purposes of comparison. Different but parallel studies could also be provided — e.g., cost/benefit calculations based on a control program that achieved a reduction in the *incidence* of the disease but did not eradicate it. Because of the possibility of the emergence of highly resistant strains, the latter kind of cost/benefit analysis would be the most useful, though Klarman unfortunately did not provide it.

Consider as a second example the issue of proposed standards for occupational exposure to the carcinogen benzene — a case under study by OSHA because of reports of excessive leukemia deaths related to benzene in industrial manufacturing plants. In his testimony in this case Richard Wilson argues both that "an average level of benzene in the workplace of 10 parts per million is much more acceptable than many other actions" and that the social benefits of the manufacture of benzene at these levels outweigh the risks associated with such production [13]. Wilson recognizes that benzene is a carcinogen and that we must be cautious about the level allowed. His point is that we *will have to settle* for a conservative estimate of the risks, as determined largely by dose levels based on animal studies. If he is correct, we have no rational choice but to accept a dose level in the vicinity of that point at which it cannot scientifically be demonstrated that benzene in such doses produces cancer, even though it demonstrably is a carcinogen. The entire hazard cannot be banned because too many significant benefits (not directly related to health) would be lost. Gasoline, for example, would have to be banned. Moreover, compliance costs at levels less than 10 ppm would be in the hundreds of millions of dollars — thus rendering manufacture nonprofitable, and without any evidence that workers would be more protected.

Although in this case risks beyond the testable level are not known, Wilson's reasoning is not remote from decision analysis that is required elsewhere, for example, in the case of the implantable heart. In both cases we must ask how much society should pay to reduce these risks, which are continually reducible to lower levels at increasingly greater financial costs. Yet in both cases the risk of death itself can never be eliminated. What we want, I suggest, is an acceptable level of risk, where acceptability is determined by what must elsewhere be given up in the way of harms and benefits in order to achieve the appropriate level. It is the *level of acceptability* that cost/ benefit analyses can provide, or at least can help us approximate. This claim should not be construed to mean that all costs and benefits can be fully quantified and all uncertainties about risk eliminated. Rather, it means that principles and standards operative in risk/benefit decisions can often be stated in considerable detail so that *unclarity in the judgmental process is reduced*. It is this reduction of intuitive weighing in the formulation of policy that I find of greatest significance in the cost/benefit approach — especially for the expensive and critical business of controlling biomedical technology.

III

An impressive set of philosophical objections to utilitarian and cost/benefit reasoning have been developed by Alasdair MacIntyre. In his essay "Utilitarianism and Cost-Benefit Analysis", [9] MacIntyre offers five criticisms, all of which he also believes to be objections equally applicable to utilitarianism and its stepchild, cost/benefit analysis. In brief, MacIntyre's five criticisms are as follows:

First, he argues that decision makers are always confronted with a large range of possible alternative courses of action (assuming that *all* the possible long-term and short-term consequences are considered). This range is so extensive that one could never seriously consider all the possible options. Some "principles of restriction" therefore must be employed to limit the number of open options to those one actually could and should consider. Such principles cannot be utilitarian, according to MacIntyre, because "we should have to find some principle of restriction in order to avoid paralysis by the construction of an indefinitely long list of principles of restriction. And so on" ([9], p. 221). In the case of practical decisions about technology in government and business, it will not do, by MacIntyre's lights, to argue that the alternatives are inherently restricted by a context — for example, by arguing that profitability limits goals and options in a business context. The goals in a context are themselves selected by some evaluative choice; and, moreover, MacIntyre argues, markets and goals of government are created by wants and needs, and thus some evaluative choices must be made that are not purely cost/benefit in character.

MacIntyre's second objection springs from the notorious problem for utilitarians of measuring, comparing, and weighing the merit of alternative courses of action. He argues that there is no scale on which alternatives can be weighed: "If this is true of pleasures, how much more complex must matters become when we seek to weigh against each other such goods as those of restoring health to the sick, of scientific enquiry or of friendship" ([9], p. 222). MacIntyre's favored example is drawn from problems of macroallocation: how is the politician to weigh and balance the different goals of constructing a school, a new clinic, a new technology, or a new power supply source, especially when they must be weighed against the loss of a beautiful landscape? He contends that totally different and "incommensurable" items would have to be weighed. Moreover, "such a rank ordering will. . . have to be nonutilitarian. For like the principle which specified the range of alternatives to be considered it has to be adopted before any utilitarian test can be applied" ([9], p. 222).

MacIntyre is particularly concerned about the problem of calculating costs where the costs involve a shortening of human life. In some of these cases policies raise or lower the level of statistical deaths. For example, by allowing a level of carcinogens into the atmosphere, we know statistically that some lives will be affected; or, to use MacIntyre's own long-range example, by allowing the Concorde to land in the United States, the likelihood is increased that there will be an increase in skin cancer. Weighing the former convenience against the likelihood of the latter untoward event is not one that can be done in cost/benefit terms, in his judgment, because a principle of choice will be arbitrarily chosen; i.e., it will prove arbitrary how "to adopt one principle for quantifying rather than another" ([9], p. 227).

MacIntyre's third objection challenges how it is to be determined whose values and preferences are to count in the weighing and assessment of harms and benefits. The old and the young have different values and weigh priorities differently, and some persons place the absence of suffering over the promotion of happiness, while others do not – to mention only two examples. MacIntyre argues that this plurality of valuation requires that a decision be made regarding whose values shall be preeminent. Moreover, he contends, we often cannot target particular individuals who will benefit – e.g., we cannot when we have future generations or the whole class of young children in mind. Who is to decide, when chances are distributed over an entire population, who will receive a chance of harm and who a benefit? He argues that cost/benefit procedures will not prove helpful, because the choice and labelling of something as a cost (say, environmental pollution) or as a benefit (say, electric power) will itself depend upon a prior evaluative viewpoint. Therefore, as is typical of MacIntyre, he concludes that evaluation *precedes* and itself critically influences cost/benefit assessments.

MacIntyre's fourth objection probes what is to count as a predicted consequence of an action. In particular, he believes it difficult and probably impossible on utilitarian grounds to specify how much care and precision must be taken in predicting and taking account of the consequences of actions. An example in regulation and corporate decision-making is offered for our consideration. In the television industry the consequences of a business action terminate, by virtue of the social and legal context and rules of business practice, at the point where the customer has been successfully supplied. More remote consequences, such as television's trivializing a culture, are conventionally thought to be beyond the ethical scope of both a business's responsibility and government agencies. It would be utterly unrealistic to expect the electric power industry to take into account such consequences in setting its policies, in MacIntyre's view. Yet these consequences are consequences of the industry's actions, and utilitarianism seems to demand that we take account of them. Thus, in MacIntyre's view only a nonutilitarian reason can determine a reasonable cutoff point at which further consequences need not be considered, for utilitarianism cannot in principle reach such determinations.

Fifthly, MacIntyre further explores the consequence-regarding character of utilitarianism. "Time-frame" problems, he argues, will inevitably appear. For example, how much should be sacrificed in the present to benefit children in the future or even remote future generations? MacIntyre contends that this question cannot be answered in utilitarian or cost/benefit terms. His reason is that predictability over time — given social change, inflation, conceptual shifts, and unknowable historical developments — cannot be accurate. And if we *allow for* unpredictability in our ethics, says MacIntyre, we incorporate nonutilitarian principles that are independent of cost/benefit procedures — especially those that specify the length of time within which costs and benefits are to be calculated.

The five objections we have just surveyed seem to me reducible to three general problems in the application of utilitarian reasoning and cost/benefit analysis: (1) problems in the *measurement* and comparison of different cost/benefit units, (2) problems both in predicting and in limiting the scope of the consequences of an action, and (3) problems in the attempt to specify whose values, preferences, and assessments are to be counted in cases of conflict. These problems certainly are practical difficulties inhibiting the *application* of utilitarian and cost/benefit reasoning, but I do not believe they present insurmountable *theoretical* problems. I shall now argue that these theoretical problems and many of the practical problems mentioned by MacIntyre can be overcome.

IV

MacIntyre's arguments seem to be deficient in at least three respects. First, he construes utilitarianism to demand perfect predictability, something that no moral theory could possibly provide. Utilitarianism is of course a *consequentialist* theory, but one need not be able to foresee all future consequences over a time-frame that includes the contingent conceptual and historical shifts to which he alludes. It is possible to adopt a criterion of *reasonable* predictability that is serviceable for cost/benefit analysis and other utilitarian purposes, without demanding perfect predictability.

It is easy to overestimate the demands of the utilitarian moral theory. While we should attempt to make accurate measurements of the preferences of others, this seldom can be accomplished because of limited knowledge and time. Often in everyday affairs we must act on severely limited knowledge of the consequences of our action. The utilitarian does not condemn any sincere attempt to maximize value, merely because the actual consequences turn out to be less than maximal. What is important, morally speaking, is that one conscientiously attempts to determine the most profitable action, and then with equal deliberateness attempts to perform it. Since common sense and ordinary deliberation about desires and consequences will generally suffice for these calculations, utilitarians cannot fairly be accused of presenting overly-demanding moral requirements. MacIntyre's problems about how to restrict the range of alternatives to be considered, as well as his difficulties over specifying relevant consequences of actions (see objections 1, 4 and 5) are less troublesome than he would admit. Of course he is correct in insisting that some "arbitrariness" in selecting variables and principles is bound to taint human calculations ([9], p. 227). This problem is no more crippling for utilitarianism than for other moral theories that attempt answers to the problems of social control that are under consideration in this paper.

Second, MacIntyre specifies no alternative approach that leaves us with a workable methodology for public-policy purposes. The most powerful reason favoring the adoption of cost/benefit analyses is its instrumental value for deciding which alternative to pursue in nonobvious, indeed dilemmatic cases. That it provides the most reliable method and perhaps the only method for reaching this goal is a powerful justification in itself, even if the method does occasionally eventuate in minor injustices or other than perfectly just outcomes.

Third, MacIntyre fails to consider seriously two theses that are basic to recent utilitarian thinking. These theses center on the concept of utility itself and on the difference between act and rule utilitarianism. I want now to show how these two theses can be used to provide responses to MacIntyre.

(A) *The Concept of Utility*

Several of MacIntyre's objections allege that a value scheme is presupposed by utilitarians and that whose values and assessments are to count is left uncertain (see objections 1–3). MacIntyre is especially tough on the now largely abandoned theories of classical utilitarians, who accepted a hedonistic position. These alleged problems can be significantly diminished, I believe, by an analysis of the nature of utility, including a specification of whose utility is to count. In recent philosophy, the language of individual *preferences* has been employed to explicate the concept of utility: "utility" for an individual refers not to experiences or states of affairs, but rather to an individual's actual preferences, as determined by his behavior. To maximize his utility is to provide what he has chosen or would choose from among the available alternatives. To maximize the utility of all persons affected by an action or policy is to maximize the utility of the aggregate group. What is intrinsically valuable, then, is what individuals prefer to obtain; and utility is translated into the satisfaction of those needs and desires that individuals choose to satisfy. MacIntyre is thus right when he says an evaluative scheme is presupposed, but this is hardly an argument *against* utilitarians.

This modern approach to value is preferable to those of its predecessors, criticized by MacIntyre, for two main reasons. First, recent disputes about hedonism and pluralism have proved interminable, sometimes ideological, and in the view of many, irresolvable. One's choice of a range of these values seems deeply affected by personal experiences − a problem the use of preference seems to avoid. Second, to make utilitarian calculations it is necessary in some way to measure values. In the hedonistic theory espoused by Bentham and Mill, for example, it is hard to know what it would mean to measure and then compare the value of pleasure or health or knowledge as human states. It does make sense, however, to measure preferences by devising a utility scale that measures strengths of individual and group preferences numerically; and this approach has proved fruitful in recent discussions of health economics and the assessment of technology.

The preference approach nonetheless is not trouble free. A major theoretical problem for utilitarianism arises when individuals have what, according to ordinary views about morality, are immoral or at least morally unacceptable preferences. For example, if a skillful researcher derived supreme satisfaction from inflicting pain on animals or human subjects in experiments, we would discount this person's preference and would prevent it from being actualized. Utilitarianism based on subjective preferences is satisfactory only if a range of acceptable values can be formulated. This task has proved difficult and may even be inconsistent with some preference-based approaches. However, since most people are not deviant in the manner envisioned and do have morally acceptable (even if we may think odd) values, I shall proceed under the assumption that the utilitarian approach makes sense and is not wildly implausible if a theory of appropriate (nonmoral) values is provided to buttress its moral perspective. (A philosophical justification of this assumption is clearly part of a much larger defense of utilitarianism as a general moral theory – a view I am not here supporting.)

If utilitarianism could be successfully explicated along the lines just envisioned, a definite procedure for making ethical choices would be provided. We would first calculate to the best of our knowledge the consequences that would result from our performance of the available options. In making this calculation, we would ask how much value and how much disvalue – as gauged by the preferences of those affected by our actions – would result in the lives of all affected, including ourselves. When we have completed all these calculations for all relevant courses of action, we are morally obliged to choose that course of action that maximizes value (or minimizes intrinsic disvalue). Moreover, and contrary to MacIntyre's objections (2–3), any acceptable decision procedure developed along these lines would include techniques for determining whose values and preferences are to be considered, how these preferences are to be ordered, and how we are to ascertain initially that something is a cost or a benefit. I would admit that such information is often difficult to obtain and that it may not always be the only or even the most relevant information for policy purposes. (Think, for example, of the range of costs and benefits that must be considered in MacIntyre's Concorde example.) However, such information is on all occasions *a* relevant one even if not the *overriding* consideration. At present this often is all that we can expect from actual cost/benefit analyses, even though we may hope in the future for more decisive conclusions.

(B) *The Distinction Between Act and Rule Utilitarianism*

While the above reply to MacIntyre does not resolve all the problems that he mentions (in objections 1–3), a second distinction will both eliminate remaining theoretical problems and also will help us treat MacIntyre's other objections, which rest on the argument that we cannot determine "what is to count as a consequence of a given action" and that such consequences as "the trivialization of a culture by the major television works", though ethically significant, generally must go ignored or be discounted because only the wants of consumers are to be considered (see objections 4–5) ([9], pp. 223, 23). This criticism ignores a distinction that MacIntyre himself acknowledges during the course of his essay – viz. that between act and rule utilitarians. This distinction has emerged through controversy over whether the principle of utility is to be applied to particular *acts* in particular circumstances in order to determine which act is right or instead is to be applied to *rules* of conduct, which themselves determine which acts are right and wrong.

The act utilitarian considers the consequences of each particular act, while the rule utilitarian considers the consequences of generally observing a rule. Accordingly, the act utilitarian asks, "What good and evil consequences will result from this action in this circumstance?" and not "What good and evil consequences will result from this sort of action in general in these sorts of circumstances?" Thus, according to rule utilitarians, rules themselves have a central position in morality and cannot be disregarded because of the exigencies of particular situations. Because of the substantial contributions made to society by the general observance of rules of truth-telling, for example, the rule utilitarian would not compromise them for a particular situation. Such compromise would threaten the stability of the rule itself, and a rule is selected in the first instance because its general observance would maximize social utility better than would any alternative rule (or a situation without rules). For the rule utilitarian, then, the conformity of an act to a valuable rule makes the action right, whereas for the act utilitarian the beneficial consequences of the act alone make it right or wrong.

This distinction is of vital importance for cost/benefit assessments. Utilitarian rules function to provide what in the cost/benefit literature are often called "constraints" on the use of *single* cost/benefit studies for single occasions. For example, in this literature it is said that there are physical and legal, as well as social, institutional, and environmental constraints on the immediate use of single cost/benefit analyses [5]. A rule utilitarian would say that there are *moral* constraints as well, as determined by relevant moral rules. MacIntyre ignores this built-in utilitarian constraint on cost/benefit analysis in arguing that utilitarians cannot decide which effects are to count as consequences and that utilitarian decisions are "not evaluatively neutral" ([9], p. 323, 73). It is certainly true that these choices are not evaluatively neutral, and no utilitarian would deny it. Values enter either at the level of subjective preference, or as MacIntyre correctly says (but without damaging utilitarianism), at the level of established preferences and agreements in a culture. Consequences are projected on this basis. But if a particular cost/benefit study would lead to actions that abridge a rule-governed constraint, we would not accept the study as determinative. In short, there is no morally satisfactory way to isolate cost/benefit analyses from the restraining control of moral rules, and that fact must straightforwardly be recognized. However, as this position is precisely the one espoused by rule utilitarians, MacIntyre's arguments fail against the most prevalent species of utilitarianism, which is the rule variety.

V

Opponents of cost/benefit analysis, including MacIntyre I should think, might reply to my contentions as follows: At least some cost/benefit analyses will reveal that a particular health measure or new technology will prove highly beneficial as compared to its costs, and yet provision of this benefit might function prejudicially in a free-market economy by denying more basic medical services to the most disadvantaged members of society. But, as a matter of justice, the disadvantaged ought to be subsidized, either in terms of health services or financial awards — no matter what cost/benefit analyses reveal. Robert Veatch, for example, has stated his conviction that planning efforts employing cost/benefit analysis "are mistaken", because they are utilitarian and thus "cannot account for our sense of justice" [12]. He in effect proposes an analytical framework that reverses the priorities of the one I have proposed. For him utilitarian reasons of efficiency may be called upon to restrict justice-regarding considerations only on rare occasions, whereas I hold that nonutilitarian justice-regarding considerations will not prove *sufficient* to require that we modify utilitarian conclusions (subject to one qualification I make in the final section below).

There is some point to this line of objection, though in the end I believe it does not succeed. For the reasons advanced in the previous section, it would not always be permissible to follow the dictates of *single, short range* cost/benefit calculations. For example, suppose that crop dusting were done with a new and technologically marvelous pesticide that significantly increased the profits of an agribusiness over the profits that would be realized by use of a less toxic and less effective pesticide. But suppose the far more profitable pesticide kills, on the average, 2 of every 295 farm workers exposed to the spraying for more than a year. It would be immoral to use the pesticide, even if statistical calculations indicated a highly favorable overall cost/benefit equation. There is a lower limit of risk of harm that can be permitted by the utilization of immediate cost/benefit calculations, and we cannot pass below this limit without abusing justice. This I do not deny.

One the other hand, these examples — which represent a common variety of counterexamples thrown up against utilitarians — are not compelling, for several reasons. First, *all* of the entailed costs and benefits must be considered. These would include difficulties in hiring new workers, losses in insurance schemes and strikes, impairment to social ideals, effects on the family, etc. Second, as I argued in the previous section, sophisticated utilitarian analyses never suggest that single cost/benefit determinations be accepted, because such utilitarians propose that general rules of justice ought to constrain particular actions or uses of cost/benefit analysis in all cases. Moreover — and here emerges the apparent difference between my views and those of Veatch, MacIntyre, and others — I think choices between justice-regarding reasons and utilitarian cost/benefit reasons will not be forced upon us. Utility in the form of cost/benefit analysis itself provides an *appropriate* (material) *principle of distributive justice*, though utilitarian rules of justice constrain single, cost/benefit outcomes. Therefore, utilitarian considerations of justice (i.e., rules of justice grounded in utility) will suffice if individual cost/benefit conclusions are shown "unjust".

VI

In conclusion, it is worth mentioning that my defense of a utilitarian material principle of distributive justice is intended neither as a defense of utilitarianism as a general philosophy nor as a defense of a utilitarian theory of justice. My argument stands or falls independently of arguments for and against more general utilitarian theories. This claim can be supported by reference to John Rawls's nonutilitarian account of justice, for his views are in no respect inconsistent with my utilitarian argument. Simply stated, my theory makes a claim only about the use in a special social context (the control of biomedical technology) of a material principle of justice, whereas Rawls's theory has no bearing on special social contexts, and he does not propose specific material principles. I shall devote this section to a demonstration of this claim.

Whereas most writers on distributive justice have developed a theory based on allocative principles ("to each according to _____"), the allocative conception of justice is emphatically not Rawls's enterprise ([10], pp. 7, 88; 303–9). Instead, he is interested in social justice as embedded in what he calls the basic structure of society. He writes as follows in *A Theory of Justice*:

For us the primary subject of justice is the basic structure of society, or more exactly, the way in which the major social institutions distribute fundamental rights and duties and determine the division of advantages from social cooperation. By major institutions I understand the political constitution and the principal economic and social arrangements. Thus the legal protection of freedom of thought and liberty of conscience, competitive markets, private property in the means of production, and the monogamous family are examples of major social institutions ([10], p. 7).

In his later article, "The Basic Structure as Subject", Rawls attempts to explicate more carefully what he means by the "basic structure". There he argues that the basic structure is the "all-inclusive social system that determines background justice" [11]. He provides several abstract but nonetheless helpful characterizations of the ingredients of the basic structure as an inclusive system. It includes the set of rules governing legal institutions such as the Supreme Court, the set of rules establishing permissible marital and familial relationships (e.g., rules requiring monogamous families), rules establishing permissible property relationships, and rules establishing permissible social and economic inequalities ([10], pp. 2–5, 61, 84). Rawls sees the structural components comprising the all-inclusive system as critical because of their pervasive influence over what he refers to as natural, social, and historical contingencies. His contention is that abilities, talents, expectations, beliefs, opportunities, etc., are all heavily influenced by the form a given society takes. To the extent that background conditions in society are themselves unjust, individuals will be adversely affected both presently and in the future. In Rawls's view it will do little good to tinker with distributional outcomes through material principles such as need, merit, effort, and utility assessments if the background conditions creating the problem are unjust. No amount of adjustment through such allocative principles will, in his view, eliminate the problem if it resides deep in the basic structure.

Rawls's favored example is that of voluntary market transactions. Imagine that the structure of the system of markets is not fair because only those born wealthy are able to engage in investments, while investments alone permit a high standard of living and those not born into wealth are systematically excluded from possibilities of investment. This situation of advantage and disadvantage could be adjusted by redistributing wealth in accordance with a principle of need or in accordance with utility. Wealth could theoretically even be distributed so as to equalize individual income. Yet the social system would remain unjust because the background conditions generating the problem have not been adjusted. To the extent that these background conditions are themselves the cause of unjust incomes requiring compensating actions, they are unjust – no matter which compensating measures are introduced.

It is exclusively these background conditions that concern Rawls in his work. However, he also believes that almost all general theories of justice rely on what he refers to as secondary principles, or mere precepts, of justice ([10], p. 47). The utilitarian material principle I have proposed would be an example, *if it were turned into* a general theory of justice. Because of the focus in these theories on allocative principles, Rawls believes these conceptions of justice tend to overlook the basic structure. His own strategy in dealing with the problem of the proper place of such principles devolves from Mill's perceptive treatment of the subject in *Utilitarianism* (Chapter V). Mill argued that common sense precepts or principles such as "to each according to effort" or "to each according to need" lead to conflicts of principles and to contrary moral injunctions. The principles themselves also assign no relative weight to their own demand when they conflict with other principles. Consequently, they are useless when a judgment of relative merit or over-ridingness must be made. These precepts thus fall short of providing a general theory of justice, for at least one higher principle is needed to arbitrate their conflicts.

Mill of course proposed the principle of utility as the higher unifying principle. Rawls's theory suggests two nonutilitarian principles instead. I have suggested neither alternative in this paper, which explains why my utilitarian views on allocative justice are compatible with both utilitarian and nonutilitarian *theories* of justice. Rawls again handles the issue of the role specific allocative principles are to play in his system through the example of a competitive market economy operating within the framework of a just basic structure. He argues that in this setting it is easy to see

how the various precepts of justice arise. They simply identify features of jobs that are significant on either the demand or the supply side of the market, or both. A firm's demand for workers is determined by the. . . net value of the contribution of a unit of labor. . . . Experience and training, natural ability and special know-how, tend to earn a premium. Firms are willing to pay more to those with these characteristics because their productivity is greater. This fact explains and gives weight to the precept to each according to his contribution. . . . Similarly jobs which involve uncertain or unstable employment, or which are performed under hazardous and unpleasantly strenuous conditions, tend to receive more pay. . . . From this circumstance arise such precepts as to each according to his effect, or the risks he bears, and so on. . . . Given the aims of productive units and of those seeking work, certain characteristics are singled out as relevant ([10], p. 305f).

Rawls thus regards common sense precepts as the natural outgrowths of pervasive social contexts. No general theory of justice can be built on such thin foundations, in his view, because problems both of conflict among principles and of indeterminate relative weight are bound to recur if a basic structure is actually governed by multiple principles of heterogeneous and uncoordinated origin. Whether the utilitarian principle I have proposed can actually be *coordinated* with others in a larger system remains to be demonstrated, but the possibility of such an integrated system of principles is far from having been disproven. My purpose in this section, however, has merely been to suggest that the utilitarian arguments found in this paper are, in principle, compatible with Rawls's and perhaps with most general theories of justice that are nonutilitarian.

VII

My argument in this paper has been that less objective methods of appraising the acceptability of allocations and technological growth than those of cost/benefit analysis are subject to the indecisiveness and personal preferences of those responsible for the formulation of public policy. I have argued that the many untidy problems of limited resources and technological expansion should be managed by designing the most comprehensive, discerning, and impartial cost/benefit analyses possible, accepting the dictates of these analyses almost come what may. This utilitarian hypothesis seems to me unrefuted by contemporary philosophy and is of great significance for federal and state policy.

Georgetown University
Washington, D.C.

BIBLIOGRAPHY

1. Beauchamp, D. E.: 1976, 'Alcoholism as Blaming the Alcoholic', *International Journal of Addictions* 11, 41–52.
2. Beauchamp, D. E.: 1976, 'Public Health as Social Justice', *Inquiry* 19, 3–14.
3. Coates, J.: 1974, 'Some Methods and Techniques for Comprehensive Impact Assessments', *Technological Forecasting and Social Change* 6, 341–357.
4. DHEW: 1973, *The Totally Implantable Heart: A Report of the National Heart and Lung Institute*, DHEW Publication No. (NIH) 74–91.
5. Eckstein, O.: 1961, 'A Survey of the Theory of Public Expenditures Criteria', *Public Finances*, Princeton University Press, Princeton, New Jersey.
6. Fenn, S.: 1974, 'Dilemmas for the Regulator', in P. Sethi (ed.), *The Unstable Ground: Corporate Social Policy in a Dynamic Society*, Melville, Los Angeles, pp. 191–203.
7. Klarman, H. E.: 1965, 'Syphilis Control Programs', in R. Dorfman (ed.), *Measuring Benefits of Governmental Investments*, Brookings Institution, Washington, D.C., pp. 367–410.
8. Kohlmeier, L.: 1974, 'Effective Regulation in the Public Interest', in P. Sethi

(ed.), *The Unstable Ground: Corporate Social Policy in a Dynamic Society*, Melville, Los Angeles, pp. 181–190.

9.   MacIntyre, A.: 1977, 'Utilitarianism and Cost-Benefit Analysis: An Essay on the Relevance of Moral Philosophy to Bureaucratic Theory', in K. Sayre (ed.), *Values in the Electric Power Industry*, University of Notre Dame Press, South Bend, Ind., pp. 217–237.

10. Rawls, J.: 1971, *A Theory of Justice*, Harvard University Press, Cambridge, Mass.

11. Rawls, J.: 1977, 'The Basic Structure as Subject', *American Philosophical Quarterly* 14, 159–165.

12. Veatch, R. M.: 1976, 'What is a "Just" Health Care Delivery', in R. M. Veatch and R. Branson (eds.), *Ethics and Health Policy*, Ballinger, Cambridge, pp. 127–153.

13. Wilson, R. (testimony): in re *Proposed Standards for Occupational Exposure to Benzene*, OSHA Docket No. #-059.

BERNARD TOWERS

RIGHTS AND RESPONSIBILITIES IN MEDICAL SCIENCE

It seems to me that there might be something worthwhile to be gained if I, a medical scientist, clinician, and teacher, try to engage in dialogue with modern Luddites who, despite, or perhaps because of their ignorance of the *practicum* of clinical medicine, seem intent on destroying not only the evident advantages that modern medical technology has provided for the common weal, but also on inhibiting the potential for future advantages that will accrue to mankind if technological and scientific enquiry does not become totally enwrapped in a jungle of bureaucratic and moralistic red tape. The thicket of do's and don't's elaborated by self-appointed bioethicists and politically-appointed legislators threatens to strangle us. Franz Ingelfinger sounded a note of concern in 1975, with his paper on "The Unethical in Medical Ethics", [2], and, to quote Tom Beauchamp, "Philosophers interested in public policy would do well to start in the midst of policy problems" ([1], p. 60). I will paraphrase that, and say, "philosophers, lawyers and legislators interested in medical problems and the application of medical research, would do well to start in the midst of clinical problems by participating in the activities of emergency rooms and intensive care units." Ever since Plato, philosophers have been reluctant to get their hands dirty for fear of polluting their minds. The ivory tower is a perfectly valid option, but it obliges one to refrain from advising on the conduct of practical affairs. This has been recognized throughout the centuries. But today, in the area of biomedical ethics and the morality of control and regulation of biomedical research, some speculators are assuming rights of control without the formal responsibility for the practical results of their speculations.

I titled my paper "Rights and Responsibilities in Medical Science". I am well aware that rights and responsibilities do not always go hand-in-glove in the society. There are many members of the community who have rights (the most pressing, urgent, and often least-acknowledged rights, entailing little responsibility), such as infants, fetuses (at least in relatively late stages of intrauterine development), and the handicapped. Those who are handicapped, whether physically, socially, mentally, emotionally, economically, or racially, have a special claim to "rights without too much responsibility", which the well-endowed ignore at the peril of the future of the society.

77

William B. Bondeson, H. Tristram Engelhardt, Jr., Stuart F. Spicker and Joseph M. White, Jr. (eds.), New Knowledge in the Biomedical Sciences, 77–85.
Copyright © 1982 by D. Reidel Publishing Company.

It would be hard to argue that members of the medical profession, or practitioners of Medical Science are, in general, handicapped in any of these senses except perhaps, ironically enough, insofar as their own health is concerned. There have been many studies which indicate that, age for age (especially in middle years) and profession for profession, we in medicine suffer more ill-health than do other groups. We are more prone to physical illness, to mental breakdown, marital breakdown, alcoholism, drug addiction, and other handicapping disorders, than are most of our contemporaries. It is hard to judge the extent to which such problems are endogenous to the group that has elected of its own accord to work in the "healing profession", and to what extent they are caused, exogenously, by the very nature of the work we do, the risks that we take and the pressures to which we are sub-jected. Medicine is a high-risk profession, to a degree that goes entirely unrecognized.

But I am going to suggest that whatever right may be enjoyed by, or should be accorded to, practitioners of medical science, they are rights that are acquired precisely by the recognition and the exercise of the responsi-bilities incurred by virtue of membership in what was once, and might be yet again when current storms have abated, regarded as one of the learned profes-sions. It is these rights that are currently being trampled on by a throng of philosophical and religious moralists, disputative lawyers, and ignorant lay people, politicians, and legislators.

The responsibilities of any member of the medical profession, by the exercise of which he/she acquires kinds of rights, are many and varied. In addition to our ordinary personal responsibilities to self and family, to colleagues and employees at the office and in the department, school, or university in which we may operate, we in medical science develop special professional responsibilities which often override those common ones just mentioned. These include: responsibilities to individual patients, first and foremost (at least in the traditional view); responsibilities to the 'patient community' both present and future to attend to and act in the behalf of the present and anticipated health needs responsibilities to personkind to pursue at times, with utmost vigor, a concept or scientific hypothesis we think beneficial to members of our present or future generations; and respon-sibilities, moreover, towards human evolution as currently expressed in the neverending quest of modern man to explore, to discover, to turn in on and try to understand the processes that occur in nature and the process of evolution itself [4, 5, 6].

If practitioners of medical science had met their responsibilities, then we might have avoided the crisis of confidence that is currently upon us. It would be foolish not to recognize that there *is* a major crisis of confidence between the general public and its elected representatives on the one hand, and the health-industry on the other. Opinion polls which ask respondents to rate the degree of trust or confidence they have in various professional groups have shown a steady erosion of confidence in the medical profession in recent years. Interestingly enough, as a Rand Corporation Study demonstrates, the confidence that individual patients have in the satisfaction they feel about their personal medical care remains very high. That may be simply the result of relief from the sense of personal vulnerability and dependency that one experiences when one is ill; sickness is a frightening and debilitating affair, during which it is natural that one should experience psychological regression. This is the basis for the "parentalist role" that physicians have traditionally played — and that they have been encouraged to play by many of their patients. One of the powerful social forces currently in motion is the rejection by many people of all authority-figures or parental-models in favor of self-sufficiency, self-respect, autonomy, and independence. That is all to the good. It works very well until, unexpectedly, one is felled by a bacterium, or an atherosclerotic plaque on a coronary artery, or by a neoplasm, or by a demyelinating disease of the central nervous system. Then, some degree of psychological regression is almost inevitable, and with that a feeling of gratitude towards the helping physician. Though some of us in medicine today encourage mutual openness and frankness, mutual responsibility for therapeutic management, and development of a genuine peer-relationship between patient and physician, it would be foolish not to recognize that the situation is bound to be unequal from the start, in that the one is sick and in need of therapeutic help and the other is, at least presumptively, well and able to give that help.

Although the individual patient is reasonably content with the care received, the opinion-polls show increasing discontent with the profession generally. It is as though patients think that, though their own doctors take their responsibilities seriously and exercise skill and compassion in their practices, they nevertheless suppose that they themselves just happen to have been fortunate, and that the "general" public is being badly treated, at enormous cost, by a greedy and arrogant profession. That is what they are told in newspapers and on TV, and have come to believe.

To this point, nothing peculiar to the current phase of the explosion of new knowledge has been said. Similar views about individual physicians and the profession generally have been expressed throughout the ages: by Chaucer,

by John Owen in the 16th century, by Molière, and George Bernard Shaw.
We all have a love-hate relation with our doctors, as we do with our parents.
Sometimes, as with Shaw, the hatred can be very persistent. Shaw was a
robust and healthy man, who had little need for medical care.

The sense of vulnerability induced by sickness often leads one to expect
or hope for a miracle from God, or some God-substitute such as a parent or
a physician, shaman, guru or other health-care provider. Such expectations
are often misguided and foolish. They are not, for instance, the kind of
expectations that physicians themselves tend to have concerning supposed
"miraculous" powers of their medical colleagues. We in the profession do not
expect miracles from our colleagues. We tend towards scepticism and non-
compliance. We notoriously make "bad" patients unless we are prepared to
allow ourselves the luxury of regression to an infantile, dependent state.
One must be prepared to relax, with a temporary "suspension of disbelief",
in order to permit the parent-figure to work the expected magic of cure.
Fellow-practitioners find that difficult to do themselves.

But if that has always been so in the past, we now, all of us, patients and
physicians alike, have been exposed in recent decades to remarkable advances
in new knowledge, and to increased sophistication of new technologies
developed (since the end of the Second World War) with great speed and a
sense of urgency. Hopes for extraordinary developments in the cure of diseases of every kind have never been so high as they were in the period between
the late 1940's and the late 1960's. But the more you expect, the more
profound is the loss of confidence when your expectations are unfulfilled.
The sober *Wall Street Journal*, on July 5, 1977, carried an editorial on the
shortcomings of medicine and medical science under the headline "When
Gods Fail". Now there is an indication of expectations if you like!

People seem to expect miracles to occur daily in medical science. It is
as if they had concluded that if we can put a man on the moon (a great
technological achievement, but simple in comparison with the complexities
of the physiology of sickness) we can "conquer" cancer or heart-disease, old
age, or even death! Nobody really came out front and protested at the fairy-
tale miracles wrought nightly on television by medical and surgical whizkids,
at the time when hospital-based shows were drawing their high Nielsen ratings.
Nobody in the profession protests at the daily string of deceptions to which
the public is exposed, for example, those concerning the effectiveness of pain-
relievers claimed to be "tested in a hospital", or vitamins, decongestants
or unguents for hemorrhoids that are "recommended by doctors". The
public has been led to believe that science has or soon will have a cure for

every disease. They naturally expect to receive the appropriate cure. So who is surprised that they become disappointed and angry? Physicians should know better than to endorse so many fradulent or unproven remedies. They should be ashamed to flaunt their M.D.s on garish book jackets advertising their own particular nostrum for "total health". At the height of the popularity of the television medical sit-coms, when the doctor was portrayed as a white-coated, god-like figure of authority, we in the profession did not protest. Some doctors became paid advisers to TV producers so as to make sure that everything on the show would look and sound "right". Thereby the profession passively and actively endorsed these deceptions. Those of us who were not directly involved nevertheless basked in the reflected glory. We did not disabuse the public of its fantasy that miracles were readily available, that all diseases, including death itself, would shortly be curable if only enough money were poured into biomedical research. Some still encourage this attitude, and seduce the public with talk of incipient "breakthroughs", when there really is very little to report except very hard though unproductive work in the laboratory or on the wards.

Far and away the greatest proportion of the vast sum of money that *has* been poured into biomedical research has gone into research conducted within the paradigm of the 19th-century reductionist or bioengineering model of disease. Medicine has always been a conservative profession, and properly so. No part of its history, I venture to suggest, will appear, to future historians of science, more conservative than the last thirty years of technical research and technical application. It never ceases to surprise me how *like* some of my colleagues are, caged in their tight little paradigms of the "biomedical model", to those classical Newtonian physicists of the late 19th century who firmly believed that by the end of the century everything that there was to know would be known about the physical structure of the universe − past, present and to come! The social, political and economic power that was wielded by physical scientists in the late 19th century is only equalled by that acquired by biomedical scientists during the middle decades of the 20th century. Power may not necessarily corrupt; but it does at the very least tend towards the development of dangerous *arrogance*. Physical scientists of the last century were arrogant to a degree. Theirs was a false arrogance, in that they did not recognize that they were looking at but one small part of the organization of the physical universe, and that small part only under special conditions. The same can be said of 20th-century biomedical scientists. We have considered the part to be more important and even more "equal" than the whole. By restricting ourselves to the biomedical or bioengineering model, we have earned the same fate as that which came to exponents of classical physics at the turn of the century. Not that what we have achieved will be considered to be *wrong*, exactly, but merely that it will be seen to have been grossly *inadequate*.

We have put too much trust in biomedical technology alone, without adequate reflection on the appropriate end of technology. Let me remind you that medicine really is an art, and that *technē* or technology is, by definition and etymology, art in the best sense. There is no such thing as "pure science" in medicine — if indeed there is "pure science" anywhere. The traditional "art" of medicine has nothing much to do with being good-hearted, or humanitarian in the "bedside manner" sense. Good medicine *is* good *technē* (good technique), based on sound knowledge, and practiced with care and compassion.

In recent years we have become so impressed with the sheer cleverness of sophisticated scientific techniques that we have forgotten what it is that technique is supposed to serve — namely, the real needs of the patient. In an essay published a few years ago I described the kind of feelings I had upon witnessing, on television in December 1966, a "surgical scientific miracle", as it was called. My statement came after a rather detailed discussion of the meaning and implications of the famous Sixth Hippocratic Precept, which says, in translation, "Where there is love of man, there also is love of the art (of medicine)." The Greek words are *philanthropiē* and *philotechniē*. The passage reads:

One doubts, sometimes, whether or not it is the health and happiness of others (which is what anyone imbued with *philanthropiē* would wish for his fellows) that many of our most earnest and dedicated technocrats of medicine today are primarily concerned to promote. I personally will never forget the anxiety I felt when watching, on television, the smiling face of Mr Washkansky, the first of the South African cardiac transplant patients. There he was, cracking his boiled egg and joking with the nurses; telling the crowding camera team how well he felt with his 'new' heart (as indeed he surely did, with the initial relief from chronic breathlessness); praising for all he was worth the medical services he was getting. And yet to anyone who had any biological insight, any knowledge of the inevitable tensions that had been created in his body, here was a man with only two possibilities ahead of him, both of them involving an early death: either his new heart would be rapidly rejected by the body's immunological mechanisms, or else those mechanisms, including defence against infection, had been eliminated before the operation. In that more likely case, here was a totally defenceless man, being paraded and exposed for publicity purposes, beseiged on all sides by crowds of people and their attendant microorganisms. His death sentence was already made out, and yet there he was, laughing and joking, pathetically secure in his trust in the modern experts in medical technology. Where now was the Hippocratic precept, that supposed equation we noted between love of man and love of the medical art? Where really was 'love' for Mr Washkansky, where was the real understanding, the *caring*, that he had a right to expect? Let us remember that this was no isolated example, even though it was the first; other cases followed it quickly enough, all over the world wherever the technical facilities for the simple transplant of hearts (a much less sophisticated operation than many others in the field of heart surgery) were available. Daily we followed, in press and television, macabre accounts of sick and dying people being rushed in and out of operating theatres for splenectomy and blood transfusion, bowel resection, dialysis for kidney disease, artificial respiration, and all the other life-saving (or, in these and countless other cases, 'death-prolonging') techniques now available. The last days of some of these patients must have been spent in the very depths of pain, humiliation and despair. And yet both *philanthropiē* and *philotechniē* require, as first essentials, respect for human dignity, whether in the living or in the dying process, and a basic concern for human justice [3].

That was my response to the heart-transplant mania of the 1960's. The most obscene example, in more recent years, of the *opposite* of the primary medical precept *primum non nocere* was the spectacle of Generalissimo Franco being rushed in and out of operating rooms for weeks on end. Horrendous news bulletins were issued daily to the people, eulogizing his brave fight with death, supported by no fewer than 36 physicians. The whole scenario was reminiscent of a rather badly-organized Spanish bull-fight. When Franco finally died, and thus released himself from the clutches of medical technologists who were doubtless functioning under great duress, I felt that the most appropriate gesture would have been to cut off the general's ears and present one each to the chief surgeon and chief physician.

We have lost much of our sense of human values in medicine. If *we* do not take our responsibilities seriously, we have no entitlement to the right (to freedom and the pursuit of happiness free of constraints and bureaucratic harassment) that a learned profession should be able to expect.

University of California
Los Angeles, California

BIBLIOGRAPHY

1. Beauchamp, T. L.: 1982, 'Morality and the Social Contract of Biomedical Technology', this volume, pp. 55—76.
2. Ingelfinger, F.: 1975, 'The Unethical in Medical Ethics', *Annals of Internal Medicine* 83, 264—269.

3. Towers, B.: 1971, 'The Influence of Medical Technology on Medical Services', in G. McLachlan and T. McKeown (eds.), *Medical History and Medical Care*, Oxford University Press, pp. 159–175.
4. Towers, B.: 1977, 'Ethics in Evolution', in S. F. Spicker and H. T. Engelhardt, Jr. (eds.), *Philosophical Medical Ethics: Its Nature and Significance*, D. Reidel, Dordrecht, Holland, pp. 155–168.
5. Towers, B.: 1977, 'Toward an Evolutionary Ethic', in H. T. Engelhardt, Jr., and D. Callahan (eds.), *The Foundations of Ethics and Its Relationship to Science, Vol. II, Knowledge, Value, and Belief*, Hastings Center, New York, pp. 207–224.
6. Towers, B.: 1978, 'The Origin and Development of Living Forms', *Journal of Medicine and Philosophy* 3, 88–106.

EDITORS' NOTE

It is worth noting the quite practical force of the Hippocratic precept concerning love of man and love of the art. It has come traditionally to be interpreted by individuals, including Sir William Osler, as connecting medicine's devotion to mankind with the physician's love of the art of medicine. This is surely an important moral point. However, the original meaning of this precept in the short cento *Precepts*, dating from some time in the first century B.C. or later, is worth stressing. It extends even further the focus of Bernard Towers's argument. The phrase in the original meant "where there is love of man, men will love the art" [1]. One can see this fairly clearly if one reads the entire sixth chapter of *Precepts* and attends to its quite practical thrust.

I urge you not to be too unkind, but to consider carefully your patient's superabundance or means. Sometimes give your services for nothing, calling to mind a previous benefaction or present satisfaction (your present reputation). And if there be an opportunity of serving one who is a stranger in financial straits, give full assistance to all such. For where there is love of man, there is also love of the art. For some patients, though conscious that their condition is perilous, recover their health simply through their contentment with the goodness of the physician. And it is well to superintend the sick to make them well, to care for the healthy to keep them well, but also to care for one's own self, so as to observe what is seemly [2].

The author is interested in sustaining the reputation of medicine and of individual physicians, and in the therapeutic force of the well-being generated by not overcharging and by giving treatment free to the indigent. In short, he enjoins the physician to resist short term advantage, because over the long run, showing love of man will have greater benefits.

This point can be transferred to the problem of public policy with respect to new knowledge in the biomedical sciences. If the application of new knowledge is done with care towards the feelings and economic situation of those influenced by such applications, the reward will be a better regard of medicine and the biomedical sciences. This can be cast, in fact, as a rule utilitarian maxim. Where there is *philanthropiē* in this introduction of new medical technologies, there will in general be *philotechniē*, positive regard of technology.

BIBLIOGRAPHY

1. Edelstein, L.: 1967, 'The Professional Ethics of the Greek Physician', in O. Temkin and C. L. Temkin (eds.), *Ancient Medicine*, Johns Hopkins Press, Baltimore, pp. 319–348.
2. 'Precepts', in W. H. S. Jones (trans.), *Hippocrates*, Harvard University Press, Cambridge, Massachusetts, p. 319.

MARY CRENSHAW RAWLINSON

HEALTH, JUSTICE, AND RESPONSIBILITY*

The issues raised by Beauchamp and Towers join in an important and power-ful way. Beauchamp articulates clearly the problem of distributive justice facing us. In discussing the issue of the fair allocation of health resources, we tend to talk about *our* obligations as a society, and we are, I think, tempted to forget that *our* obligation is always in the end *my* obligation and *your* obligation. *Our* obligation is not anonymous, but personal. Towers's discus-sion involves just this issue. He calls us to recognize our own responsibility for our health or lack of it: physical, professional, and moral. My remarks deal for the most part with Beauchamp's essay, but my conclusions, I hope, answer Towers's call.

A solution to the problem of distributive justice outlined so clearly by Beauchamp requires answers to both *empirical* questions about what resources are actually available and the probable consequences of employing those resources, and *moral* questions concerning whose interests are to be con-sidered in our analyses, what is to be determined as constituting a benefit, how various benefits are to be comparatively evaluated and ranked, and what rights, obligations, and principles of fairness must necessarily be considered as governing or at least as served by our cost-benefit analysis procedures. The questions which Beauchamp poses for us are these: first, how are resources to be distributed among major social undertakings, such as preventive medicine, personal health care, or biomedical research, such that distribution is *fair*, that is, such that certain persons or groups of persons do not, because of greater political, financial, or social power, receive a disproportionately large share of resources, while others, because of weakness or the mere circum-stances of nationality, sex or race, receive less than is their right? Second, this general question is made particular. How are those resources available for the maintenance and improvement of health to be fairly distributed? The utilitarian response involves considerations of both what ends are worth obtaining and across what population those ends can and should be extended, so as to achieve the greatest good.

The problem is clearly stated, but the proposed solution requires criti-cism. The essential thesis of Beauchamp's essay is surely that cost-benefit analysis provides a *"utilitarian* ethical justification" ([2], p. 161) for policies

87

William B. Bondeson, H. Tristram Engelhardt, Jr., Stuart F. Spicker and Joseph M. White, Jr. (eds.), New Knowledge in the Biomedical Sciences, 87–102.
Copyright © 1982 by D. Reidel Publishing Company.

addressing the *moral* question of how our health resources *ought* to be allocated. "Cost-benefit analysis", it is claimed, "provides an *appropriate* (material) *principle of distributive justice* . . . " ([2], p. 72). As he presents his project, then, Beauchamp is attempting to establish a principle of distributive justice adequate to serve as a principle of allocation in resolving conflicts of interests and claims with regard to goods and services related to health. He criticizes Dan Beauchamp, however, for offering just such an argument ([2], pp. 58–60). Tom Beauchamp is careful to point out that he is not simply criticizing Dan Beauchamp's theory in particular; rather, he rejects it as an *example* of an "approach taken to problems of macroallocation and regulation" in which appeal is made to principles of distributive justice ([2], p. 58). One wonders what the significant difference is between his own approach and that of Dan Beauchamp.

Tom Beauchamp seems to attempt to address just this objection. He states emphatically that his "*theory* makes a claim only about the use in a special social context . . . of a material principle of justice", and that he has offered no defense of any general theory of justice ([2], p. 72). He puts much weight on a distinction between principles and theories, and between general principles and *material* principles, and in Section VI he appeals to the work of Rawls, claiming that the *principle* for which he has argued would be compatible with (among other theories) Rawls's (nonutilitarian) theory of justice. There seems to be a worrisome confusion here about the relation of principles to theories, and concerning the nature of the principle Beauchamp is proposing. As Beauchamp rightly claims,

In Rawls's view it will do little good to tinker with distributional outcomes through material principles such as need, merit, effort, and utility assessments if the background conditions creating the problem are unjust. No amount of adjustment through such allocative principles will, in his view, eliminate the problem if it resides deep in the basic structure ([2], p. 73).

Such principles only reflect the justice or injustice following from the larger theory of justice of which they are specifications. We may agree that individual decisions ought to be made fairly and consistently rather than capriciously; however, the claim has little moral import if the policy to be enacted is itself unjust. Beauchamp has, in discussion, characterized his project as an *internal* critique of present systems of allocation which accepts the given general social and economic structure, as distinguished from an external critique which questions the "basic structure" determining the justice of social and economic relations. He seems to affirm this determination here in explicating the difference *and compatibility* of his own project and that of Rawls. It is clear that Beauchamp is not disagreeing directly with Rawls for he is not directly addressing the same problem, namely that of a general theory of justice; however, Rawls indicates that the justice or injustice of material principles of justice cannot be determined if they are isolated from the larger context in which they occur. Yet, it is in just this way that Beauchamp has argued for cost-benefit analysis.

Beauchamp's appeal to Rawls is doubly odd, because he has, in fact, rejected the sort of project Rawls has engaged in as useless — at least in the practical order to which Rawls surely intends it to apply. As long as philosophers try to do ethics and social philosophy by designing and arguing from a grand "basic structure", they will be of little use to anyone but themselves, according to Beauchamp. "Since Plato", Beauchamp tells us, philosophers have held the mistaken belief that "general philosophical considerations can determine how to resolve dilemmatic social problems and policies" ([2], p. 60). It is, in fact, Beauchamp claims, "impossible to apply abstract principles of justice to minute areas of social policy" ([2], p. 60). Surely *some* abstract principles, for example, "do good and avoid evil", are useless to us because they are so vacuous as to be impossible to apply in any systematic way. That simply means it is a poor abstract principle, though, *not* that all abstract principles are equally vacuous or useless. *Other* abstract principles, Rawls's difference principle, for example, propose precisely a specific method for obtaining the just state of affairs.

It is, however, precisely, the special *usefulness* and practicality of cost-benefit analysis which Beauchamp offers as one of two reasons supporting his claim that this procedure offers the best means of adjudicating conflicts of interest and solving dilemmas of allocation. Cost-benefit analysis — being no "abstract principle" — treats precisely the "financial exigencies" and "political realities" in which we find ourselves, and yields clear and definite answers to the question of what course of action ought to be pursued in these given circumstances. In criticizing this claim I repeat problems which Beauchamp himself raises. How are we to convert risks and benefits into acceptable quantitative units? How are we to delimit the scope and range of our analyses, and to describe the complex interrelations of particular cost-benefit analyses? These problems have, as Professor Beauchamp mentions, generally left the economists, like the philosophers Professor Beauchamp chided, with an elegant theory, perhaps, but with little to show for it in practice. But, this is just the situation from which the methods of cost-benefit analysis was supposed to deliver us. Beauchamp, in considering MacIntyre's objections to the cost-benefit approach, summarizes these objections as problems of measuring costs and benefits for purposes of comparison, problems in predicting outcomes, and problems in defining what is to count as a cost and as a benefit. We are told that while these surely constitute "practical difficulties inhibiting the *application* of utilitarian and cost/benefit reasoning" they do not "present insurmountable *theoretical* problems" ([2], p. 66). But, were we not at least in part urged to accept the cost-benefit analysis approach because it would work for us in the practical order? It seems to me that at this point in his argument, Beauchamp has forgotten his earlier claim that one criterion by which we must appropriately judge any theory of distributive justice is its efficacy in solving the real dilemmas in which we find ourselves regarding allocation of scarce resources. And, that is a claim which we ought not to forget. Perhaps the cost-benefit analysis approach, while imperfect and suffering its own problems of applicability *is* our "best hope" for solving dilemmas of allocation, but that is precisely what must be shown, *not* that these problems are merely ones of application, rather than theory.

Beauchamp's complaints about general theories and abstract principles are, I think, so much sand in our eyes. He states that he does not want to argue for a general theory of justice, but only for a material principle; however, as Rawls argues, the actual justice or injustice of that principle cannot be determined without some consideration of the larger system of principles and historical context in which it occurs. For Rawls, the sort of proposal that Tom Beauchamp makes will be ineffective in obtaining justice if the "background conditions" are themselves unjust. As Rawls argues in Section 47 of *A Theory of Justice*, to which Beauchamp refers:

... different conceptions of justice are likely to generate much the same common sense precepts ... however, the weights that are assigned to these precepts will not in general be the same. It is here that conceptions of justice diverge .... Thus the contrast between conceptions of justice does not show up at the level of common sense norms but rather in the relative and changing emphasis that these norms receive over time [in virtue of] the principles regulating the background system and the adjustments which they require to current conditions ([4], pp. 306–307).

Furthermore,

There is no way, then, to give a proper weight to precepts of justice except by instituting the surrounding arrangements required by the principles of justice ... no inference about the justice of the final distribution can be drawn from viewing the use of any precept in isolation. The overall weighting of the many precepts is done by the whole system ([4], p. 308).

Thus, precepts of justice or particular allocative principles reflect the justice or injustice of the background conditions in which they occur; and their justice or injustice can only be determined in reflection on those background conditions, and in terms of their relation to other precepts. Thus, Beauchamp's material principle of distributive justice might in one case be just and in another unjust, according to Rawls, depending upon how the background system required it to be instantiated, weighted, and adjusted according to changing conditions. True, it is perhaps compatible with a number of theories; however, if we are interested in its justice or injustice as we surely are here, we must look not simply at the isolated principle but precisely at the particular theoretical context in which it occurs.

Beauchamp, in fact, can understand his own proposal as something besides the "tinkering" Rawls describes *only* because it is his judgment that the moral problem regarding the allocation of resources does *not* reside "deep in the basic structure". We must "accept the situation in which we find ourselves", Beauchamp tells us; and, this does not simply mean assuming a realistic attitude toward the facts and the possibilities for altering them. It means, rather, that we ought to accept the given political and *institutional* situation. Within this framework, then, we can institute a methodology for decision-making which will yield less arbitrary and less capricious results. As Beauchamp states, he does

... not subscribe to Louis Kohlmeier's view that "the flaws in the regulatory process are fatal and [they are not] trustworthy repositories of the public interest" ... [he does not believe] that these agencies are inherently political nor that they have been "captured" by industry. The problem is rather that they need but do not possess a methodology that frees them from capture by either political or industrial interests, while at the same time enabling them to carry out their assigned duties with efficiency ([2], p. 57).

Beauchamp finds such a proposal significant, even if only a very small moral step forward, because he accepts the "basic structure of market justice". The qualifications on his own project now become clear: he does not argue for a general theory because, in fact, he has already accepted one, and he is simply engaged in the limited task of working out one of the finer and more specific principles within that theory. Beauchamp seeks to counter this characterization of his proposal, and it is true that cost-benefit analysis might be coherently employed at some very specific level in a society structured by the sort of background principles which Rawls, for example, outlines; however, the justice or injustice of the results obtained by those procedures depends at least to a crucial degree if not entirely on the context in which they are employed. We cannot rightly avoid, then, becoming critical of the system which Beauchamp simply assumes. Cost-benefit analysis *in itself* cannot provide an adequate principle of distributive justice, material or otherwise. The justice or injustice of principles of distribution of health care resources cannot be determined in isolation as Beauchamp insists on doing, but can only be treated in relation to other issues of distribution and, in fact, in relation to the entire system of earning and deserving. Furthermore, one cannot merely assume that the background structure is just; rather, that is the crucial and decisive issue.

Beauchamp accepts the "basic structure" of the American economic and governmental systems and their institutional manifestations, not simply because it would be impractical not to, but because he thinks the problem resides elsewhere, in the methodology, or lack of one, which individual decision-makers employ. Dan Beauchamp, on the other hand, argues that the very project of protecting the public's health itself requires that we reject the concept and practice of "market justice" ([1], pp. 7–9). He does not argue, as Tom Beauchamp claims, from the assumption of a general theory or "basic structure" of social justice to more specific principles; rather, he argues that the goals of public health policies necessarily conflict with the tenets of market justice and, thus, if we are to make sense of the project of protecting the public's health, we require some new foundation for and account of our commitments. It is Dan Beauchamp's argument that the idea of public health and the limited public health measures now in effect, already instantiate principles of social justice. His proposal involves an extension of these principles, rather than an introduction of them. The "new ethic" arises not in the imposition of abstract theory upon the public community by abstruse philosophers, but in public health coming to understand itself and its project appropriately. "What is required," Dan Beauchamp claims, "is for the public to see that protecting the public's health takes us beyond the norms of market-justice categorically, and necessitates a completely new health ethic" ([1], p. 6). Dan Beauchamp differs in his thinking from Tom Beauchamp, not by greater abstractness, nor by attempting to impose an elegant theory on all too recalcitrant empirical problems, but in his determination of what the problem in fact is. The project of public health — controlling environmental hazards to prevent death and disability through organized collective action in which burdens are shared fairly — *requires* conflict with present economic and administrative structures because "the public health ethic is [in itself] a counter-ethic to market-justice and the ethics of individualism as these are applied to the health problems of the public" ([1], p. 7). Tom Beauchamp attributes to Dan Beauchamp the belief that "general philosophical considerations can determine how to resolve dilemmatic social problems and policies" ([2], p. 60) and argues against him on these grounds. Such is, however, inessential to Dan Beauchamp's argument, as his claim is that the very project of guarding the public's health itself requires a recognition of the principles of social justice. Thus, Tom Beauchamp does not address Dan Beauchamp's proposals and arguments, and he fails to do so both because he misunderstands Dan Beauchamp's claims *and* because he begins himself with the assumption that the problem does not reside with the "basic structure".

The qualifications which Tom Beauchamp has placed on his original statement of his thesis, namely that the principle for which he is arguing is a *material* one and that he is not defending any particular *general* theory of justice, do not alter its susceptibility to criticism. *If* cost-benefit analysis can function as a principle of distributive justice, then it is subject to the same sort of criticism as any other such principle, and, as I have argued, that includes an analysis of the theoretical and empirical context in which it is proposed. Thus, I find unacceptable Beauchamp's project of arguing for a material principle in isolation. Furthermore, I want to continue my argument to show that not only does cost-benefit analysis employed as a principle of distributive justice merely reflect the justice or injustice of the background conditions, but also that, while cost-benefit analysis may reduce the capriciousness of our decision-making, it is appropriately employed only *after* the critical moral decisions concerning whose interests are to count and how interests are weighted have already been made. It can never itself provide answers to those moral problems.

The second reason Beauchamp offers in support of his "utilitarian hypothesis" is that by employing the procedures of cost-benefit analysis, "unclarity in the judgmental process is reduced", that is, the approach allows for a "reduction of intuitive weighing in the formulation of policy", and it is this advantage of the approach which Beauchamp claims is of the "greatest significance" ([2], p. 63). As I understand it, it is to this advantage which Beauchamp refers when he describes the cost-benefit analysis approach as more "objective" and more "impartial" than other theories and proposals concerning how resources ought to be distributed. Presumably, this procedure is more "objective" at least in part because it is quantitative, and because questions usually understood as evaluative ones are reinterpreted as empirical questions concerning the real satisfaction of actual preferences or desires, and the probable consequences of certain courses of action. More "objective" here surely means as well less arbitrary and fairer, that is, more just. By adopting the methods of cost-benefit analysis, we will be, Beauchamp suggests, less easily "subject to the indecisiveness and personal preferences of those responsible for the formulation of public policy" ([2], p. 75). I would argue, however, that not only does the cost-benefit analysis approach fail to relieve us of the burden of making difficult moral decisions about the nature of rights and obligations and defining principles of fairness, but also, if understood and used in the way suggested here, it constitutes a dangerous example of "bad faith" in that what are, in fact, moral judgments are presented as mere empirical descriptions. Beauchamp states, again in response to MacIntyre's objections, that

... [this] decision procedure ... would include techniques for determining whose values and preferences are to be considered, how these preferences are to be ordered, and how we are to ascertain initially that something is a cost or benefit ([2], p. 69).

That it can treat such "information" in a clear and systematic way is the virtue of the cost-benefit analysis approach. But preference, values, and *their relative orderings* do not constitute "information", mere descriptions of matters of facts. Beauchamp, later in his essay, recognizes this; furthermore, he points out the way in which certain moral rules not derivable from the cost-benefit analysis itself, such as requirements of promise-keeping or absolute prohibitions against certain forms of harm, must constrain the cost-benefit analysis ([2], pp. 70–72). Before we begin the cost-benefit analysis procedure, then, we must make certain value judgments about what constitutes a benefit or risk, whose interests are to be considered, how the costs, benefits, and interests are to be weighted, and what moral rules will constrain our analyses. Beauchamp, as I said, seems to recognize this; however, I remain perplexed. I do not understand why this does not call into question his central claim that cost-benefit analysis *in itself* provides an adequate principle of distributive justice and that we should then "accept the dictates of these analyses almost come what may" ([2], p. 75).

In addressing the problem of defining what is to count as a benefit, Beauchamp offers the modern reinterpretation of the concept of utility as "an individual's actual preferences". What counts as a benefit, then, in our analyses would be that which, in fact, satisfies the desires and preferences of those individuals whose interests we have already decided we must take into account. Again, this is, I think, an example of dangerous bad faith. What are really value judgments are considered and accepted *uncritically* as matters of fact, and an unjustified presumption is made in favor of the *status quo*. Once more, Beauchamp anticipates my objection; he states:

A major theoretical problem for utilitarianism arises when individuals have what, according to ordinary views about morality, are immoral or at least morally unacceptable preferences . . . . Utilitarianism based on subjective preferences is satisfactory only if a range of acceptable values can be formulated. This task has proved difficult and may even be inconsistent with some preference-based approaches ([2], p. 68).

The cost-benefit analysis approach here appears to be hardly the "most objective" and in itself adequate theory of distributive justice; rather, the most negatively *subjective*, dependent for its objectivity upon prior *and uncritical* decisions about rights, obligations, and hierarchies of values constituting the sort of theory of distributive justice to which the cost-benefit analysis approach was supposed to be an alternative. My point is that the cost-benefit analysis approach does not provide in itself an adequate principle of distributive justice, nor can any principle or set of principles of distributive justice be derived from it; rather, any time we employ these procedures we do so with a theory of distributive justice already in hand.

The criticisms of relying on actual preferences to define the notion of benefit Beauchamp dismisses by suggesting that "most people are not deviant in the manner envisioned and do have morally acceptable values" ([2], p. 68). Without launching into a discussion of the very real possibilities of finding ourselves in a so-called "sick" society or the subject of unhealthy and immoral desires, I can simply point out that it was from reliance on just these sorts of individual moral intuitions and value judgments that the cost-benefit analysis approach was supposed to deliver us. In fact, it not only requires that we rely on them, but that we remain uncritical of them.

Towers has described quite well what results when one group of persons, say patients, attempts to give up the responsibility for their own well-being, while another group of persons, say physicians, is seduced into attempting to be ultimately responsible for providing and maintaining well-being in others. The point is well taken here. Handing over our problems to the "experts", in this case, the cost-benefit analysts, will not relieve us of the responsibility for the normative decisions their policies reflect.

At this point, Beauchamp has every right to consider me one of those students of philosophy who does a lot of criticizing and theorizing and not much helpful proposing. It is my turn to put myself "at risk" and admit forthrightly that I find the moral problem residing in the background conditions themselves, and to confess that the sort of "social justice" theory which Beauchamp specifically criticizes seems to me to be the adequate and acceptable theory of distributive justice. In supporting my own position, I want to agree with and attend to two claims which Beauchamp makes: First, that

"Philosophers interested in public policy would do well to start in the midst of policy problems" ([2], p. 60), and, second, that the social justice theory, like *any* theory of distributive justice, involves certain claims regarding the nature of individual interests and rights.

The starting point ought to be in the midst of the real problems regarding the allocation of scarce resources. Right! But, what is the problem in which we find ourselves? Is it the problem of deciding between investing in cancer research or producing the Totally Implantable Artificial Heart (TIAH), between the development of exotic new medical technologies or the funding of local mental health centers; or, is the problem really one of deciding at least for the immediate future, between, on the one hand, the relief of hunger and the provision of the most basic forms of health care in those areas of our country *and* the world where malnutrition, infection, and disease are a way of life, and, on the other hand, the proliferation of present sophisticated medical services and technologies, the development of new exotic medical technologies, and the pursuit of advanced research for the benefit of the health care industry as it is now organized and for the community it now serves? I suggest that the situation in which we find ourselves is the latter, and that if we are to follow Beauchamp's well-spoken dictum we must start here, with the recognition that decisions about *what* sort of medical resources should be developed are also already decisions about *who* should receive them. *Who* will be affected by certain allocations of resources, who will be included and excluded from that sphere in which the benefits accruing from certain investments of our resources may be enjoyed, and what is the kind and degree of suffering which will be relieved by those investments? Whose needs are to be considered, and which needs are to prevail?

Our discussion thus far involves, I think, an assumption about the boundaries of our moral community. We worry with the decision between investing in the production of the TIAH or allocating more funds for cancer research in the context of a society in which most though not all persons are well-nourished and enjoy at least a minimal access to at least basic health care. I want to suggest that there is no good *moral* reason for failing to consider the interests, preferences, or needs of *everyone*. And, by everyone, I mean, *everyone*; that is, the problem in which we find ourselves regarding the allocation of scarce resources is an international, not a national one. There is no good *moral* reason why only the interests of those persons who happen to be members of our political community ought to be considered in determining how we allocate our resources, or why the benefits accruing from those allocations ought to extend only as far as our political boundaries.

Such a claim obviously contradicts the fundamental tenet of a social contract theory, namely, that social and political relations between persons are established in virtue of a contract, and that the contract describes the limits of specific moral obligations. Certainly, my claim requires as its foundation an account of the way in which that which is ontologically and morally ultimate is not the individual, but the community. I cannot adequately review here Hegel's analysis of the master-slave dialectic and his account of the way in which self-consciousness itself is made possible only by a mutuality of recognition, though that analysis is certainly the background for my claims. Let me ask you simply to consider the possibility that you are not first an individual and *then* secondarily a member of a community, that is, an individual who decides for practical and prudential reasons to contract with other individuals in order to form a social order; rather, that you are an individual only by virtue of being a member of a human community, that your being an individual is a social and historical event constituted in and through participation in the community.

Moral discourse most often centers on conflicts of interests, either on conflicts between individual interests or on the way in which the interests of the individual conflict with those of the community. I am suggesting that our interests are a great deal more mutual than we have been willing, perhaps for reasons of immediate personal advantage, to recognize. Surely adherence to the kind of social justice theory of distributive justice which has been discussed here will require me to sacrifice some of my particular personal interests, but it serves, I think, our most fundamental interest, viz., the preservation and nurturing of the human community and a respect for persons.

What I am suggesting is that an individual, as Hegel says, "*is* only by being acknowledged or 'recognized'" ([3], p. 229). The gaze of the other is a "mirroring" in which I find my own free subjectivity reflected. I find myself in the other who is like me; I see his actions as possibilities for me; I am constituted as an identity only in differing from the other; I discover the objectivity of *my* world in the inter-subjectivity of *our* world. If Hegel is right, if an individual discovers himself in the other in this way, then, in denying or ignoring the other he denies himself. To negate the freedom and worth of the other is to negate his own. If I enslave the other, I am as bound by the relation of slavery as the slave is, though in a different way.

Violating this relation of mutual recognition and dependence can consist in transgressions of the other's rights, or, and perhaps more commonly, it consists simply in *divesting* the other of his rights. The other objectified, divested of his personality, no longer requires of me a mutuality of active respect. We would not think of turning away the starving man or woman at our door, but we live quite comfortably with only occasional wailings and moanings over the "suffering mass", the hundreds of thousands of individuals suffering severe malnutrition in a variety of countries.

Beauchamp suggests that the difference between "market justice" and "social justice" consists in a different account of individual responsibility, and he is right in making this claim ([2], p. 59). Market justice rests on the view that individuals are responsible for and to themselves and, in fact, are or ought to be capable of taking care of themselves. Social justice, Professor Beauchamp suggests, rests on the contrary view that individuals are not responsible for themselves or are, through no fault of their own, incapable of taking care of themselves. This is, I think, an inadequate statement of the notion of individual responsibility implicit in a theory of social justice. The claim is, rather, that the individual is responsible for himself *as a member of the community*, that is, that he is responsible for the way in which he participates in and nurtures the welfare of the whole.

Again, I would remind you of Towers's remarks concerning individual responsibility. I am certainly not suggesting that a few ought to take care of the many, though there are some persons who, because of certain debilitating conditions which must be carefully spelled out, ought to be accorded, as Towers states, "rights without too much responsibility" ([5], p. 77). I am suggesting that being properly responsible for ourselves involves being properly responsible for the other, interested in his welfare and in maintaining and nurturing his freedom and well-being. Such an interest includes *restraining from usurping* his responsibility for himself; that is, we are required in the mutuality of respect to avoid the paternalism, or in Towers's appropriate coinage, "parentalism", which divests the other of the very thing which distinguishes him as human, his ability to act freely and rationally.

That is all to the good, [Towers states] . . . until, unexpectedly, one is felled by a bacterium, or an atherosclerotic plaque on a coronary artery, or by a neoplasm, or by a demyelinating disease of the central nervous system. Then, some degree of psychological regression is almost inevitable . . . it would be foolish not to recognize that the situation [between doctor and patient] is bound to be unequal from the start, in that the one is sick and in need of therapeutic help and the other is, at least presumptively, well and able to give that help ([5], p. 79).

Towers suggests that one must recognize the way in which being ill necessarily involves a "vulnerability" and a "dependency" which constitute some degree of "psychological regression". Surely illness obstructs our encounter with the world; it incapacitates, isolates, and often humiliates. Do these debilitations, however, in any way necessitate or justify the establishment of a parentalist relation between patient and doctor? The essentially debilitating character of illness requires that we define careful limits for the kinds of decisions a physician may appropriately make on behalf of his patient, while confronting the tender problem of identifying those instances in which a patient's judgment, his capacity to choose freely, is so impaired that another ought to intervene for him to protect his interests. The problem consists in maintaining appropriate respect for the patient's integrity and autonomy while recognizing his necessary (in virtue of his illness) dependence upon the physician or the health care team. The problem is solved or *dis*solved in recognizing that the dependence essential to the relation of physician and patient, is of a specific and limited sort which neither necessitates nor justifies any encroachment upon the autonomy of the patient. I would argue that the dependence obtaining between physician and patient by virtue of that relation, consists in the reliance of one on the other for certain knowledge and skills, a dependence characteristic of many professional relations and one which does not itself limit the patient's right to make normative judgments. Futhermore, I would suggest that the tendency to understand the relation of physician and patient as peculiar in the dependence it requires and as, therefore, presenting peculiar moral difficulties, arises from a misunderstanding of the nature of autonomy itself.

We have agreed that illness debilitates; so does ignorance. As a teacher, my students depend upon me to share with them a certain kind of knowledge and expertise which will, if I am any good at my job and they at theirs, enable them to write and think more clearly and more critically, skills needed to pursue their academic and professional careers. They depend on me, and that dependence has often caused the teacher's role to be likened to that of the parent. We teachers are said to function *in loco parentis*. But the *special* dependence of the student is only a dependence upon my performing my professional duties competently. He agrees to submit to my lectures three or four times a week because he expects that he will learn something it will be good or useful for him to know. He or she may be especially impressionable and dangerously subject to my influence, or timid in the face of what is identified as authority and like many patients vulnerable, frightened and submissive, but it is my responsibility precisely to refrain from acting in ways which foster those conditions or take advantage of them, not only because that is essential to good teaching, but because I am morally obliged not to encroach on the integrity of the other in that way, even if he or she out of some weakness invites me to do so. My students have every right to expect that I will teach them how to recognize a good argument or a good reason, and as well that I will *refrain* from telling them what they must believe. The point is that the very real relation of dependence is *limited by* a relation of mutual respect, such that the central integrity and autonomy of the student is never threatened.

Admittedly, the stakes are usually higher in medicine; however, I think the relation of dependence is not essentially different. The patient is dependent upon the special knowledge and expertise of the physician for a more or less critical medical care. Like the ignorant person who cannot read, the patient often finds himself incapable of performing a variety of ordinary tasks due to his illness and he depends upon the physician to alleviate that condition. As Towers states, the situation is "bound to be unequal from the start". The question is what is the exact nature and extent of the inequality, and does any relation of parentalism *necessarily* follow from it. Need the physician become a "parent-figure", which as Towers points out is so often the case? I think not if we recognize that the dependence of the patient *qua* patient on the physician *qua* physician consists only in the need for certain information and the services of certain skills. This dependence, however, does not inherently involve relinquishing to the physician or improperly burdening him with responsibility for the quality and course of one's own life. Any physician who has ever tried, for example, to convince his patient that he cannot take the phenobarbital which he needs if he continues to drink alcohol, knows this. The debilitations of illness make understandable, perhaps, the parentalism so often characteristic of the doctor-patient relation, but they do not justify it except, perhaps, in those cases in which the patient is literally incompetent to make decisions. And, in those cases the purpose of the treatment ought to be, at least in part, to restore in the patient just that capacity. That someone becomes in some specific and limited way dependent on us need not mean that we gain power over them; it certainly does not mean that we are justified in assuming and maintaining power over them, though it may present the possibility for doing so. My point is that proper medical practice involves the establishment of a relation of mutual respect between peers which contains and bounds the relation of dependence.

There is simply something wrong-headed in understanding this relation of dependence as something peculiar to medicine though that case surely has its peculiar features. Hegel's argument concerning the necessity of the recognition of the other in being a self, yields the conclusion that human persons are *essentially* subject to relations of dependence, and not simply when they are ill or poor or ignorant. There is nothing in the relation of dependence itself which necessitates or justifies an encroachment upon or relinquishing of the autonomy of the patient. Autonomy is not incompatible with dependence but, in fact, is itself established only mutually. Autonomy is not independence, but *inter*dependence. What leads us to think that the dependence necessarily characteristic of the relation between physician and patient necessitates or at least justifies limitations on the autonomy of the patient is precisely the false equation of autonomy with independence. To be properly responsible for the other means to protect and nurture his autonomy, our interdependence. Our interests are mutual, for being a free, rational human being is necessarily a *social* event.

I think this sort of mutuality of interest, the reciprocity of interest between individual and community, is precisely what Mill meant by "enlightened interest" or "higher pleasure". "Enlightenment" requires precisely a recognition of the way in which individual interest is neither subordinate, nor super-ordinate to the communal interest, but is, in fact, coherent with and constituted by the interest of the community. I think Mill would agree that the appallingly unequal distribution of resources now obtaining diminishes the quality of my life, not only if I am one of those who haven't enough to eat, but simply and most profoundly because the most fundamental interest I have is that of being a responsible member of a just human community.

But, have I not now forgotten that dictum of Beauchamp's to which I promised I would attend: that philosophers ought not to naively put forward, perhaps, inspiring but, in fact, practically useless principles of justice, that we must begin with the real dilemmas in which we find ourselves. No, I have not forgotten! A theory of social justice and the account of the mutuality of interests which underlies it issue in proposals which are at least as specific and practical as those of the cost-benefit analysis theory. The problem is not that the social justice theory is more abstract or that it fails to issue in specific proposals, but that the policies which it requires *will* be more difficult to implement because they will, in fact, most probably be resisted by those who now own the resources and possess the political and financial power. A theory of social justice will require the sort of specific proposal concerning the delivery of health care which Dan Beauchamp outlines, and which Tom Beauchamp rightly points out it will be difficult to implement. Such a theory requires, I think, even more specific proposals about how you and I ought to spend a portion of our paychecks, limit our consumption of certain resources, and share our skills. That these proposals will be difficult to implement does not, however, make them any less right or just. And that is where he began, with the problem of how we could in very specific and pressingly real situations achieve justice.

State University of New York
Stony Brook, New York

NOTES

* I would like to thank Ernest Loevinsohn and Mark Sedler for their very helpful advice and criticism.

[1] Tom Beauchamp also claims that few will readily accept Dan Beauchamp's proposals, but that is a *political* point which does not weigh against the justice of his claims.

[2] Dan Beauchamp explicitly states that he does not argue for the extension of these principles beyond the area of health care, nor for social justice as a background theory. See, e.g., ([1], p. 11). This central claim is that "making the ethical foundations of public health visible only serves to highlight the social justice influences at work behind pre-existing principles".

BIBLIOGRAPHY

1.   Beauchamp, D. E.: 1976, 'Public Health as Social Justice', *Inquiry* 19, 3–14.
2.   Beauchamp, T. L.: 1982, 'Morality and the Social Control of Biomedical Technology', in this volume, pp. 55–76.
3.   Hegel, G. N. F.: 1967, *The Phenomenology of Mind*, Harper and Row, New York.
4.   Rawls, J.: 1971, *A Theory of Justice*, Harvard University Press, Cambridge, Mass.
5.   Towers, B.: 1982, 'Rights and Responsibilities in Medical Science', in this volume, pp. 77–85.

SECTION IV

BIOMEDICAL KNOWLEDGE: LIBERTARIAN *VS.*
SOCIALIST MODELS

GERALD WEISSMANN

THE NEED TO KNOW: UTILITARIAN AND ESTHETIC
VALUES OF BIOMEDICAL SCIENCE

When a practicing scientist faces an audience concerned with the ethics of
his discipline, he feels somewhat like an author being asked out to lunch
by his editor. In the long run, to paraphrase G. K. Chesterton, it is always
the author who pays. And I suspect that, when a philosopher asks "What new
knowledge is needed in the biomedical sciences?" the scientist is expected
to pay by agreeing that the question *can* be answered. But I doubt that it
can be answered, suspecting that there is no way of determining in advance
what shall or shall not be known, what knowledge we do or do not need.
Therefore, I will not be able to predict for you whether what we need to
know is in the realm of manipulative genetics, the reconstitution of cell
membranes, or even the conquest of neoplasia. I should like, instead, to
consider those values which, for a working experimentalist, underlie our
need to know.

These considerations will be based upon a recent classification of values
by Thomas Nagel, who suggests that

There are five fundamental types of value:
first, there are specific obligations to other people or institutions: *obligations* to
patients, to one's family, to the hospital or university at which one works, to one's
community or one's country.
The next category is that of constraints on action deriving from *general rights* that
everyone has, either to do certain things or not to be treated in certain ways.
The third category is that which is technically called *utility*. Utility includes all
aspects of benefit and harm to all sentient beings not just those to whom the agent has
a special relation, or has undertaken a special commitment. The general benefits of
medical research and education obviously come under this heading.
The fourth category is that of *perfectionist ends* or values. By this I mean the intrinsic
value of certain achievements or creations, apart from their value *to* individuals who
experience or use them. Examples are provided by the intrinsic value of scientific discovery, of artistic creation, of space exploration, perhaps.
The final category is that of *commitment* to one's own projects or undertakings,
which is of value in addition to whatever reasons may have led to them in the first place.
It is partly a matter of justifying earlier investment of time and energy, and not allowing
it to have been in vain. It is partly a desire to be the sort of person who finishes what
he begins ([5], pp. 281–282).

I will use the third category of values just as Nagel does, calling it the

105

*William B. Bondeson, H. Tristram Engelhardt, Jr., Stuart F. Spicker and Joseph M. White,
Jr. (eds.), New Knowledge in the Biomedical Sciences, 105–112.*
Copyright © 1982 by D. Reidel Publishing Company.

"utilitarian", but will lump his fourth and fifth categories of values (perfectionist ends and private commitments) under the term "esthetic". And I do so because it is likely that perfectionism and private commitment describe common ends with a kind of esthetic sensibility shaping both.

My major argument is quite simple. Until recently, the biomedical scientist has been quite certain that any new knowledge acquired as to the nature of living things could not help but be useful to the general welfare, and that such "utilitarian" values constituted a moral guarantee for his intrusion upon the natural world. In consequence, he was required only to follow his "esthetic" concerns for the elegant experiment, the beautiful proof, the unshakable theory. Recent events have unsettled this agreeable view, but I am arguing here that there is life in it yet.

There is ample support for the idea that "science for its own sake", the esthetic view, yields utilitarian benefits. Research oriented not to disease, but into the nature of soil fungi, gave us streptomycin, inquiry into the nature of cells in culture led to the Salk vaccine, and studies of the cell cycle in onion root tips have eventuated in the rational treatment of leukemia. Such examples, and at least three-score others which decorate our recent history, have reassured the community of biological scientists that our general enterprise is intrinsically benign. As a corollary, the scientist is persuaded that if he performs his task professionally by doing *well* , he is doing *good*.

His doubts relieved as to ends, he concentrates on means. And what magnificent means are available! The toyshops of technology, and the purses of our government, have provided him with electron microscopes to view single cells peeled and split like oranges, centrifuges which hurl viruses at gravitational forces 100 000-fold that of the earth, X-rays which display the molecular symmetry of our tendons, and spectrophotometers which scan the uncoiling of our genes.

By these means, the game of science has been played in obedience to a set of rules which has remained uncluttered by any ethical stricture save one: thou shalt not fudge the data! The professional code of the scientist has been a stringently esthetic one. It has rewarded the individual imagination for coming up with reproducible experiments. And that kind of imagination has, until recently, been considered by one and all to resemble that of the creative artist, no more − and no less − in the service of temporal, social mores. W. H. Auden has summarized this attitude, removing this creative effort to another realm: "Both science and art are primarily spiritual activities, whatever practical applications may be derived from their results" ([1], p. 78).

This state of affairs — still quite satisfactory to me — has now become so strongly challenged that the esthetic values of biomedical research have been edged into disrepute. Indeed, even the utilitarian ends of our science — the manipulation of nature for the eradication of what we perceive as its errors — have been attacked by environmentalists, humanists, and the new theologians. Energized a decade ago by the folly of our technology in Viet Nam (organic herbicides against the tropical forest, psychoactive drugs in the hands of the CIA), critics from without have been joined by the disenchanted young from within the perimeter of science.

The disenchantment of scientists and their lay critics culminated in the fuss over recombinant DNA which has moved from the shores of Asilomar to the halls of Congress. What began as a brave, internal effort to face the ethical problems raised by gene-splicing has slowly developed into a broad social movement, in the words of June Goodfield: " . . . 'to blow the whistle', to taper off that curve of infinite environmental manipulation" ([4], p. 178).

For the first time in recent democratic history, there is a good chance that some, perhaps benign, authority will legally declare to the biological scientist: thou shalt not do this experiment, because it is *morally* wrong to muck about with our genes!

Now I think it unprofitable to rehearse here at length the compelling scenarios of gloom that opponents of DNA recombinancy have plotted. In the picturesque words of Bernard Davis, they re-tell three popular myths: the Andromeda strain fantasy, the legend of chimaeras, and the creation of the Golem. Nor need I detail the overwhelming evidence that they are unlikely to be realized. Indeed, their reification becomes more improbable with each new issue of *Science* or *Nature*, as the solid experimental advances of January render pointless the regulatory legislation drafted in October. Instead, let us return to June Goodfield whose recent book, *Playing God*, brilliantly recounts the history of the genetic debate, and elaborates upon its larger meaning. Admitting that "it is so hard to produce a rational argument for one's moral qualms about DNA research" ([4], p. 169), she nevertheless encapsulates the less-than rational ones which are so much more powerful:

What bothered us so about the new technology? Three things came to mind: the slow erosion of that which up to this point in our history has gone to make us uniquely human, or what we have considered to be human; the latter-day assault on personal autonomy and integrity; and the increasing sense that individuals are losing control over the conduct and direction of human affairs ([4], p. 170).

I hope it is not fanciful to point out that the first of these worries is a restatement of the Golem fantasy, the second a rephrasing of the chimaera myth (assault on personal integrity), and the third reflects a modest confusion between *Brave New World* and *The Double Helix*. But this reduction of Goodfield's arguments does not render them less cogent. Scientists share with humanists these worries as to the remote, unpleasant, utilitarian consequences of gene-splicing, even as they exult over their recent capacity to turn bacteria into engines for the production of insulin or somatostatin.

But the most striking extension of these social and ethical anxieties is yet to come, for as A. J. Ayer has suggested: "ethical terms do not serve only to express feelings. They are calculated also to *arouse* feeling, and so *to stimulate action*" [my emphasis] ([2], p. 108).

The action which is called for conflicts with both the utilitarian and esthetic values of biomedical research. It is the imposition, by means of external authority, of a professional code upon the scientist. Such a code, arrived at by the usual democratic process, and with the usual degree of consent by the regulated, will guarantee – we may presume – that after his successful pursuit of the Golden Fleece the researcher will not come home to Medea. These professional codes (as fairly arrived at as the codicils of Internal Revenue) will not only enlarge the number of degree-bearers now legislatively responsible for the products of their endeavors, but also submit these to prospective, moral scrutiny.

We return to Goodfield's book on DNA recombinancy. In it we can discern that the moral imperative for regulation comes from the potential abuse which may result from our capacity to fiddle with genes, from our "playing God". Dr Goodfield's analysis of professionalism is straightforward:

The scientific profession has a relationship with society quite unlike that of any of the other professions. All professions have a number of identifying characteristics, many of which the scientific profession shares. The practitioners engage in their work full-time, in a manner long accepted by their particular tradition. Admission into the profession is conditional upon a demonstrated mastery of the accepted skills and competences, to which an apprentice binds himself to conform. Professions are self-governing: they alone determine what will be the criteria for recognized accomplishment and the hierarchies of authority and eminence. Indeed, they establish the very procedures whereby authority is recognized and eminence bestowed. If a person decides to enter the profession for the status or the cash that may come his way, this is his own business, but the profession itself was not constituted for those ends. Professional activity is not only concerned with individual rewards but with something transcendental too: whether it is improved health care or a more realistic interpretation of the law or better education for the young or, as in the case of the scientific profession, the discovery of truth. With the sole exception of the scientific profession, one other thing unites them all: services to the public are their chief object, cemented by a contractual relationship. Because of this contract the competence of a professional is appraised both internally, by his contemporaries, and externally, by the public ([4], p. 78).

This argument goes on to urge not only that the professional scientist be governed by some sort of professional guild, like the American Medical Association or the American Bar Association, but that he be subject to the laws of malpractice. Goodfield describes the unregulated state of science prior to our recent, ethical concerns:

Save for the expenditure of society's funds, however, the (scientific) profession was still accountable for nothing. The law in no way held them to the highest degree of care: they were never sued for malpractice nor for misapplication of their work. The only set of ethical principles that ever concerned them were those concerned with protecting the good name of the profession and its "sublime" methodology. They were in no way concerned with the needs of society . . . ([4], p. 89).

It is this argument that conflicts with the two sorts of values we have been discussing. For the argument assumes that the utilitarian output of the scientist's profession has some "unique" social implications, and that these implications require society at large to set some limit on his esthetically motivated quest. But are the social consequences of scientific research different "in kind" from those of other scholarly pursuits or the creative arts? Professional historians offer their narratives to gain an understanding of the present; professional philosophers (of some schools, at least) believe in the usefulness of their metier for proper conduct; and social scientists agree that their analyses are of use in the amelioration of political problems. But can we say with certainty that the contributions of Fichte, Nietzsche, and Spengler had less grave consequences for the orderly flow of social progress than even the most lurid results imaginable of our biologic inquiries? Should the esthetic motivations of Pound, Celine, or the Marquis de Sade have been modulated at the source by a morals committee? Cyril Connolly has quipped: "Le coeur a ses raisons — and so have rheumatism and the 'flu" ([3], p. 53). Since some of us look into the reasons of rheumatism for the reasons of our heart, is it extravagant for the sciences to claim — at least with respect to subject matter — a measure of the license granted to the arts? Like it or not, we are discussing censorship when we liken the profession of science to the profession of law or of medicine. Malpractice rules are written to ensure that the practitioner conforms to the general level of professional practice in the community — surely this is not the standard of the creative scientist, nor of the innovative scholar in any field. The possible misuses, in the utilitarian sense, of his knowledge should not lead to pre-emptive rules as to the kind of inquiry the professional may engage in. A scientist, in the best interpretation, is not only a professional in the sense that a lawyer or a doctor is. In the very best sense, he is a professional in the way of a historian, a poet, or an artist.

In 1968, Erwin Chargaff addressed the rebelling students at Columbia who complained that the results of all scientific research were capable of perversion by the military-industrial complex: consequently, scientists were not to be trusted. Chargaff suggested that if the Pentagon could eliminate the Viet Cong by incessantly playing the B Minor Mass, its perverse use of Bach would still not give the students the right to burn his scores. Does this imply that I advocate complete license, complete liberty with respect to what kind of new knowledge we biomedical scientists should pursue? Let me advance this claim, as phrased by Auden:

> Liberty is prior to virtue; i.e., liberty cannot be distinguished from license, for freedom of choice is neither good nor bad, but the human prerequisite without which virtue and vice have no meaning. Virtue is, of course, preferable to vice, but to choose vice is preferable to having virtue chosen for one ([1], p. 221).

Such a completely libertarian view is clearly counter to the temper of our time. We must, indeed, accept the rational bases for the general disenchantment of our culture with the products of science pursued for its own ends. The wonderful folks who gave you (however indirectly) the bomb of Hiroshima, the laboratory of Auschwitz, and the psychiatry of the Gulag archipelago are not generally trusted to keep their new genetic tools locked safely in the academic cupboard.

But from where did the counter-forces arise to these overt excesses? To a large extent, scientists themselves, acting in response to a code of moral values they share with others, have "pulled the whistle" on more of these outrages. The atomic physicists, by means of their Bulletin, have resisted the proliferation of their monster, biomedical scientists have propagated the Helsinki Declaration, and the psychiatrists have exposed the social mischief of the mental health commissars. The motivating force behind these ameliorative actions has been, I believe, the sense of humane ethics in which our society at large is impregnated. It may be useful to remember that ηθικος (and its Latin progeny, *mores*) originally meant "character" in the singular, and "manners" in the plural. The character and manners of our scientists are probably determined more by the general culture of which they are a

THE NEED TO KNOW

part than by any unique sense of scientific ethics. A society gets not only the government, but the science, it deserves.

Our only guarantee that new knowledge will not be gained at the expense of human values is the integrity of that network of values in which all our inquiries are enmeshed. This is to argue that we should impose no pre-emptive restrictions on the *kinds* of new knowledge to be sought. If we wish, for example, to prohibit certain investigations on human subjects by our physiologists because their Nazi counterparts violated any reasonable code of behavior, we may be granting the Nazis a posthumous victory they do not deserve. Of course, our science should not design experiments that are trivial, dangerous, or dehumanizing. However, these adjectives are best defined by the consensus of society at large. And if that consensus be justly derived, we can expect that the community of scientists, as citizens, will agree.

It has recently been argued that "truth at any price" — unrestricted inquiry into anything at all at any time — is an over-riding *cultural* value of our sort of civilization. It may well be, but only to the extent that it does not entirely conflict with those values of society that the scientist himself has introjected. There are many "truths" and many kinds of knowledge — and if we want to be sure that the scientist (following his own esthetic bents) does not come up with chimaeras or Golems, we'd be well-advised to make certain that our society as a whole doesn't want such fantasies realized. The alternative — the proscription of those lines of inquiry which could possibly lead to chimaeras or Golems — is based on the assumption that only the *worst* consequences of an experiment are to be expected. Many of us over forty would not be alive today if that assumption had been dominant in the last century.

Finally, I am convinced that the culture of science, which engages at least as much of our population as does the humanist culture, is worth nurturing for its own sake. The unravelling of the genetic code, the elucidation of cell structure and metabolism, our analysis of how nerves make muscles twitch or speech possible, constitute, I submit, cultural achievements no less imposing than the mosaics of Ravenna or the cathedrals of France. At a time when the arts of our decade are devoted to the production and analysis of works related to self — inquests into narcissism — the objective triumphs of our science are perhaps even more to be cherished. We will, I daresay, not achieve the utilitarian ends of our science: freedom from hunger and disease, less anxious youth and sturdy old age, without adopting the risky, libertarian view that there shall be no bounds as to what scientists need to know. Motivated by esthetic considerations to reach the aims of utility, our new biomedical knowledge will come (in the words of Lewis Thomas) "if the air is right . . . in its own season, like pure honey".

New York University School of Medicine
New York, New York

BIBLIOGRAPHY

1. Auden, W. H.: 1963, *The Dyer's Hand*, Faber & Faber, London.
2. Ayer, A. J.: 1936, *Language, Truth and Logic*, Victor Gollancz, London.
3. Connolly, C.: 1947, *The Unquiet Grave*, Viking, New York.
4. Goodfield, J.: 1977, *Playing God*, Random House, New York.
5. Nagel, T.: 1977, 'The Fragmentation of Value', in H. T. Engelhardt, Jr., and D. Callahan (eds.), *Knowledge, Value and Belief*, Hastings Center, Hastings-on-Hudson, pp. 279–294.

MARX W. WARTOFSKY

MEDICAL KNOWLEDGE AS A SOCIAL PRODUCT: RIGHTS, RISKS, AND RESPONSIBILITIES

1. PRELIMINARY REMARKS

Let me sketch the program of this paper at the outset. I will begin with some scene setting: a brief account of the crisis in medicine. Then I will pose a problem: the need for a theoretical model of medicine in terms of which to approach the crisis. I will go on to analyze the problem in terms of some of the fundamental concepts involved in the construction of the theoretical model — specifically, the nature of medical knowledge, and the rights, risks and responsibilities which are involved in its acquisition, possession, and use. Finally, I will suggest the direction of a resolution of the crisis, in terms of the theoretical model. In effect, I am offering a foray into some conceptual philosophical muddles which characterize the systematic thought concerning these questions.

2. THE CRISIS IN MEDICINE

Modern medicine is in a crisis. The older traditional structures of medical practice, the comfortable and familiar models of patient-physician relationships, of one-to-one curative medicine, the straightforward economies of private practice, or even the more complex economies of group and institutional practice — have all been put in question. Apart from the more obvious stresses and strains of an inflationary economy, and the growing demand for health care beyond the limits of presently available resources, medicine faces a host of special problems. Medicine must meet the challenges of federal and state regulation, legislative and judicial incursions upon the heretofore sacrosanct preserves of medical decision-making in such traumatic contexts as abortion, terminal care, and limited access to new diagnostic and therapeutic technologies. Medicine must consider the specter of patients' rights, the ethical and epistemological complexities of informed consent, fee-setting by the insurance industry, the impending periodic review of licensure, the prospects of national health insurance, the record-keeping explosion, the national maldistribution of health care facilities and medical personnel, and the malpractice mania. All of those and more are symptoms of a systemic

113

William B. Bondeson, H. Tristram Engelhardt, Jr., Stuart F. Spicker and Joseph M. White, Jr. (eds.), New Knowledge in the Biomedical Sciences, 113–130.

disorder. Yet, in the midst of these difficulties, major policy decisions demand to be made: decisions such as allocating resources, setting priorities in research and in clinical treatment, designing, purchasing, and utilizing new and expensive medical technologies, introducing new legislation affecting medical decision-making, establishing new organizational and administrative structures to decide, review, or consider major questions of principle and ethics, and in effect, to reshape the ideology of the profession. The diagnosis of the crisis cannot be limited to what can be reconstructed *ad hoc* from the signs, symptoms, and complaints. Rather, what are needed are some theoretical models of medicine itself as a practice. What is involved in the present crisis is neither simply the economics, nor the internal organization of medicine, but rather a question of what the norms of this practice are, and what they ought to be. Fundamental to the question of norms is the notion of rights, and the concomitant question of responsibilities. But fundamental to the question of rights and responsibilities are the grounds for these rights, and the sources of these responsibilities. This is not an "ethical" question, in some abstract sense, but is a theoretical question concerning the very nature of medical practice. The question of the norms of medical practice, and of rights, risks and responsibilities is, in this sense, a question of the ontology and epistemology of medicine, of what medicine *is*, and what constitutes medical knowledge.

I want to argue that medicine is fundamentally a cognitive practice or activity: that it is, in a broad sense, *knowledge*; that it is a *teleological* practice — i.e., it is the acquisition, use and transmission of this knowledge to some end; further that this knowledge is a *social* product, and that the analysis of rights, risks and responsibilities has to be grounded in this social nature of medical knowledge. I do not pretend that such a theoretical model provides the answers to the questions raised by the contemporary crisis in medicine. I do want to claim that without the development of some such model, the response to the crisis will remain *ad hoc*, incoherent, and anarchic. It will remain at the level of primitive, empirical, rule-of-thumb folk-medicine. The alternatives are neither *ad hoc* poultices nor totalistic panaceas, but rather a formulation of some coherent bases, some theoretical models of the disease, from which to approach its diagnosis and cure.

In my discussion, which suggests one such approach, I intend to address three sorts of questions: First, what is the nature of medical knowledge, and how is it acquired and used? Second, what rights are involved in the acquisition and use of this knowledge, and what are the correlative duties and responsibilities that accompany these rights? And further, on what are such rights and duties grounded? What legitimates them? Third, in light of the answers to the first two questions, what model of medicine, theoretical and practical, is appropriate to, or derives from such an analysis of the nature of medical knowledge, and of the rights and responsibilities involved in the acquisition and use of this knowledge?

I will propose a social model of medical knowledge – i.e., a model of medical knowledge as a social product, and of medical practice, whether research or clinically oriented, as a social activity. By this I mean an activity and its product which cannot be understood except in terms of social interaction among agents, and the historical (and historically changing) forms of social organization within which these interactions occur.

The considerations will therefore be (1) *epistemological* – having to do with the nature of this knowledge, (2) *social* – concerning its acquisition, organization, utility, and its institutional forms, and (3) *normative* – having to do with the goods or values which such knowledge represents, and with the rights to these goods.

I will begin with a characterization of medicine as a fundamental human practice. Within this framework, I will then proceed to address the three sorts of questions I posed at the outset, and to develop the normative model of how medical knowledge ought to be used, what rights and responsibilities are involved in its acquisition and use, and to whom these belong.

3. MEDICAL KNOWLEDGE AS A SOCIAL PRODUCT – BACKGROUND DISCUSSION

Medicine is one of the fundamental social practices that characterize the human species. Like science, art, law, and religion, it is a mode of cognitive praxis, a form of human activity by means of which the species preserves and develops itself, adapts itself to an historically changing environment of needs, wants, and purposes.

Broadly speaking, medicine is at the same time a form of production. Like the productive activity by means of which human beings transform nature, by creating those artifacts required for their biological existence (e.g., food, clothing, shelter) and those concomitant human artifacts through which such primary production takes place – (language, tools, social organization, the technology of skills and practices, and the cognitive technology by means of which knowledge is acquired, preserved and transmitted) – so too, medicine produces a fundamental value required for species-life, namely the means for dealing with disease and injury, and for preserving and enhancing the health of individuals and thereby the good of society.

Medicine, then, is essentially a means. To say that medicine is a teleological activity, then, is to say that it is defined as a value and in terms of its activity, relative to some end, but not as an end in itself. I will want to characterize the activity of medicine as a cognitive practice, that is, *knowledge*. It is this knowledge, — its acquisition, use, preservation, transmission, and growth — which serves as the means to the ends of medicine, i.e., to the prevention and treatment of disease, the alleviation of suffering, the maintenance and care of the ill, and the preservation and enhancement of health.

I will therefore define medical knowledge as such a means, in a broad way, to include three main components: (1) theory, (2) technique, and (3) ideology. The theoretical component involves what is typically included as the didactic component in medical education, and more: the theory of the human organism — i.e., anatomy, physiology, pathology, epidemiology, the theories of disease and health, the basic natural scientific disciplines — biochemistry, biophysics, pharmacology, and the relevant formal disciplines, mathematics, statistics, the logic of medical reasoning in the contexts of clinical judgment and experimentation; and also the supporting social scientific disciplines which bear on the relation of medicine to law, to society, to technology and the policy sciences, to administration. The technical or *applied* component includes the clinical aspect of medical education, the skills and techniques of medical practice, the rules of art, the technology of instrumental artifacts designed and used in diagnostic and therapeutic activity, and the soft or cognitive technology of the analytic practices of epidemiology, preventive medicine, and public health.

The *ideological* component includes the norms and beliefs which characterize both the medical community and the society at large, with respect to the principles of right action, the concepts of the person and of society, the notions of obligations, duties, rights, and responsibilities, of justice in the procedures and decision-making activities — (including, therefore, all the considerations usually labelled "medical ethics" though I think this is too narrow a term, and also a misleading one). This component is not explicitly included in the medical curriculum, but has always been a part of traditional medical education, transmitted either by precept or example, or tacitly understood and learned as ideology. It is, more and more, becoming an explicit part of the supplemental medical school curriculum, in courses, symposia and programs in medical ethics, community medicine, philosophy of medicine, or in so-called 'medical humanities', or in considerations of medicine and values.

For analytic purposes, these three components may be characterized linguistically and epistemologically as (1) propositional knowledge — i.e., "knowing that . . . ", (2) skills — i.e., "knowing how", and (3) propositional attitudes — i.e., beliefs. The second and third, at least, may be said to have, in Polanyi's terms, a tacit dimension [1]. I would argue that the first does, as well, but will not press the point here.

In view of this characterization of medical knowledge, what does it mean to say that medical knowledge is a social product? At the simplest level, it is to say that it is produced socially, i.e., that its production involves the participation and cooperation of many individuals, and that these individuals enter into specific forms of social relations in producing it. Like any social product, then, medical knowledge represents, in its very coming into being, and in its structure, the social relations and processes involved in its production. To use a simple analogy, any product of human activity of this sort, say a food product, or a bridge or an automobile, involves the cooperative activity of designers or planners, producers of the raw materials (e.g., food growers, miners), fabricators or processors and transporters, merchandisers, etc. These activities in turn involve the whole network of support functions — social and legal structures, educational systems, other forms of production — e.g., machine tools, or the production of the means of production — within which food production, bridge-building, or automobile manufacture take place.

But here we are concerned with *knowledge* as a product, and specifically with medical knowledge, i.e., not simply with the production of things. That such knowledge is a *product of human activity* means that it is "made", i.e., brought into being by cognitive activity. it does not simply exist in nature, but is a social artifact. How shall one characterize it? Does it "exist", so to speak, in the minds of the people who possess it? Or is it instead the record or imprint of the results of cognitive acquisition in, e.g., books? Is it a "set of facts", whatever those are, or "a set of true statements", i.e., is it a linguistic entity? Or again, if we distinguish so-called propositional knowledge or knowing that some proposition or statement is true, from practical knowledge or skill — i.e., knowing *how*, does such practical knowledge "exist" *in* the acquired skills of practitioners, embodied, so to speak, in their know-how? Further, how is such knowledge acquired, how is it preserved, how is it transmitted or taught? Short of a fuller epistemological theory of cognitive acquisition and cognitive *praxis*, I want only to point to the social character of this knowledge, in all of these contexts. Only individuals use knowledge. But such individual human beings are essentially social, in their cognitive praxis, whether in learning to walk, to speak a language, or in acquiring social or technical skills — and certainly, in acquiring theoretical understanding, or propositional knowledge.

The point of these general considerations is to establish that medical knowledge, like any other, is not only a social artifact, in its genesis or coming into being, but is, in its acquisition and use, a social activity. And the importance of this for my subsequent discussion is that it sets the frame-work for the analysis of rights and responsibilities with regard to such knowl-edge. Let me proceed then to a more specific analysis of this knowledge as a social product in *medicine*, and of the social character of the cognitive activity in which it is acquired and used.

4. GENESIS, USE AND TRANSMISSION OF MEDICAL KNOWLEDGE: A MODEL OF SOCIAL INTERACTION

An ontological analysis of what medical knowledge *is*, what sort of entity it is, may characterize it as embodied in the rational understanding and in the skills of those who study and practice medicine. We may say that it is *possessed* by the medical community, and that it is this very possession that demarcates or defines the medical community. The social means by which such possession is attested to is the certification of the practitioner or re-searcher, i.e., the social decision to permit someone to practice medicine. Now of course, one may acquire and possess this knowledge, and even use it in practice *without* certification, e.g., the M.D. degree and license. But the organization of medical education and the regulation of requisite competence as a condition of practice has always functioned, in varying historical periods and in different cultures, as the social means of defining medical knowledge itself. And therefore, these institutional forms of medical education and medical practice have come to shape the definition of what is properly called medical knowledge. Now this, as it turns out, is an interesting fact, because it means that what *will* be considered a part of medical knowledge, in one setting, will *not* be so considered in another. For example, so-called "folk medicine", in Western cultures, is not considered, as such, part of medical knowledge proper; and the current inclusion of both traditional and "Western" or "scientific" medicine in the medical curriculum in China now incorporates, as medicine "proper", what was at one time excluded. So too, alternative or even rival traditions of what is properly medical knowledge have vied with each other, for hegemony, throughout the history of medicine, in the charac-terization of this knowledge. The very definition of what constitutes medical knowledge then may be seen to be *not* simply an epistemological question, context free, but a normative question of what it is that is requisite to certify competence and to license practice.

It may be seen to follow, then, that such socially and historically differential determinations of medical knowledge proper yield alternative epistemologies of medicine. That is to say, where medical knowledge is regarded as the acquisition and possession of an institutionalized group, i.e., the profession of medicine, as it is defined in a given society, or a given culture — and where such an institutional group comes to determine the conditions of certification and licensure, the dominant epistemology of medicine will reflect a certain view, or an ideology, of the nature of that knowledge itself.

Specifically, if medical knowledge is treated as that which is acquired and used by those individuals who constitute the certified professional group, then the role of those outside this group, in the acquisition and use of such knowledge, will be ignored, or denied. The social interaction in which medical knowledge is attained will be seen to consist solely in the infra-professional activities of medical education and training, and in the research of biomedical scientists or the clinical practice of physicians.

What alternative is there, however? Let me examine a different model of the *genesis* of medical knowledge, to make a point. The interaction in which medical experimentation and therapeutic practice takes place includes not only the researcher or clinician, and not even only supporting staff, e.g., laboratory assistants, nurses, but obviously, the research and clinical subjects — those who are either experimental subjects, or patients. Now it seems patently odd to claim that such subjects contribute to the acquisition of medical knowledge in any way, except as sources of information for the actual cognitive activity of researchers and physicians. The subject's or patient's contribution is passive here, and even the etymology of the terms "subject" and "patient" suggests and reinforces this view. The consequence is that the conditions of the *acquisition* of this knowledge also set the terms for defining its *possession*, and thus also, its *control*. Yet, though one may argue that the subject's contribution makes some claim to participation in the acquisition of this knowledge, even if in a passive way, it would be odd to say that such subjects "possess" the knowledge. There is, presumably, no deliberate cognitive acquisition on the part of subjects or patients.

Now one may make two small, but important points here: first, that experimental subjects and patients sometimes do come to learn something from participation in experiments and from clinical treatment. Moreover, where information is not simply available as signs, or as somatic data, but is symptomatic and is available only through the subject's or patient's verbal reports, whether in experiments, in history-taking, or diagnostic procedure, some cognitive contribution is being made. Moreover, there is no intrinsic limit to what subjects or patients may come to understand, or learn, by way of more sophisticated knowledge of a medical situation, or more sophisticated judgment in the offering of data. Second, the cognitive concept "possession of knowledge" is not essentially linked to the concept of control of this *as a possession*, i.e., in the derived sense of a claim to control over its use, or as proprietary right. Yet, in point of social and historical fact, cognitive possession of medical knowledge has come to be taken in modern capitalist societies as a basis for proprietary right to the control and use of this knowledge — or more sharply still, such knowledge has come to be regarded not as *social* property, but as the private property of its possessors. One may argue that it is the medical community as a *whole* which possesses and dispenses this knowledge; but in fact, in clinical practice where the still dominant mode of treatment is the one-on-one, physician-patient relation, and where a fee is paid, the possession of this knowledge as private property, and the sale of its use as a service, marks off the social character of this knowledge as owned by, and dispensable by *individuals*. To the degree that treatment is given by a group of physicians, or by a clinic, or comes under some plan of medical insurance, this simpler private model is mediated. But in general, one may say that medical knowledge, though it is socially produced, is privately owned and the use of it dispensed as the private property of the physician.

These two points, concerning the contribution of experimental subjects and clinical patients to the social product, and the transformation of cognitive possession of medical knowledge by individuals, to the economic possession of this knowledge as private property, and sale of its use as a service, i.e., as a commodity, provides a wedge for some of the more perverse things I wish to say.

What is said here about the social character of the genesis or production of medical knowledge may be elaborated with respect to its use and its transmission. For example, the use of medical knowledge may be seen to involve the network of consultative and group practices, the interdependence of physicans, nurses, paraprofessionals, social workers, and, especially in institutional practice, clinics, hospitals, community health centers, etc., a wider interdependence on maintenance and operational staff, community resources, administrative structures, etc. Here too, patients and their families, the community funding and regulative agencies all participate in the practice, i.e., in the uses of this knowledge either directly, or as facilitating it, in various degrees, from the center to the periphery. With respect to the preservation and transmission of medical knowledge, here too the cognitive artifacts — books, libraries, laboratories, medical schools, supporting liberal arts and technical education, and public education in health care, i.e., in preventive and therapeutic resources — all constitute a social matrix in terms of which acquired knowledge is stored, taught, disseminated.

Thus, in these three aspects of medical knowledge, its genesis or acquisition, its use, and its preservation and transmission, the context is inescapably social, and becomes more and more so. The individualist model of the lone physician in an office practice, as the locus of medical knowledge in these three respects, was always a myth or, at best, a radical abstraction; but it is no longer viable even as a vision of the golden age of medicine.

The social model serves, then, as a basis for an examination of the relation of the "possession" of medical knowledge to the question of the rights, risks and responsibilities of the "possessors".

Let me present my argument briefly, first, so that its outline is clear:

The possession of medical knowledge becomes the ground for the right to use and control this knowledge, when such cognitive possession becomes transformed into the social and economic reality of proprietary right. The physician has become, paradigmatically, the owner, agent, and dispenser of this knowledge, and this activity then is taken to constitute the practice of medicine. However, the *social* character of this property, despite its apparent privatistic form, makes itself felt in at least seven important ways:

(a)   through the internal guild-character of the medical profession, inherited from medieval models of professional, trade and craft practices;

(b)   through the regulative agency of the state, including its legislative and judiciary functions;

(c)   through the growth of institutional forms of medical practice — the clinic, the hospital, the research center, the community health center, the group practice, and through the administrative hierarchies which are correlated with such institutional forms;

(d)   through public funding of medical research, medical education, hospital-construction, insurance and welfare programs;

(e)   through the very development of specialization, which makes the individual physician, surgeon, nurse, health worker, part of a collective, both in consultative and in applied contexts — (e.g., the medical team). One may characterize this as the socialization of medical practice, through the growing interdependence of medical practitioners on each other;

(f)   through the rapidly developing interdependence of so-called scientific medicine, or biomedical and pharmaceutical research and clinical practice; and the growing dependence of medical practice on biomedical technology;

(g)   through the development of patients' rights, and of the social, political, and economic roles of patients (and of prospective patients, namely, the public at large) in setting limits on, and participating both in medical decision-making and in decision-making about medicine.

Thus, the contemporary private forms of medical practice, i.e., of the use and control of medical knowledge, come into sharper and sharper conflict with social modes of medical practice, internally; and with social influences and constraints upon this practice, externally. This sets the context for a reexamination of rights, risks, and responsibilities. And here too, medicine has a mixed historical heritage. At one time, rights were granted, risks assumed, and responsibilities assigned by the profession itself. It was, on the surface at least, self-regulating, and self-legitimating. Of course, the guild itself often had its patents and privileges conferred by a king, or a ruling body, or in theocratic societies, by claimed descent from a god (e.g., Apollo). But the legitimation of the authority and relative autonomy of the profession, and of its individual practitioners, was based on knowledge, i.e., on cognitive competence in the theory and practice of medicine. The intrusion upon this authority and autonomy, insofar as it characterizes the present crisis, derives from the increasingly explicit social character of medical knowledge. Therefore, a reassessment of rights and responsibilities starts from an analysis of these very *grounds* for the legitimation of these rights and the assumption of these risks and responsibilities.

My argument is that such rights and concomitant responsibilities are based on the property-forms which have come to characterize the possession of medical knowledge. Therefore, I will proceed to sketch three such property-forms which have historically defined the rights of possession and use of medical knowledge, and which continue to exist simultaneously in contemporary practice. I will go on to argue that these property-forms are often in conflict. More importantly, I will argue that the property-form of medical knowledge is in radical transition; and that therefore, an assessment of the emerging property-form demands a radical reassessment and reformation of rights and responsibilities in medicine, as they are now understood.

To the question of rights, then:

First, a general remark. Rights are relations. A right inheres in a person or some entity, but it is a right against another person or thing, or a right to something. Therefore, a right is a relation of some entity (and I would hold that only persons have rights) to some other entity. In legal theory, the distinction is made between rights against persons and rights against things; i.e., *jus ad personam* and *jus ad rem*. Without entering into the issue here, let me simply state that I will take all rights to be rights against persons, and that rights against things translate into relations of right and duty among persons. This is important since property-rights are often regarded as rights *ad rem*, but I will regard these also as rights *ad personam*, i.e., describable in terms of social relations among persons, even when these relations are embodied or reified as relations of persons to things, or in relations to institutions, or among institutions. The reason for this insistence should become clear, since I will argue that rights, their concomitant responsibilities, and their correlative duties depend on the concrete, historical property-forms, and that in medical contexts, it is the property-form which the possession of medical knowledge takes which determines the rights, duties, and responsibilities.

One may ask: If rights and responsibilities are based on possession of medical knowledge, this account refers only to the rights and responsibilities of medical practitioners and researchers; but then, where do the rights and responsibilities of patients, or of society come in? Surely, these are rights against those who have the knowledge, and cannot therefore derive from possession of this knowledge. For example, the right to health, if there is one, does not require, as its foundation, the possession of medical knowledge; nor does the right to treatment. These may derive from the general character of human rights, or social rights. I will argue, against such a view, that the *right* to health or to treatment remains an abstract and ungrounded right, if it is approached in this way. Rather, such rights derive their concrete character from the correlative duties of medical practitioners. Abstract "rights", where no claim can be made against a correlative duty or obligation, remain empty rights. The right to health without the means to satisfy this right is no right at all or remains an empty formal right or is at best a right to the creation of such means.

One more distinction, by way of introducing this discussion: We may distinguish duties from responsibilities in the following way: In the relation between persons, A has a right against B where B has a correlative duty to A. But in having a given right, A also assumes a concomitant responsibility in the exercise of that right, *if* (and perhaps *only if*) the right is embedded in a teleological context. For example, the right to practice medicine entails the responsibility of practicing medicine to some end, if medicine is defined as an essentially teleological practice. Where the end of medicine is taken to be the prevention and cure of disease, the care of the ill, the alleviation of suffering, the maintenance and enhancement of health, then the right which the possession of medical knowledge grants, to use and control this knowledge, in one or another of the social forms of property rights, carries with it the responsibility to use it to these ends, and presumably, to do so in some optimal or just way. Thus, the use of medical knowledge in the service of any other ends is not the fulfilling of the concomitant responsibilities. Such other ends may be benign – e.g., earning a living, satisfying one's curiosity, etc.; or may, in turn, be subsidiary ends which are instrumental in fulfilling the larger end, as, e.g., the satisfaction of one's curiosity may be instrumental in improving medical care or increasing medical knowledge to the benefit of health. But such activity *in itself* does not fulfill the responsibility. Where such other ends are in *conflict* with the ends of medicine, then of course, they are malignant. So, for example, the use of medical knowledge for the sake of social domination, or to the detriment of the health of patients, or use which does not aim at improving their condition, is not, properly speaking, the practice of medicine at all, since it does not accord with the norms which define that practice. (Here, I am borrowing from Alasdair MacIntyre's definition of the norms of a practice.) The insurance company physician or the manufacturing company doctor, whose end is principally the screening of eligible and ineligible insurance risks, or workers for a job, is working for the ends of the company, and not those of medicine. Whether his/her activity is benign or malignant depends of course on how these other ends are characterized; but properly (and normatively) speaking, such a doctor is not practicing medicine in the sense of realizing the responsibilities which are entailed by the rights conferred by an essentially teleological practice.

As against duties, therefore, responsibilities inhere in the claimers of rights, with respect to the exercise of these rights. Duties, by contrast, inhere in those against whom someone else has a claim, by virtue of the right which this other person has. A, as a medical practitioner, has a right to the use of his or her medical knowledge and a concomitant responsibility in the exercise of this right, to fulfill the ends which the norms of the practice command. B, as a patient, or as "society at large", i.e., as any person bound to respect A's rights, has the duty to permit A to practice, *and* to see that the conditions for this practice are provided.

Now this latter duty derives from the fact that the ends of the practice are not simply those of the practitioner, but the common ends shared by both practitioners and patients or prospective patients, i.e., society at large. Medicine as a social activity, or medical knowledge as a social product, is therefore an activity which is engaged in by the society *as a whole*, with respect to the human need for medicine, and not simply by medical practitioners. The practice of medicine, in this sense, is a social practice defined by the *relations* of medical personnel to patients (and to the public at large, with regard to prevention) by correlative duties on the part of the rest of society. But the patients' or the public's rights are likewise matched by correlative duties which the medical practitioner, or the possessor of medical knowledge, has to patients and the public; and these duties also express the responsibilities which physicians have in the exercise of their rights as physicians.

The question of rights depends, as I have said, on the nature of possession of the knowledge; but possession in turn depends on the mode of acquisition of this knowledge. We may make a distinction between possession and property here. "Possession" refers to the actual "having" of medical knowledge in epistemological terms, i.e., having acquired the theory, skills and ideology, which mark the ability to practice medicine, to make competent judgments, to know how to proceed in a medical situation, and to act in accordance with the norms of the practice. "Property", by contrast, concerns the right to use and/or to control the use of these means. For medical knowledge is here considered not an end in itself, but rather a means to an end. It is essentially instrumental, and its acquisition is for the sake of its use towards that end. Thus, if we separate the concept of possession from that of property, it may be the case that a possessor of such knowledge may not, in fact, have a right to its use, or control over its use. He or she may simply be an instrument, controlled by or at the disposition of another person or institution. On the other hand, one's possession of this knowledge may lead to a right to its use, not as one's own property, but as a fiduciary, i.e., as someone who has been entrusted with the use of this property, under an agreement as to the conditions of such use. In this case, the right to use or practice is in effect a privilege, which may be withdrawn upon failure to meet the fiduciary conditions. Finally, the possession may be identical with the right, in which case possession and property are extensionally identical. In this case, having the knowledge gives one the right to its use and control as one's private property. It may then be put at the disposition of others at the choice of the owner, as such private property; or disposition of its use may be sold as a commodity.

If there is suspicion of an analogy here, between these three forms of property-right and social or economic systems of property-right, the analogy is purely intentional. One may draw the analogy in the following terms: the first form of possession may be seen as akin to slave systems in which the slave has no possession but his/her own body, and no property right to that possession or to its use. The slave is an *instrumentum vocis*, (a speaking instrument), in Aristotle's terms, and the property of another. The second form is that of communal or feudal property, in which individual use, e.g., of land, is on the condition of certain obligation to the commune or the feudal lord, and the right to use of one's possession is a fiduciary right. One is "elected" to this right by membership in the commune or the fief. Medieval guilds institutionalized this mode of "right to practice" one's profession or trade, and it remains a dominant mode, at least formally, in the professions, e.g., law, medicine, education. Thus, either the guild itself, or in other more centralized forms, the community as a whole, or its ruling group, i.e., the state — licenses and regulates the practice, and may withdraw such a right to practice if the agreed-on conditions of the use of one's professional knowledge are violated. The third form of private or individual ownership, with the concomitant right to use, or control the use of medical knowledge, is in fact the classic model of the free-exchange system of capitalism, where property exchanges for property through the medium of money, by the consent of exchangers. Medical knowledge or rather disposition over its use in this context is a commodity, exchangeable for a fee, in the market-place.

The peculiar thing about medical practice is that it is caught up in all three of these forms of property-right and represents a complex historical palimpsest of these modes. For example, nursing, as a component of medical practice, is to a great extent still caught in the "slave economy" of purely instrumental use: the exercise of the nurses' functions remains under the control of the physician or the hospital administration. The possession of knowledge in this case is not the same as control over its use, as property. Yet at the same time, the nurse, working for a wage or a salary, is free to choose or refuse the position in which this knowledge is used, and is at the same time licensed to use this knowledge, and thus falls under the fiduciary model as well. The practicing physician is identified with membership in a guild, which is self-regulating and self-legitimating, in setting conditions of certification. At the same time, the society, or its ruling bodies (i.e., the state, the legislature and the courts), are also involved in regulation, licensure, and review, so the social characteristics of possession and use of medical knowledge are revealed in the criss-crossing jurisdictions of the guild and the society. In addition, medical insurance, private or public, also intrudes upon the exercise of the proprietary rights of practitioners. In effect, then, medical practice, the exercise of medical knowledge as a human activity, may be characterized, in systematic terms, as an eclectic mess: Social in its modes of production and practice; private in its explicit proprietary form; in a process of transformation under the influences of a mix of social jurisdictions (the guild, the state, the populace at large), and by its interactions with technology and science.

In the consideration of rights, then, I have argued that such rights are grounded in the social nature of the production and possession of medical knowledge, and of its use and transmission. We may now summarize the schema I have been proposing, in reply to three questions: (1) What are rights? (2) Who possesses rights? (3) What is the appropriate property form of this possession?

(1) Rights are social relations among persons, coordinated with concomitant responsibilities and correlative duties.

(2) Individuals therefore have rights, duties and responsibilities — but obviously only *in* such relations to other individuals. But because such relations are social, and take on their concrete historical forms as property rights, the appearance is that rights also inhere in institutions (e.g., in corporate bodies, which represent practices or common interests or purposes, and which embody the norms of such practices); or that society *as such* has rights. These are hypostatizations of the social forms of relations of rights among individuals.

(3) The appropriate form of the possession of rights is grounded and derives its legitimation from the social nature of the production and possession of medical knowledge. I have argued that medical practice is an activity of a whole society, i.e., a network of individuals *in* social relations, and that the exercise of the use of this knowledge by, e.g., physicians or health professionals generally is only a part of that activity. Thus, in the relations of rights, in medical contexts, the right of possession is a right of the society as a whole, as the social producers, users, and participants in the use of this knowledge. The appropriate property form is therefore no longer either that of the "slavery" model, in which the possessor has *no* rights in the possession, but is merely an instrument of the use of this knowledge which belongs as property to someone else (the "owner", whether an individual, or an institution, or the state);

nor is the appropriate property form the medieval guild form whose
normative structures and functions are still preserved in contemporary
medical practice. That is to say, the production and possession of
medical knowledge does not simply give the practitioner a fiduciary
right to exercise this knowledge, or to participate in the practice
as a privilege or right of licensure or membership in the guild.
Further, the early capitalist model of private ownership of this
knowledge as a commodity, and the private control over the use
and exchange of this commodity, as the product of one's own
individual acquisition, is also no longer coordinate (if it ever was)
with the appropriate property-form.

Instead, I am proposing a model of medical knowledge as social property,
both as it is socially produced, socially used and participated in, and socially
transmitted.

That is about as perverse as one can get, I think. For it proposes not
"socialized medicine" (though this may be one possible form of the practice,
and there are wildly alternative and even mutually exclusive models of such
a form); but rather *socialist medicine*, which is a different and more fundamental conception.

Now let me allay some fears and ward off some misinterpretations. Socialist medicine does not mean state control, since I draw a sharp distinction
between "state" and "society". It also does not mean "free medical care"
or "free medical education" or "free malpractice insurance", since what
has a value has a price, in the system of social exchange, which is not likely
to be replaced even in a socialist economy. Nor am I naïve enough to suppose
that socialist medicine can be practiced in a capitalist economy. It is not
even clear how it could be practiced in a socialist economy. I am not proposing an *applied* model, of the reorganization of medical practice; but
rather the norms which would guide the formulation of such applications,
given changed circumstances and the possibility for the implementation
of such applications. What I am proposing is a normative model — i.e., a
theoretical model of how the property-relations or property-forms of medical practice can be brought into conformity with the emerging and already
existing nature of this practice as essentially social — both in the applied
forms of medical practice and in its institutional structures, but *not yet* in
its property-forms.

I believe that the current crisis in medicine cannot be resolved by *ad hoc*
or patchwork measures. But I also believe that the crisis will require, and

cannot avoid, piecemeal reforms, changes, restructurings, and innovations, in each of its component parts.

I also believe that a fundamental resolution of the crisis does require a fundamental social change in the property-forms of the society as a whole and that without this, the crisis will simply deepen, or if resolved in one respect, will reappear in another form. But that is a question for a major treatment of the political economy of medicine, and I do not pretend to even begin to offer that here. Instead, I mean only to make a foray in the interests of putting such questions on the agenda and articulating some of the conceptual issues. It seems to me that in dealing with specific and concrete aspects of the crisis in medicine, the emergence of a coherent normative model of medical knowledge, in the broad definition I have offered of it here, as theory, technique and ideology, will help to show how one aspect of the crisis relates to the others; and therefore, that a coherent model is needed as a guide to the understanding of the ontology and the diagnosis of the crises, and the therapeutic measures which are needed to resolve it.

5. CONCLUSIONS

The model of medical knowledge as a social product leads to an analysis of rights, risks and responsibilities in terms of this social character. This does not give answers to the questions raised by the contemporary crisis of medicine which I posed at the outset. Rather, what I have attempted is a sketch of a systematic approach to these questions in terms of the social model; not an attempt to impose a social or socialized matrix from above, but rather an explicit recognition of the pluralistic and often conflicting character of the social jurisdictions.

But *if* medicine is a teleological practice whose end is the health of individuals, and through this, the well-being of society, then the *normative* character of this knowledge commands a normative characterization of rights, risks, and responsibilities with regard to *this* end. The question to be asked, then, is not "Is it good for the profession?" or "Does it serve to ensure social stability?" but rather "Is it good for people? Does it provide for the delivery of high quality health care maximally to the greatest number?" The right to the acquisition, use, control and transmission of medical knowledge is a *social* right; the risk is a social risk; the responsibility a social responsibility. The forms which such social relations (rights, risks and responsibilities) will take, therefore have to be measured against the values of the practice, defined in these social terms.

Boston University
Boston, Massachusetts

BIBLIOGRAPHY

1. Polanyi, M.: 1958, *Personal Knowledge*, University of Chicago Press, Chicago.

KENNETH F. SCHAFFNER

BIOMEDICAL KNOWLEDGE: PROGRESS AND PRIORITIES

1. INTRODUCTION

In the present essay I am going to begin with some comments on the essays
of Professors Weissmann [24] and Wartofsky [22]. I will then go on to
develop the outlines of what I take to be a more realistic and adequate
picture of the process of genesis, dissemination, and application of biomedical
knowledge in the context of the current system of health care and in medical
research institutions.

The essays of Weissmann and Wartofsky are two rather different approaches to the common theme of biomedical knowledge. Weissmann considers the *conditions* of new knowledge, especially the moral, or better, the
"esthetic" conditions, and argues for the moral freedom of basic scientific
research. Wartofsky, on the other hand, analyzes the *process* of knowledge,
namely its generation, dissemination, and practical application. He then goes
on to consider the moral implications of his account of the process of medical
knowledge for both health-care delivery and the reward structure of the
health-care system. Both papers are essentially normative and are also clearly
utopian. Both represent idealized and, as I will argue, overly narrow perspectives of the conditions, the process of generation, and the practical and
clinical applications of newly acquired biomedical knowledge.

2. WEISSMANN'S ESTHETIC VIEW OF THE BIOMEDICAL SCIENCES

At the beginning of his essay, Weissmann expresses his doubt that the scientist can answer the question, "what new knowledge is needed in the biomedical sciences?" In place of that question he proposes "to consider those
values which, for a working experimentalist, underlie our *need* to know".
In this section I will primarily address myself to this latter question, but will
return to the suppressed question in Section 6.

Following and modifying Thomas Nagel's five-fold typology of values
[16], Weissmann distinguishes between "utilitarian" and "esthetic" values
[24]. The former encompasses practical consequences: benefits and injuries
to all sentient beings. The benefits of medical research are taken as typical

131

*William B. Bondeson, H, Tristram Engelhardt, Jr., Stuart F. Spicker and Joseph M. White,
Jr. (eds.), New Knowledge in the Biomedical Sciences, 131–151.*
Copyright © 1982 by D. Reidel Publishing Company.

of such utilitarian values. "Esthetic Values", on the other hand, are instantiated by "the elegant experiment, the beautiful proof, the unshakable theory". Weissmann's central thesis is that the traditional view – the view that pursuit of esthetic concerns by a scientist, *"or science for its own sake"*, generates new knowledge which "could not help but be useful to the general welfare . . . " – is still a viable position. This is the thesis that basic research should not be constrained by practical considerations or encumbered by legal guidelines. Taken to its logical (but actually illogical) extreme, such a view merges with the late Jacques Monod's *ethic of knowledge*, by which human existence is authenticated by a pursuit of knowledge for its own sake ([15], pp. 140–142).

Weissmann does not go as far as Monod; he tempers his argument for scientific autonomy by ultimately admitting toward the end of his essay that "of course, our science should not design experiments that are trivial, dangerous, or dehumanizing". I suspect that this qualifier introduces a potential inconsistency into his main argument, but I shall postpone comment on this point until later.

Weissmann is quite concerned about the attack on the traditional freedom of science to follow its own esthetic bent. The attack, he notes, comes from a variety of sources – environmentalists, humanists, and the new theologians – and it has culminated in "the fuss over recombinant DNA". The recombinant DNA debate does raise the specter of a governmental authority laying down proscriptions concerning what types of experiments it is permissible to perform. Weissmann is critical, correctly I think, of those who create "scenarios of gloom", but he is also opposed to any "professional code" which might be imposed on research scientists. His criticism is specifically directed against a suggestion by June Goodfield that scientists might consider creating a professional guild and in addition become subject to the laws of malpractice [7]. Weissmann takes exception to this proposal for singling out scientists, since he believes that we cannot say for certain that "the contributions of Fichte, Nietzsche, and Spengler had less grave consequences for the orderly flow of social progress than even the most lurid results imaginable of our biologic inquiries . . . ". He suggests that professionalizing science along the models of medicine or law would be tantamount to censorship – for the creative scientist cannot be bound by traditional rules which is the role of malpractice rules.

3. CRITICISM OF WEISSMANN'S POSITION

It is here that I part company with Weissmann's congenial libertarian thesis.

In my view, scientists are already subject to malpractice rules, viewed in their most general form — as evidenced by the application of the law of torts to actions which result in harm to person or property through negligence on the part of scientists. If the preponderance of evidence indicates a causal chain of events resulting in such harm can be traced to a scientist's experiments; if the scientist negligently violated usual safeguards, and was a proximate cause of harm to person and/or property; and if it can be shown that the scientist was negligent in controlling a hazardous experiment, for example, then suit could be brought.[1]

It has been argued in several recent articles that neither ethical principles nor constitutional law, nor traditional constraints of academic freedom, are persuasive bases for complete scientific autonomy. Hans Jonas has pointed out that

the boundaries between theory and practice have become blurred . . . . The two are now fused in the very heart of science itself, so that the ancient alibi of pure theory, and with it the moral immunity it provided, no longer hold [11].

Harold P. Green writing in the *Newsletter on Science Technology and Human Values* [8] has pointed out that scientific freedom can have no greater claim than the First Amendment freedoms of press and of speech, and these we know are construed as limited and constrained by other constitutionally guaranteed rights. Walter P. Metzger, in a searching historical inquiry into the concept of "academic freedom", does *not* find that this notion extends to and supports complete and unlimited freedom of scientific inquiry [14]. Rather, he argues, scientific freedom is a separate species involving rights and limits of its own. Such rights and limits, Metzger claims, would be based on scientific freedom's *own* theoretical formulation, with "its own machinery and procedures for detecting and reproving an offense" ([14], p. 108). Metzger does not, however, provide any detailed suggestions for such machinery and procedures.

Would such machinery and procedures amount to censorship and severely retard scientific progress? The question is a difficult one and for the foreseeable future there will be competing answers. My own reply, to be developed in more detail in Section 6, is that some guidelines are desirable. The NIH has issued such guidelines and has several times altered the guidelines as well as the machinery to implement them. Authority for initial approval of recombinant DNA experiments is now delegated to institutional committees.

This appears to follow the precedent established for research on human subjects, where initial approval has to be obtained from the Institutional

Review Board (IRB) designed to protect human subjects. Having audited a number of these meetings at different institutions, I know that such committees are far from infallible and that they do at times introduce some delays. They are, however, necessary. Whether IRB's for recombinant DNA research will turn out in the long run to be as necessary is questionable, but it would seem wise to begin such work cautiously.

In his reflections on the need for *some* controls restricting science from designing experiments that are "trivial, dangerous, or dehumanizing", Weissmann maintains that "these adjectives are best defined by the consensus of society at large". "And", he adds, "if that consensus be justly derived we can expect that the community of scientists, as citizens, will agree."

This position suggests that Weissmann needs to elaborate on what for him constitutes a *justly derived consensus* in the recombinant DNA debate. For example, is the working out of guidelines through the NIH and the political process a necessary and/or sufficient condition for such "just derivation"? I believe Weissmann needs to specify such mechanisms and criteria in order to outflank a potential inconsistency between his fundamentally libertarian position and his admission that some control over research is required.

This need for elaboration is consistent with a thesis which I have argued for previously [2] and which is also espoused by other commentators on the issues of scientific progress and priorities, such as Harvey Brooks [1]. Basically, the thesis maintains that scientific progress can only be adequately understood if it is perceived from a *unified* internal and external point of view. Here I will understand by "internal" considerations those elements of scientific decision-making having to do with the stage of maturity of a theory, the sophistication and precision of experimental techniques, and various criteria of choice affecting these elements, such as relative simplicity. By "external" considerations I intend those elements such as political proscription, societal needs, a religiously engendered ethics, economic developments, patterns of funding by various foundations and agencies, and possibly even the peer pressure which judges some scientific areas as more exciting than others, though this factor begins to move toward the "internal" side. Weissmann's analysis is, according to the view I wish to defend in more detail, somewhat one-sided and utopian. Such a relatively narrow view can never fully present the conditions of scientific advance since it leaves out the social-support mechanisms without which science would cease to exist. Weissmann might rejoin that societal benefits have always flowed naturally from science following its own "esthetic" goals, but this would beg the question and is worse yet probably false. An examination of national funding patterns, both pre-World

War II and post-war, indicates that some perceived national need, such as a cure for cancer, national security or prestige, or an "energy crisis", is required to generate large-scale support for basic science research, support which is usually derivative of mission-oriented work.[3]

4. WARTOFSKY'S THEORETICAL MODEL OF SOCIALIST MEDICINE

Wartofsky's analysis leads us through "a brief account of the crisis in medicine" and into an argument for the need for a new *theoretical model* of medicine. This model focuses on "the nature of medical knowledge and the rights, risks, and responsibilities which are involved in its acquisition, possession and use". In his conclusion, Wartofsky suggests how the crisis in medicine with which he begins might admit of some resolution in terms of his new theoretical model.

Wartofsky's account of the "crisis in medicine" is an array of problems associated with contemporary health care delivery. To recapitulate his summary, he notes that the elements of the crisis are (1) the questioning of the traditional concepts of the doctor-patient relationship, (2) the increases in demand for health-care services "beyond the limits of presently available resources", as well as a series of "special problems". These special problems are multitudinous and include

federal and state regulation, legislative and judicial incursions upon the heretofore sacrosanct preserves of medical decison-making in such traumatic contexts as abortion, terminal care, and limited access to new diagnostic and therapeutic technologies. ... the specter of patients' rights, the ethical and epistemological complexities of informed consent, fee-setting by the insurance industry, the impending periodic review of licensure, the prospects of national health insurance, the record-keeping explosion, the national maldistribution of health care facilities and medical personnel, and the malpractice mania. ([22], p. 113).

Wartofsky believes that the problems affecting contemporary medicine are "symptoms of a systemic disorder" and contends that "the diagnosis of the crisis cannot be limited to what can be reconstructed *ad hoc* from the signs, symptoms and complaints. "Rather," Wartofsky stresses, "what are needed are some theoretical models of medicine itself as a practice" ([22], p. 114).

Wartofsky's theoretical model is idealized and normative. It is based in part on a concept of a "teleological practice" and, in part, on Wartofsky's perception of the *social* character of medical *knowledge*.

A teleological practice is one which is a *means* to some (normative) end.

Medicine, to Wartofsky, "is a teleological practice whose end is the health of individuals, and through this, the well-being of society . . . " ([22], p. 129). This end, then, taken as a *value*, is the basis of "a normative characterization of rights, risks, and responsibilities" which are found in medical practice ([22], p. 129).

Medicine, however, is also a *cognitive* practice and one which is quintessentially *social*. From genesis to application, medical knowledge is located in interrelations among individuals and institutions. For example, in considering the *genesis* of medical knowledge, Wartofsky writes:

> The interaction in which medical experimentation and therapeutic practice takes place includes not only the researcher or clinician, and not even only supporting staff, e.g., laboratory assistants, nurses, but obviously, the research and clinical subjects − those who are either experimental subjects, or patients. Now it seems patently odd to claim that such subjects contribute to the acquisition of medical knowledge in any way, except as sources of information for the actual cognitive activity of researchers and physicians ([22], p. 119).

Wartofsky sees certain tensions or contradictions between the way in which medical knowledge is generated, passed on, and applied on the one hand, and the way it is *possessed* on the other. "In general," he writes, "one may say that medical knowledge, though it is socially produced, is privately owned and the use of it dispersed as the private property of the physician" ([22], p. 120). Wartofsky wishes to use this *social* dimension of medicine as the basis for a critique "of the 'possession' of medical knowledge [and its relation] to the question of the rights, risks and responsibilities of the 'possessors' " ([22], p. 121).

Wartofsky devotes a significant part of his essay to a discussion of rights, duties, and responsibilities, and also considers various property forms which can be found in contemporary medicine. I will not address myself to the details of these analyses except where the distinctions seem to affect centrally the main thesis of his essay. I take his thesis to be that the social nature of medical knowledge has important implications for an optimal form of medical practice.

Wartofsky argues that the end or goal of medicine enjoins certain general responsibilities on its practitioners:

> Where the end of medicine is taken to be the prevention and cure of disease, the care of the ill, the alleviation of suffering, the maintenance and enhancement of health, then the right which the possession of medical knowledge grants, to use and control this knowledge, in one or another of the social forms of property rights, carries with it the

responsibility to use it to these ends, and presumably, to do so in some optimal or just way ([22], p. 124).

This formulation does not exclude other ends, e.g., earning a living or satisfying one's curiosity from medicine, but the fulfillment of the responsibility is not accomplished by these other adventitious ends.

Medical practice can be realized in a number of different forms of property right, of which Wartofsky distinguishes three: (1) slave-economy, (2) communal, feudal, or guild-like, and (3) private or individual ownership. Wartofsky sees contemporary medicine "as a complex historical palimpsest of all three of these modes" and "as an eclectic mess" ([22], p. 126).

The central thesis of Wartofsky's essay, if I can isolate it from a number of reformulations, is that:

The appropriate form of the possession of rights is grounded, and derives its legitimation from the social nature of the production and possession of medical knowledge. I have argued that medical practice is an activity of a whole society, i.e., a network of individuals *in* social relations, and that the exercise of the use of this knowledge by, e.g., physicians or health professionals generally is only a part of that activity. Thus, in the relations of rights, in medical contexts, the right of possession is a right of the society as a whole, as the social producers, users, and participants in the use of this knowledge ([22], p. 127).

Wartofsky is, in his words

proposing a model of medical knowledge as social property, both as it is socially produced, socially used and participated in, and socially transmitted ([22], p. 128).

This, he contends, is *socialist* medicine, which he is concerned to distinguish from *socialized* medicine.

5. CRITICISM OF WARTOFSKY'S VIEWS

My criticisms of Wartofsky's paper fall into four parts: First, I shall question his general global approach to a diagnosis of the ills of contemporary medicine, suggesting instead that a more piecemeal approach is needed to these complex and multifaceted problems. Second, I shall question whether his own account of socialist medicine is sufficiently developed to determine, even in outline, what the conclusion of his analysis is, and whether it meets any conceivable conditions of adequacy. Third, I shall raise a question concerning the necessity of a "socialist" approach, pointing out that by the conditions of his own arguments, non-socialist forms of health-care delivery might well satisfy his sketch of the "norms" of medical practice. Fourth and finally, I shall ask if his argument is really sufficient to convince us of the socialist character of medicine, by comparing medicine with law; I shall contend that, though all the relevant features of medicine and law are identical, his argument that we need a "socialist" law is hardly convincing.

(a) Wartofsky argues that the development of a new theoretical model of medicine is a necessary condition for providing "the answers to the questions raised by the contemporary crisis in medicine". "Without the development of some such model," he maintains, "the response to the crisis will remain *ad hoc*, incoherent and anarchic. It will remain at the level of primitive, empirical, rule-of-thumb folk-medicine" ([22], p. 114).

Recall the range of items which constitute the contemporary crisis of medicine. As an alternative to Wartofsky's suggestion that a *unified* answer is a necessary condition, I suggest that contemporary medicine's crisis is a complex of independent and partially interdependent problems. An analysis of the source of the public's increasing expectations concerning medical care will not necessarily share a common cause with the rise of judicial incursions into medical decision-making. Problems with the allocation of scarce resources, such as kidney transplants, are largely independent of shifts in the doctor-patient relationship. To be sure, there are important interdependencies in health-care delivery problems: The increase in third-party payment coverage and the rapid increase in health care costs are such examples. However, it is not clear to me that a careful analytical and historical dissection of the array of problems which constitutes Wartofsky's contemporary crisis with an eye to determining where, in point of fact, there are such interdependencies is not a precondition to an adequate solution. In her scholarly and informative work, *American Medicine and the Public Interest* [21], Rosemary Stevens shows how the complex, contemporary health-care system arose out of various influencing factors and agencies, such as the U.S. Congress, the American Medical Association, the Flexner Report, the Association of American Medical Colleges, the various Blue Cross and Blue Shield Plans, the Medicare and Medicaid Acts, the National Institutes of Health, the Medical Specialty Boards, and numerous powerful individuals and pressure groups. An adequate "theoretical model" must be able to do justice to the rich complexity of our current health-care delivery system, and it is not clear that a number of *quite different theoretical models* will not be required to analyze the problems which face contemporary medicine.

(b) It would be useful to compare Wartofsky's socialist medicine model with some alternatives to determine how well the theoretical model might explain the source of the problems afflicting contemporary medicine, and to consider what solutions such a model might suggest. The reader of Wartofsky's essay will, however, find difficulties in any such attempts. The theoretical model is not, in my view, sufficiently well-developed to allow such comparison and assessment. It is very difficult to determine what socialist medicine amounts to in detail. Wartofsky has given us an interesting argument leading to an incompletely specified conclusion. I believe it behooves Wartofsky to fill in at least the outlines and contours of his theoretical model, in more detail than he has thus far, in order to enable his readers to appreciate the model and to ascertain the adequacy of his concept of socialist medicine.

(c) In the account which Wartofsky gives of the theoretical practice of medicine and its norms, he points out that the ends of medicine are "the prevention and treatment of disease, the alleviation of suffering, the maintenance and care of the ill, and the preservation and enhancement of health". These ends, together with his analysis of medicine as a social system, lead him to suggest that a socialist medicine will fulfill the ends of medicine most appropriately. The difficulty with this claim is that it does not constitute an argument but only a statement. An argument would show that there were (1) contradictions between any other model (say an individualistic private model) and the social character of medical knowledge with its specified ends, or (2) that a socialist model met more desiderata and met them better than did any other competing model.

It is unclear, however, that the best available (and affordable) medical system which meets the ends of medicine is *not* a socialist model but rather some "mixed economy" model. There may well be valuable features in certain traditional forms of health-care delivery and economic structures. For example, the individual doctor-patient relationship for primary care is thought to be very desirable by a number of patients. Also the traditional payment systems, for example, fee-for-service (for non-catastrophic illness), may provide the most equitable control on medical costs.

The point I want to make under this heading is that Wartofsky has not provided us with a sufficiently persuasive argument for a socialist model, even given his characterization of the end of medicine as a teleological practice.

(d) I argued that Wartofsky did not provide an argument for the *necessity* of a socialist model even given his premises. I now want to argue that, given his premises, they are *not sufficient* to license a socialist model. Rather, I would argue, the *plausibility* of the argument is largely based on covert intuitions, largely held by contemporary academics and many others, that health-care is sufficiently enough of a "right" that some socialist machinery is obligatory to translate that right into action. To put the thesis another way, arguments to the conclusion of the necessity of some form of a socialist medicine, I would submit, are dependent on a perception that the medical care system is sufficiently different from other professions because of the *type of service* it delivers, *not* because of its *structure*. Police and fire protection would be good examples: freedom from bodily and property harm are taken to be sufficiently basic rights that some type of socialist system providing for equitable protection is seen as mandatory. Wartofsky argues, however, from structure or form, and not from content. I claim that the argument will not go through without some additional covert premise, e.g., "health care is a right and ought to be provided by a socialist model." This, however, would be close to begging the question.

To see that the social structure of medicine is not sufficient to entail a socialist model of medicine, consider the same argument with the profession changed. This could be done with architecture or engineering, but perhaps the law is closer.[4]

We can first examine Wartofsky's argument for the genesis of medical knowledge. He begins by pointing out that knowledge arises not only from the activities of the researcher or clinician, but also from the activities of the supporting staff *and* from the patients. In law, the plaintiff and defendant (the legal analogues of the patient) are also involved as are the lawyer, judge, jury, and supporting staff. The plaintiff and defendant contribute to the law and are served by it (for example, Brown in *Brown vs. the Board of Education*, or Bakke in his recent case), as is the patient by the physician, even in the process of the generation of new knowledge. A similar argument could be made concerning the client of the engineer.

Secondly, we can examine Wartofsky's "seven ways" in which medical knowledge is *social*. In what follows, I will quote from his essay and place in parentheses the legal analogues.

Wartofsky notes (a) the guild character of the medical profession (Bar associations), and also (b) the regulative agency of the state (Bar examination for lawyers). Wartofsky also comments on (c) the institutional forms of medical practice — the clinic, the hospital, the group practice (the courts, the law firm), and on (d) the public funding of medical research (and of the judiciary system, and public prosecutors and public defenders). Wartofsky notes the development of specialization, the physican, surgeon, nurse, social worker, which makes each part of a collective (lawyer, corporate law specialist, clerk, court recorder). Wartofsky points out the interdependence of scientific medicine on science and technology (the analogy here would be to the dependence of the law on jurisprudential articles and ethics, for example Rawls's *A Theory of Justice* was cited in the Saikewicz decision).[5] Finally, Wartofsky maintains that the patients'-rights movement and the increasing role of the public in medical decision-making (rights to legal protection, store-front lawyers) underscores the social character of medicine.

I believe the analogy between law and medicine is complete in all relevant aspects: the question is whether a socialist model of law is entailed by such premises. I would contend that it is not and that we would not feel that a set fee-for-service system, for example, would be inappropriate in the legal context (in fact, it might even seem to be a consumer advance over the percentage system used in a number of cases) whereas we often have concerns about such a system in the health-care area. The difference, then, between law and medicine, if I am correct in my view, is based on the *product* rather than the *social structure*, and an argument based on the social structure of a profession is then not sufficient to entail a socialist structure for that profession.

I would readily grant the appropriateness of advances in legal practice which now provide public defenders for those accused individuals who are unable to pay, but note that such advances are based on the context of the service *and* the perceived seriousness of the situation and our collective sense of fairness, and not on the social structure of the law. The analogue in medicine would be the suggestion that some form of medical service be provided for individuals too poor to afford it, i.e., the State medicaid systems.

6. THE NET OF BIOMEDICINE

I shall now develop the skeleton of a complex schema of the biomedical sciences. Fleshing out this skeleton would require several major monographs, but I think that even in the rough outline form to which the space available restricts me, I can indicate that both Weissmann's and Wartofsky's perspectives are somewhat one-sided. In addition to developing this skeleton, which I shall argue is a complex interconnecting network of "internal" and "external" factors, I want to propose three theses. First, I shall maintain that the net of biomedicine is structured from modes of activity and strands of influence which involve both "internal", "external", descriptive, and prescriptive (or value-laden) features. Second, I shall argue that what *is decided* to be desirable new knowledge in the biomedical sciences arises from a partially designed, partially serendipitous interplay among many of the groups and actors represented as nodes in the net, and involves conceivable alternatives, desired options, possible actions and outcomes, and judgments of feasibility and likelihood, as construed by many different parties. Third, I want to propose that the most appropriate means of resolving contradictions, managing competition, and allocating intellectual and financial resources, will require further development of a pragmatic theory of valuation and its institutional implementation, and that neither a dogmatic libertarian nor a rigid socialist approach is likely to be adequate.

A. *The Value-laden Structure of the Net of Biomedicine*

Wartofsky is certainly correct when he stresses the complex social character of the biomedical sciences and underscores the many individuals — patients, researchers, and others — who are involved in the genesis of new knowledge in biomedicine. The structure and functioning of biomedicine is also shot through with normative features, which is congruent both with Wartofsky's notion of "teleological practice" and the important role of "esthetic values" discussed by Weissmann. Just how complex and interactive the net of bio-medicine is can perhaps best be presented by providing a figure schematized by those features that have traditionally been construed as "internal" and "external" to an analysis of science. In Figure 1, I have depicted the skeleton of the net and, where it was unclear if a factor was internal or external, I have placed it roughly midway between the two extremes.

The value-laden feature of those factors which condition research direc-tions and biomedical progress should be evident by inspection of Figure 1. "Esthetic values" or values or norms "internal" to the workings of scientists can be found at the left of the figure. "Esthetic values" cannot be pursued, however, without the cooperation of more external factors: projects must be funded, IRBs must approve of various activities, patients must be willing to participate in a study, and so on. Decisions made by those groups listed under the "external" rubric involve both descriptive aspects, for example the demography of diseases, as well as prescriptive features, for example, ethical and legal principles.

B. *What New Knowledge is Desirable in the Biomedical Sciences?*

It would be a gross oversimplification to locate a lone decision-making entity in the net of biomedicine. Decisions as to which research project to pursue are, of course, made by individual researchers, but such decisions

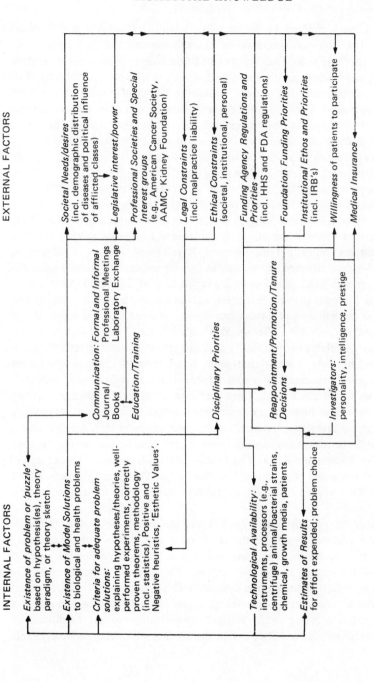

Fig I. The net of biomedicine. Not all possible arrows of influence have been entered, nor have the influences of differing strength been quantified. However, a sufficient number have been depicted that the net-like character and values and cognitive interactions should be evident.

are significantly affected by features like scientific feasibility and financial support. The political elements in biomedicine are also not controlling, since for anything more than short-term projects they require some tangible scientific and health-care results, whether such results be directly related to the project's original goals or be serendipitous fallout of considerable interest in their own right. It would not be to the point here to enter into an analysis of applied or mission-oriented research versus basic research. Suffice it to say that students of the history of the National Institutes of Health [19] have always noted that the significance of "practical advances" − such as the antibiotics and the discovery of the Salk and Sabin polio vaccines, or the hope of such practical advances as a cure for cancer − usually enter into decisions taken to fund basic research in the biomedical sciences.

A good example of the complex interaction of the various depicted factors in the net of biomedicine affecting the course of a basic science research project can be found in James Watson's *The Double Helix* [23]. Watson's interest was conditioned to an extent by his education under Luria. His meeting up with Crick was a complex result of post-doctoral support conditions and his own research interests, as was his meeting with Wilkins and attendance at Wilkins's seminar when Watson realized that the secret of the gene might be tractable: "Before Maurice's [Wilkins] talk", Watson wrote, "I had worried about the possibility that the gene might be fantastically irregular. Now, however, I knew that genes could crystallize; hence, they must have a regular structure that could be solved in a straightforward fashion."

Readers of Watson's book know just how complex the "straightforward fashion" was, and how the exigencies of personality, brilliance, serendipity (as well as the relentless "internal" constraints provided by the X-ray photographs and the tinker-toy atomic models) led first to failure and then to success for Watson and Crick. *The Double Helix* offers a microcosmic instantiation of a number (but not all) of the factors sketched in Figure 1, and supports the complex character of decision-making that affects biomedical progress.

It should be evident from Figure 1 and the double helix story that new biomedical knowledge will be the result of a large number of conditioning and causative social factors. What is less clear is how one decides *morally* what new knowledge should be pursued. The pursuit of purely scientific interests or essentially economic interests will not necessarily result in determining moral priorities of research projects. Neither, however, can such a realistic moral ordering occur without consideration of the likelihood of scientific interest and success, nor in the absence of an economically viable project, whether such economic conditions are direct (for example, immediate economic payoff) or indirect (via available grant support for the project). Weissmann's answer is, on my view, too simplistic, but an alternative is rather difficult to articulate clearly. I now turn to what types of feasible alternatives may exist in contrast to Weissmann's position and how priorities might be legitimated.

C. *The Need for a Theory of Valuation in Biomedical Science Policy*

I believe that the contributions of Weissmann and Wartofsky represent, in microcosmic form, the problems which attend attempts to generate a moral biomedical science policy which would articulate reasoned priorities or safeguards for biomedicine. Both Weissmann's and Wartofsky's positions are too narrow: they exclude too many of the determinative factors. To defend them by terming them "normative" is also insufficient, since except for staunch deontologists, the moral nature of actions is affected by the descriptive conditions and consequences of such actions.

From my point of view, what is lacking at the national (and international) level is sufficient attention to the amalgam of internal *and* external factors which condition biomedical progress, and a critical analysis and weighing of these factors individually and in concert. The biomedical scientist who desires to pursue a research program on purely "esthetic" grounds, without regard to any ultimate utilities and dangers, is as unrealistic as a Congressman mandating a victory in five years in the "war on cancer". Both points of view are necessary, however, and may even be pursued by individuals, but to be effective in the long run they can function only as initial positions — as partial inputs into a more comprehensive rational science policy.

It would be utopian to begin to sketch the outlines of a moral research policy for the biomedical sciences. On the basis of what has been argued to this point, an enormous amount of descriptive data must be analyzed and function as input before such a policy could emerge, and many contributions must be considered from the "external" side. I would, however, propose that a satisfactory and convincing moral policy can only be developed on the basis of an adequate moral epistemology and methodology. Such knowledge must function in tandem with concrete instantiations possessing the requisite details of data and arguments. My last point, then, will be to outline on what methodological and epistemological basis a moral policy can be constructed which takes into account the internal-external, and normative descriptive manifolds depicted in Figure 1.[6]

Basically, the theory of valuation I wish to urge comes from the natural-istic, humanistic, and pragmatic schools of philosophical inquiry, and is indebted to suggestions made in various places by C. S. Peirce, John Dewey, and C. I. Lewis. Let me first outline the general position very briefly. I shall then develop it in more detail and apply the theory of value to the issues of the present essay.

We can, following Dewey, distinguish between "prizings" and "appraisings". (The words are not important, though the concepts to which they refer are.) "Prizings" are those aspects of our experience toward which we gravitate and aim prior to critical and reflective thought; they are intuitively perceived as values. "Appraisings", on the other hand, are likings which are the outcome of a multilevel complex of prizings subjected to conscious scrutiny in which the conditions and consequences of possible actions are considered. The "good", that at which one *should* aim, is *constructed*: It is *defined* as "good". This process of *intelligent* choice, it can be argued, yields maximal individual and social *satisfaction*. The ethical theory is thus eudaemonistic in a very general sense. The approach considers given values as continually subject to scrutiny. It is a public approach in which arguments about the desirability of values and conflicts between incompatible values can be entertained.

Let us now attempt to develop and defend this position in some detail, and also to anticipate some objections. This elaboration will primarily draw from a number of Dewey's ethical writings, but will, I think, be congruent with similar pragmatic positions developed by C. S. Peirce and C. I. Lewis.

It is most appropriate to begin an elaboration of a pragmatic theory of valuation by noting that it ultimately rests on an *intuitionistic* basis.[7] Contrary to Lewis's intuitionistic position, however, the intuitions which one has of values are for Dewey — I think correctly — both *fallible* and *corrigible*, and also what I will term *multilevel.*

For Dewey, intuitions of value are "tertiary qualities" of nature, a term he borrowed from Santayana. In a defense of his moral theory against H. W. Stuart, Dewey wrote:

Instead of presenting that kind of mechanistic naturalism that is bound to deny the "reality" of the qualities which are the raw material of the values with which morals is concerned, I have repeatedly insisted that one theory of Nature be framed on the basis of giving full credence to these qualities just as they present themselves ([4], p. 580).

Common elements of these intuitions can be abstracted into what Dewey, in his *Theory of the Moral Life* [5] termed *principles*. These principles can also be given at the *beginning* of an ethical situation, being embodied in traditional moral codes, and in "legal history, judicial decisions, and legislative activity", as well as in the various sciences such as medicine, sociology, and economics, and also in rational philosophical theories of ethics ([5], pp. 22–25).

Taken as starting points, these principles can themselves be both prized and appraised in the light of other prizings and consequences. It is only if these principles take on the status of what Dewey called *rules*, that is, inflexible and incorrigible principles, that this form of intuitionism degenerates into traditional intuitionism, an ethical theory which Dewey saw as lending support to an ossified conservatism ([5], pp. 136–46).

We have, then, intuitions on the level of individual likings, and also on the level of principles. Conflicts and assessments are to be mediated by the experimental method, a method which Dewey contended is better than alternative methods such as authority, tradition, rationalism, or revelation. The experimental method is the action of intelligence such as we find employed in science. It would seen natural to conclude on the basis of the pragmatic theory of valuation as developed thus far that the *justification for the experimental method* is based on the same corrigible intuitionism which is encountered operating in the levels of concrete experience and principles.[8] If this reconstruction of Dewey's view is defensible, we are presented with a theory of valuation which is based on a multilevel and corrigible intuitionism. These "levels" are themselves almost certainly artificial divisions on the continuum of generality, certain aspects of which are at any one time presented with force, others of which are more remote. As time and experience change, different aspects of experience come more to the fore and others recede. These multilevel intuitions are thus always partial and may occasionally be flagrantly wrong, but they are not so unstable that an accretion of experience, which often passes for reflective and sensitive wisdom, is not the outcome of the process.

It is this view which I think is embodied in Dewey's pragmatic theory of value, a theory he summarized somewhat cryptically in his *Theory of Valuation* in the following manner:

These considerations lead to the central question: What are the conditions that have to be met so that knowledge of past and existing valuations becomes an instrumentality of valuation in formation of new desires and interests – of desires and interests that the test of experience show to be best worth fostering? It is clear upon our view, that no abstract theory of valuation can be put side by side, so to speak, with existing valuations as the standard for judging them.

The answer is that improved valuation must grow out of existing valuations, subjected to critical methods of investigation that bring them into systematic relations with one another. Admitting that these valuations are largely and probably, in the main, defective, it might at first sight seem as if the idea that improvement would spring from bringing them into connection with the one another is like recommending that one lift himself by his bootstraps. But such an impression arises only because of failure to consider how they actually may be brought into relation with one another, namely, by examination of their respective conditions and consequences. Only by following this path will they be reduced to such homogeneous terms that they are comparable with one another.

This method, in fact, simply carries over to human or social phenomena the methods that have proved successful in dealing with the subject matter of physics and chemistry ([3], p. 60).

The method here outlined may receive some additional support from the fact that it also appears to be the method employed by a variety of non-pragmatic theories. For example, John Rawls articulates his method for arriving at the generalizations which are to be taken as the basis for his deontological contract theory construal of ethics as follows:

In searching for the most favored description of this situation [the "original position" in which rational beings behind a "veil of ignorance" choose the ethical principles which will bind them] we work from both ends. We begin by describing it so that it represents generally shared and preferable weak conditions. We then see if these conditions are strong enough to yield a significant set of principles. If not, we look for further premises equally reasonable. But if so, and these principles match our considered convictions of justice, then so far well and good. But presumably there will be discrepancies. In this case we have a choice. We can either modify judgments, for even the judgments we take provisionally as fixed points are liable to revision. By going back and forth, sometimes altering the conditions of the contractual circumstances, at others withdrawing our judgments and conforming them to principles, I assume that eventually we shall find a description of the initial situation that both expresses reasonable conditions and yields principles which match our considered judgments duly pruned and adjusted. This state of affairs I refer to as *reflective equilibrium* ([17], p. 20).

Something like what Rawls attempts in the remainder of his book is, of course, a necessary further step in the articulation of a complete system of values. It is not my intention in these pages to present anything like a *complete* system but rather to suggest the *method* of valuation which allows for a proper perception of the value aspects of scientific inquiry in all its components.

Within the context of the history of science, this pragmatic theory of values or valuation allows one to move from (relatively) descriptive values found in historical episodes ("relatively" because though these values are based on intuitions, the complex of intuitions has not yet been adjudicated and clarified) to (relatively) normative, more philosophically sophisticated values. These would be the products of articulation, scrutiny, and debate about the aims of science in the light of detailed cases. For example, "simplicity" as a natural desideratum of a scientist can be scrutinized in the light of other goals; and from the point of view of a desirable, more precise explication, it can be tested in a series of case studies, and a reasoned normative conclusion can be reached. This process seems to accord with scientific practice and also allows for an *evolution* of the desiderata of science as a function of evolving science.

Similar arguments apply to the context of policy decisions in the biomedical sciences. For example, the debate about recombinant DNA is a good case in point in which the scientific and political factors are scrutinized and attempts to balance various values are pursued. An examination of the give-and-take as outlined in the recent *Federal Register* [6], represents an examination I believe to be in accordance with a *practical* elaboration in concrete form of the type of deliberation I am arguing also be pursued at a theoretical level.

The institutional forms through which such a pragmatic approach could be implemented are themselves a matter for further research and deliberation. In this article, I have been concerned to propose from a rather theoretical point of view only some very tentative perspectives and directions for further work which might arouse interest.

University of Pittsburgh
Pittsburgh, Pennsylvania

NOTES

[1] I base my views here on the general rationality of the law in negligence cases. For an introduction to the laws' complex reasoning processes in such circumstances see [13], esp. pp. 8–27. In addition suits could be brought under a strict liability doctrine without negligence.

[2] See my [18] and also Section 6 below.

[3] See, for example, Shannon's historical account of the development of federal support of the biomedical sciences [19].

[4] The legal system clearly contains "socialist" components, in the sense that judges and court personnel are paid and regulated by governmental entities. The main point of comparison here, however, is between the physician and the lawyer, and also between the cost-assessment procedures, which are not "socialized".

[5] See note 15 on page 430 of the Saikewicz decision [12].

6 The following section owes much to my essay on values *in* and affecting science [18], esp. pages 161–167.
7 The role of intuitionism in contemporary ethics has recently received considerable attention, due in part to a widespread perception that Rawls's theory [17] is open to criticism as an intuitionistic theory. For a discussion of these criticisms see Daniels's [2] analysis of theory acceptance in ethics and also Shaw's [20] account of intuition and moral philosophy. Of less direct relevance but still of considerable interest are Harman's recent accounts of the role of intuitions in the study of reasoning in general [9], [10].
8 See Harman [9], [10] for a different but related view.

BIBLIOGRAPHY

1. Brooks, H.: 1978, 'The Problem of Research Priorities', *Daedalus* 107, 171–190.
2. Daniels, N.: 1979, 'Wide Reflective Equilibrium and Theory Acceptance', *Journal of Philosophy* 76, 256–282.
3. Dewey, J.: 1939, *Theory of Valuation*, University of Chicago Press, Chicago, Ill.
4. Dewey, J.: 1951, 'Experience, Knowledge and Value: A Rejoinder', in P. A. Schilpp (ed.), *The Philosophy of John Dewey*, 2nd ed., Tudor, New York, pp. 18–35.
5. Dewey, J.: 1960, *Theory of the Moral Life*, Holt, Rinehart, and Winston, New York. (This is a reprint of part II of Dewey and Tuft's revised edition of their *Ethics*.)
6. *Federal Register* 43, No. 146, July 28, 1978, Part IV.
7. Goodfield, J.: 1977, *Playing God: Genetic Engineering and the Manipulation of Life*, Random House, New York.
8. Green, H. P.: 1977, 'The Boundaries of Scientific Freedom', *Newsletter on Science, Technology and Human Values* 20, 17–21.
9. Harman, G.: 1978, 'Using Intuitions about Knowledge to Study Reasoning', *Journal of Philosophy* 75, 433–438.
10. Harman, G.: 1980, 'Reasoning and Explanatory Coherence', *American Philosophical Quarterly* 17, 151–157.
11. Jonas, H.: 1976, 'Freedom of Scientific Inquiry: The Accountability of Science', *The Hastings Center Report* 6 (August), 15–17.
12. [Jones] Superintendent of Belchertown State School v. Saikewicz, 373 Mass. 728, 373 N.E. 2nd 417 (1977).
13. Levi, E. H.: 1949, *An Introduction to Legal Reasoning*, University of Chicago Press, Chicago, Ill.
14. Metzger, W. P.: 1978, 'Academic Freedom and Scientific Freedom', *Daedalus* 107, 93–114.
15. Monod, J.: 1970, *Chance and Necessity*, Knopf, New York.
16. Nagel, T.: 1977, 'The Fragmentation of Value', in H. T. Engelhardt, Jr. and D. Callahan (eds.), *Knowledge, Value and Belief*, Hastings Center, Hastings-on-Hudson, New York, pp. 279–294.
17. Rawls, J.: 1971, *A Theory of Justice*, Harvard University Press, Cambridge, Mass.
18. Schaffner, K. F.: 1977, 'Reduction, Reductionism, Values and Progress in the Biomedical Sciences', in R. Colodny (ed.), *Logic, Laws and Life*, Pittsburgh, University of Pittsburgh Press, pp. 143–171.

19. Shannon, J. A.: 1976, 'Federal Support of Biomedical Sciences: Development and Academic Impact', *Journal of Medical Education* 51, 1–98.
20. Shaw, W. H.: 1980, 'Intuition and Moral Philosophy', *American Philosophical Quarterly* 17, 127–134.
21. Stevens, R.: 1971, *American Medicine and the Public Interest*, Yale University Press, New Haven, Conn.
22. Wartofsky, M.: 1982, 'Medical Knowledge as a Social Product: Rights, Risks, and Responsibilities', in this volume, pp. 113–130.
23. Watson, J. D.: 1968, *The Double Helix*, Atheneum, New York.
24. Weissmann, G.: 1982, 'The Need to Know: Utilitarian and Esthetic Values of Biomedical Science', in this volume, pp. 105–112.

SECTION V

BIOMEDICAL ETHICS AND ADVANCES IN
BIOMEDICAL SCIENCE

ARTHUR CAPLAN

APPLYING MORALITY TO ADVANCES IN BIOMEDICINE: CAN AND SHOULD THIS BE DONE?*

1. THE ETHICS 'BACKLASH' AND THE NEED FOR SELF-SCRUTINY IN BIOETHICS

Recent disputes concerning the development and application of new knowledge and new therapies in the biomedical sciences have created a new industry of sorts — bioethics. This is not to say that advances in medical science prior to the 1960's and 1970's moved ahead with little attention to moral concerns. Nor is it to say that biomedical research and therapy prior to the 1960's was conducted in an immoral or amoral manner. Rather, as new advances in biomedicine enabled physicians to intervene with greater power in the lives of their patients, many in the health professions and the humanities found themselves increasingly concerned about the normative issues raised by the administration of new technologies to preserve or maintain the lives of the very young, the very old and the very ill.

The field of bioethics has grown rapidly since the days of its inception in the mid 1960's [13], [14], [19]. Philosophers, theologians, and physicians doing research in bioethics have gained enough legitimacy in the eyes of a concerned public so that it has become rare to see a television show on a controversial subject in medicine that does not have the benefit of the ruminations of some sort of ethics expert. Nor is it unusual to see regulatory agencies in the federal government appoint or contract with a specialist in bioethics for advice on matters of health policy.

This growth in the number of specialists dispensing moral expertise has evoked a kind of "backlash" among many health professionals against bioethics [9], [27]. One manifestation of this backlash is the claim, manifest in the papers by Weissmann [48] and Towers [44], that the medical profession can and must tend to its own house in matters moral. Other workers in biomedicine have expressed second thoughts about the value of interdisciplinary moral inquiry. Much of this backlash is fueled by the feeling among many members of the biomedical community that ethical reflection has led both to an excess of legal regulations which are impeding inquiry in the sciences, and to a diminishment in the moral authority of physicians, an authority perceived to be an essential element in achieving therapeutic success [21], [42].

155

William B. Bondeson, H. Tristram Engelhardt, Jr., Stuart F. Spicker and Joseph M. White, Jr. (eds.), New Knowledge in the Biomedical Sciences, 155–168.
Copyright © 1982 by D. Reidel Publishing Company.

This backlash comes as a surprise to many of those working in the field of bioethics if for no other reason than that the frequency of morally outrageous behavior as instanced by the notorious Tuskegee syphilis experiments and the cancer research experiments at Brooklyn Jewish Hospital [5], [28] has greatly diminished. The presence of Institutional Review Boards and informed consent requirements at all medical research centers act as powerful deterrents to flagrant violations of moral common sense. And those in bioethics take the credit for these minimal protections against ethical abuse.

Nonetheless, it may be that those in bioethics should not be all that surprised at the recent turn of events within the biomedical community. For if, as Joseph Duffy convincingly argues [16], medicine has only recently come to occupy a position of moral authority and respect in the public eye, and given the ever-present lure of non-medical therapies for American consumers, it should not be surprising that the medical community would react angrily to any challenge to its moral adequacy.

The moral authority that many physicians perceive to be an essential part of the art of medicine may, as many writers have suggested, be neither appropriate on ethical grounds nor desirable on grounds of efficacy. The notion that medical expertise confers a kind of moral license on physicians and other health professionals to determine the goals of therapy and research has come under serious question, both by those who have contributed papers to this volume [20], [44] and in numerous other books and articles [19], [45], [46]. Unfortunately, those who offer this particular critique of medical morality have not always grounded their attack on solid descriptive grounds. In order to modify medical attitudes and practices regarding the use of medical knowledge, both old and new, it may be necessary to examine more closely the values framework operating within the health professions. Without a solid descriptive base it may be difficult to know how best to convince medical professionals to mend their moral ways since socialization and custom are as powerful as rationality in forming the ethical mores present in any profession [7], [17].

While fear, greed, and defensiveness are all at work in the medical profession's growing skepticism concerning bioethics and in the regulations and legalisms it appears to have spawned, it may be that other forces are at work which are of equal importance in understanding the "ethics backlash". Some of the current discontent can be attributed to a lack of critical self-scrutiny among those involved in biomedical ethics of their own activities and methodologies. If the imposition of moral expertise is wrong in medicine, then perhaps this is because it is wrong in most other contexts as well [22], [45].

As those in bioethics begin to serve on various commissions, advisory boards, blue ribbon panels and regulatory bodies, it may be time to re-examine the models and methods that are and ought to be operative in this field. This is especially so given the potential damage that would accrue from misperceptions, misunderstandings and misconduct in regulating an area as sensitive as biomedical research [48].

2. WHAT IS APPLIED BIOETHICS?

There are few topics in bioethics about which those in the field agree. But one subject which seems to have the nearly universal agreement of all concerned is the analysis of the "applied" nature of ethics as represented by activities such as medical ethics or bioethics.

In discussing the nature of bioethics those persons writing about the field are always quick to make the point that medical ethics or bioethics are neither new nor unique theoretical endeavors. As K. Danner Clouser observes in his article on "bioethics" in the *Encyclopedia of Bioethics*:

Medical ethics is a special kind of ethics only insofar as it relates to a particular realm of facts and concerns and not because it embodies or appeals to some special moral principles or methodology. ... It consists of the same moral principles and rules we would appeal to, then argue for, in ordinary circumstances. It is just that in medical ethics these familiar moral rules are being applied to situations peculiar to the medical world ([13], p. 113).

Clouser's explication of the nature of biomedical ethics is echoed in a wide variety of texts and articles [4], [6], [28]. The model of bioethics which permeates the field is that (a) there exists a definitive and adequate set of ethical theories, (b) these theories contain a number of useful rules and principles, (c) medical activity is morally unique only with respect to its peculiar goals and unique data base, and (d) the task of the bioethicist is to apply extant theories and principles to the empirically unique world of medicine.

3. THE INADEQUACY OF THE STANDARD VIEW OF BIOETHICS

If this view really is the "be all" and "end all" of biomedical ethics, then there are good reasons for pessimism on the part of the medical profession about the possible fruits of bioethical labor [24], [27]. It is not at all obvious why those schooled in moral theory would be adept at applying their skills to moral issues in the biomedical sciences. After all, expertise in moral theory hardly qualifies one for service in the *empirically* arcane lands of biomedicine. If technical skills plus a mastery of empirical fact and scientific theory is not the stuff of which sound moral judgment is made, it is also true that a knowledge of ethics *simpliciter* is not going to be sufficient for the analysis of theory policy issues and moral choices in the biomedical sciences.

The horns of the dilemma posed by the standard definition of bioethics operative in the field are patent in making moral analyses of normative issues in and about medicine. Health professionals lack the requisite moral sophistication to do the job. Bioethical specialists are unlikely to have the technical and scientific competence to do much good.

The solutions to the dilemma are, of course, as patent as the dilemma created by the standard view of bioethics. Either assure the technical and scientific competence of the bioethicists, or educate the scientific community in all the details and fine points of moral theory. Given the fact that it is the empirical phenomena of medical science which are alleged to be the distinguishing features of bioethics, and the pragmatic fact that it is easier to teach ethics to a neophyte than to teach biomedical science to a similarly ignorant neophyte [14], it should be obvious which solution is the most reasonable. Indeed, perhaps it is the insight that it is easier to inculcate wisdom about ethical theory in biomedical scientists than it is to carry out the reverse process for bioethicists that fuels some of the current backlash against bioethics. At worst, bioethicists, on their own view of the field, will totally bungle the job of the moral analysis of medicine. At best, bioethicists can serve as the rather dull conduits for the flow of moral theory from theoretical philosophy and theology to biomedicine. Even using a best case analysis, the task of bioethics is unlikely to capture the respect of either its practitioners or its recipients.

If I am correct in laying the blame for some of the present discontent with bioethics at the door of the model of application current in the field, then perhaps there are flaws in this model. After all, one does not have to be a Nobel prize winner to see that a host of therapeutic and research procedures in contemporary medicine raise interesting moral problems. Nor does one have to possess a doctoral degree in philosophy to see that certain moral problems in medicine are occasionally amenable to analysis and solution by subsumption under a general or universal rule.

There are reasons for skepticism about the adequacy of the conception of bioethics advanced by Clouser [13] and many others [4], [6], [28]. First, it is not at all obvious that moral theorists have concocted an adequate set of moral theories. While philosophers and theologians like to joke that all of philosophy is but a long set of footnotes to Plato, the fact remains that change and even progress have occurred in the history of ethics [25]. Certain theories have been discarded as unworkable, i.e., psychological egoism. New theories are not uncommon, i.e., those of Rawls and Nozick. Those who would argue that the history of ethics is more cyclical than linear need only look to the treatment of blacks, women, children, or animals to see counter-examples. The history of ethics may not be quite the steady march sometimes attributed to the history of science [43], but it has shown movement. And there is no reason to presume that the theories on hand today are adequate either for analyzing medical quandaries or any other moral phenomena.

Moreover, not only is it doubtful that current theories of ethics are adequate, it is also unclear what kinds of structures are possible and plausible forms for an ethical theory to take. Reasons for doubt exist within biomedicine itself.

There are many ways currently in vogue for constructing and confirming theories in ethics. Some moral philosophers start with abstract idealizations of social life and moral choice and build out to the actual world of morality [36]. Others begin with various theories of human nature and motivation and attempt to construct moral views consonant with these theories [29], [18]. Deductivist strategies now dominate most discussions of moral theorizing, but other strategies are possible.

One might adopt an inductivist approach to moral theorizing. A rich base of real world moral phenomena could provide as interesting a starting point for the construction of a moral theory as an idealized, abstract imaginary world. And medicine would be a fruitful place to seek just this sort of data. The morality inherent in the practice of biomedicine might provide as much theoretical fodder as do the imaginary worlds of rootless rational beings or idealized isolated communities of egoistic souls [7], [17], [34].

Nor is it obvious that moral analysis must always proceed by applying moral generalizations or rules to individual moral case examples. Such a view of ethical theory's role in bioethics derives from the belief that for a body of claims to count as an ethical theory, they must be organized in an axiom-atizable deductive manner. All ethical theories, on this view, consist of a hierarchy of moral rules and principles with a set of axioms at the top and a set of low-level material rules at the base [4], [33].

What is troubling about this picture of theory structure in ethics is that it is a mirror-image of the model of theory structure in the sciences that until recently dominated in the philosophy of science. As such, it is susceptible to all of the many criticisms that have been levelled against the "received" view in the philosophy of science [10], [43].

For example, it is not clear that a set of moral phenomena or moral facts exists such that all moral theories can agree on a common basis for theorizing. All the problems of theory-laden description and ambiguous event individuation [32] cited against the positivist belief in a theory-free observation language can be effectively raised against the axiomatic view of theory structure in ethics. Similarly, the criticism that not all explanation in science involves subsumption under and deduction from lawlike statements [15], [40] has an exact parallel in ethics. It is not evident that normative prescription can only occur when moral facts are subsumed under general moral rules or principles.

Worries about the commensurability [41] of scientific theories are easily generated for ethical theories as well. Moral philosophers and theologians who disagree in their prescriptive analysis of medical case studies may simply be "disagreeing" as a consequence of theoretical incommensurability between, say, deontological and teleological points of view [23], [24]. In the same vein, those who argue that the structural analysis of science would benefit greatly from a closer attention to the actual history and practices of scientists [8] should quickly recognize a kindred criticism in my claim that a more empirical, inductivist approach is needed if bioethical analyses are to have pragmatic effect.

While it is, of course, true that the inadequacy of the positivist view of theories in science is not a proof of the inadequacy of a similar view of theory structure in ethics, it is at least instructive of the sorts of difficulties inherent in such a view. Without some attention to these kinds of problems, there is no *prima facie* reason to think that (a) present ethical theories are definitive and adequate, or (b) that these theories must be composed of a hierarchy of rules and principles.

Nor is it self-evident that the only distinctive characteristic of medical ethics is the distinctive character of empirical medical facts and concerns. Many writers on bioethics have noted that medicine is an area where unique normative concerns appear to be in evidence [7], [17], [20], [21], [27], [34], [42], [48]. For example, health, truth-telling and duty all have intrinsic values for the medical practitioner that may not govern the activities of those outside of medicine. Scientific values are not always the same as non-scientific values, as legislators and regulatory bodies quickly discover. While it may be true that the domain of medicine does not contain types of values that are only to be found there and nowhere else, the specific weightings and orderings given these values are sometimes at odds with those prevailing in other arenas of social life [44], [48].

Even the last part of what I have termed "the standard model of bioethics", that bioethics takes as its sole goal the application of moral theory to medical phenomena, is open to question [11]. The relationship between theory and application current in bioethics is obviously derived from that often thought to obtain between theory and application in the sciences. The theoretical aspects of ethics are seen by the practitioners of bioethics to be confined to the "pure" or basic side of ethics. Practitioners of bioethics depict themselves as being moral engineers taking theoretical insights from the basic researchers of ethics and applying them to the analysis and resolution of concrete moral dilemmas.

4. BIOETHICS AND MORAL ENGINEERING

The engineering metaphor is an important component of the standard view of bioethics. It holds out the promise of solutions to moral quandaries by the careful application of moral theory to practical problems. Indeed, Tom Beauchamp plumps for this metaphor when he chides philosophers "since Plato" for believing that "general philosophical considerations can determine how to apply abstract principles of justice to minute areas of social policy" and argues instead that "philosophers interested in public policy would do well to start in the midst of policy problems, where financial exigencies and political realities already exist and cannot be swept behind a veil of ignorance" ([3], p. 60). Moral engineering, like scientific engineering, cannot proceed without a detailed specification of boundary and initial conditions if theory is to be applied to reality.

Rawlinson [35] and Wartofsky [47] each in their own way take Beauchamp to task for his espousal of a simple engineering model for bioethics. They both argue that examining structural factors and social contexts are at least as important, if not more important, to the analysis of issues regarding the regulation and control of new knowledge in biomedicine. As Rawlinson notes, "I find the moral problem residing in the background conditions themselves ... " ([35], p. 95). The solution for her as for Wartofsky to the question of the regulation of new knowledge in biomedicine depends upon the results of an examination of science as a social and economic activity.

I think Rawlinson and Wartofsky have pinpointed an important deficiency in the standard view of bioethics. Ethical analysis of health policy issues cannot simply be the application of principles and rules to moral issues. As has been noted earlier, if this were all that applied ethics had to offer, it is not clear that philosophers or theologians would be able to contribute much toward the analysis of normative policy issues in biomedicine. They would, more often than not, lack the clinical facility in biomedicine to accurately apply moral theory [27].

Not only does the engineering model of applied ethics give a false impression of the theoretical richness involved in such work, but it often holds out promises that cannot be fulfilled. It is simply naïve to think that a well-trained philosopher can step boldly into the emergency room or neonatal unit and immediately dissolve moral conundrums by dint of expertise in moral theory. Sometimes not enough facts are available for finding fast solutions. Sometimes the philosopher does not have the foggiest idea of exactly what problem it is that should be the grist for the mill of moral theory. And it is often presumptuous to think that health professionals of moderate intelligence would fail through years and years of practice to discern solutions to moral quandaries that are capable of quick and easy resolution. It is simply ludicrous to think that all that has stood between medicine and moral insight is the application of a few key principles wielded by some moral virtuoso.

The persistence of certain moral dilemmas in medicine should discourage any thought that quick and easy solutions are to be forthcoming. While it is, of course, true that conceptual confusion and miscommunication can often be cited as the sole causes for disagreement about moral issues, achieving conceptual clarification is not the same as finding a solution to a moral dilemma. The difference becomes quickly apparent to anyone who has taken on the assignment of constructing a code of ethics, a patients' bill of rights, an intensive care unit admissions policy, or guidelines for a national health insurance scheme. While answers to these policy problems can be found, they are rarely to be fashioned solely out of the cloth of extant theory in ethics.

Perhaps the most serious problem confronting the engineering model of bioethics is the question of problem definition. The engineering model presumes that it is always evident to those involved in the analysis and solution of a moral problem or quandary that the nature and description of the problem or quandary is not in dispute. In other words, the task of describing the problem to be addressed is left to those seeking a solution from the bioethicist. One need not invoke too complex a theory of the social role of science to see that the power to define a problem is at least as important as the ability to provide an answer [45], [46]. The difficulty with a view such as Beauchamp's is that in reality it is often not apparent exactly what normative issue the applied ethicist is being called upon to grapple with. An example should help to highlight the complexities involved in the task of problem definition in the area of regulating and applying new knowledge in biomedicine.

5. THE PROBLEM OF PROBLEM DEFINITION – THE CASE OF RENAL DIALYSIS

A great deal of attention has been devoted in the literature of medical ethics in recent years to the issue of the allocation of renal dialysis to those suffering from renal failure [2], [30], [34], [37]. Indeed, the topic is something of a classic in medical ethics. The problem in such cases seems clear enough – in situations of scarcity who should be given access to the available kidney machines? Various principles of justice can be brought to bear in such cases and the literature is full of suggestions as to what criteria are morally defensible in making difficult decisions such as this [1], [4], [12], [28], [34], [37].

As dominant as the issue of just allocation was in the early days of medical ethics, however, it is not clear that the problem with respect to the allocation of scarce dialysis equipment or any other scarce piece of medical technology is or was limited to locating a just allocation criterion. Many authors have complained in the literature on this subject that, historically, white middle-class family men tended to be the primary recipients of dialysis under conditions of scarcity. This fact led many writers to suggest that unfair ethical criteria, or, more simply, bias was to be faulted for excluding the poor, the elderly, the very young, the retarded, and the sick from consideration for dialysis treatment [1], [12].

It is interesting to note how little attention was paid by those in medical ethics interested in the question of just allocation to the broader technological and political context in which renal dialysis technology evolved. A few facts are particularly salient:

Although dialysis machines have been available in medicine since World War II, the arterio-venous shunt used to gain repeated access to a patient's circulatory system has only been available since the early 1960's. This means that the procedure of *chronic* renal dialysis only really came into its own during the late 1960's and early 1970's. In essence, despite its ubiquity and familiarity as one of the success stories of medical technology, chronic renal dialysis is a relatively new procedure [39].

As a new biomedical procedure dialysis faced a number of "competitors" for the treatment of individuals with renal failure. Not only was dialysis in competition for funds and space with other technologies for other diseases, but other possible avenues for coping with renal failure existed as well — renal transplantation from living donors and cadavers, and peritoneal dialysis [22], [30]. The battle over the efficacy and desirability of transplant versus dialysis as the optimal treatment for kidney failure continues to the present day. Surgeons and nephrologists can still be heard at case conferences arguing for one procedure as superior to the other.

Given this historical climate, it should come as no surprise that those committed to renal dialysis quickly put a premium on two factors in the course of promoting dialysis technology in the 1960's. First and foremost, they wanted the procedure to work. They were greatly concerned to show the utility of dialysis as against transplantation or other procedures in terms of reducing morbidity and mortality. Second, since chronic dialysis was a relatively new procedure, they were concerned with picking up complications induced by the procedure itself. Over the years many possible complications have emerged including dementia, anemia, hepatitis, trace metal intoxication, ascites and motor neuropathy [26]. The spector of iatrogenic illness haunted all involved with chronic dialysis as the technology evolved. Both of these factors — a desire to win a technological competition and the need to monitor the effects of the procedure — played a key role in the selection of patients for dialysis [17], [39].

The issue of who gets the machine was influenced as much by the political and "technological" needs of the researchers as it was by considerations of cost or justice. Indeed, these technological considerations were at work in the selection of patients and procedures in a number of countries where dialysis was introduced, including Britain, France, and Sweden [30], which operated under variants of socialized medicine. Surprisingly, the medical ethics literature that emerged from this period — the late 1960's and 1970's — remained almost totally oblivious to the play of technological and political factors that were at work in allocating dialysis machines. Those in medical ethics simply followed the engineering model and applied various principles of justice to individual cases to see what a particular theory of justice dictated be done. Given the interest of researchers in showing the efficacy and safety of dialysis, it is not surprising that certain groups — the elderly, the very young, the non-compliant, and those with complicating diseases — fared poorly in the allocation competition. But this had less to do with the presence or absence of any particular ethical theory or theory of justice held by physicians than it did with the exigencies of promoting a new technological procedure.

The costs associated with renal dialysis were a result of the need to master a relatively new therapy. This process can be as costly in terms of equipment, personnel and time as the costs associated with basic research [38]. Without a sound understanding of the evolution and dissemination of new technologies in medicine, it is impossible to predict or assess the amount of expenditure involved in developing and reimbursing new medical techniques.

Medical ethicists misunderstood the normative problem involving renal dialysis. The real issue during the late 1960's and early 1970's was not "who should survive?" or "who gets the machine?" Instead, the issue was when should a new technology be treated as a therapy available to all, rather than as an experiment available only to a very select few? [17]. This is not to say that theories of justice or moral philosophy in general could shed no light on the issues involved in the dissemination of renal dialysis technology. Rather, the example highlights the problems involved in taking a simple engineering approach to complex policy issues that have their own unique histories and momentum.

It is not sufficient, as Beauchamp claims [3], to enter a policy problem in midstream. Some attention must be given to the historical developments preceding the policy problem at issue. Without such knowledge, ethical analysis is seriously hampered, both in method and legitimacy [31], [35].

Problems or cases for moral analysis are not served neatly on platters for moral delectation. Those in medical ethics and those interested in learning from the experiences of medical ethicists who have attended to policy issues in the analysis of new medical technologies must remain sensitive to the difficulties involved in formulating the questions to which answers are sought by legislators, scientists, and the public.

6. APPLYING APPLIED ETHICS

I have tried to argue that it would be both inaccurate and inappropriate to limit the role of the applied ethicist's contribution to the analysis of policy issues in biomedicine to that of moral engineering. However, obviously, once a moral issue has been satisfactorily individuated and defined, moral analysis becomes necessary. In thinking about the role of new technologies in medicine, this situation can only be attained by attending carefully to the historical circumstances surrounding the innovation and dissemination processes in technological diffusion. Unfortunately, our understanding of technological evolution is far from complete. Nonetheless, some salient features of this process have been identified [17], [38], [39], [47]. They cannot and should

not be ignored by those interested in the moral issues surrounding the use
and control of new technologies and therapies in medicine.

The proper application of ethics in applied contexts depends neither
on the quick and dirty analysis of cases brought *simpliciter* to the ethicist
[3], nor in the critique of existing social and economic realities [35], [41].
Rather, it consists in a careful effort to do both and more. Empirical, historical, methodological and political analysis are all key adjuncts to sound ethical
application.

Hastings Center
Hastings, New York

NOTE

* I would like to thank John Arras for his comments on an earlier draft of this essay.
I am grateful for the support of the Henry J. Kaiser Family Foundation in writing this
essay.

BIBLIOGRAPHY

1.   Adams, L. R.: 1978, 'Medical Coverage for Chronic Renal Disease: Policy Implica-
     tions', *Health and Social Work* 3, 41–52.
2.   Agassi, J.: 1980, 'Between Science and Technology', *Philosophy of Science* 47,
     82–99.
3.   Beauchamp, T.: 1982, 'Morality and the Social Control of Biomedical Technology',
     in this volume, pp. 55–76.
4.   Beauchamp, T. and Childress, J. F.: 1979, *Principles of Biomedical Ethics*, Oxford
     University Press, New York.
5.   Beauchamp, T. and Walters, L (eds.): 1978, *Contemporary Issues in Bioethics*,
     Dickenson, Belmont, California.
6.   Bok, S.: 1977, 'The Tools of Bioethics', in S. Reiser *et al.* (eds.), *Ethics in Medi-
     cine*, Massachusetts Institute of Technology Press, Cambridge, pp. 137–141.
7.   Bosk, C. L.: 1979, *Forgive and Remember*, University of Chicago Press, Chicago.
8.   Burian, R. M.: 1977, 'More Than a Marriage of Convenience: On the Inextrica-
     bility of History and Philosophy of Science', *Philosophy of Science* 44, 1–42.
9.   Callahan, D.: 1975, 'The Ethics Backlash', *Hastings Center Report* 5, 18.
10. Caplan, A. L.: 1978, 'Testability, Disreputability and the Structure of the Modern
     Synthetic Theory of Evolution', *Erkenntnis* 13, 261–278.
11. Caplan, A. L.: 1980, 'Ethical Engineers Need Not Apply: The State of Applied
     Ethics Today', *Science, Technology and Human Values* 6, 24–32.
12. Childress, J. F.: 1970, 'Who Shall Live When Not All Can Live?', *Soundings* 43,
     339–362.

13. Clouser, K. D.: 1978, 'Bioethics', in W. Reich *et al.* (ed.), *The Encyclopedia of Bioethics*, The Free Press, New York, pp. 114–116.
14. Clouser, K. D.: 1980, *Teaching Bioethics*, Hastings Center, Hastings-on-Hudson, New York.
15. Cummins, R.: 1978, 'Explanation and Subsumption', in P. D. Asquith and I. Hacking (eds.), *PSA 1978*, Volume I, Philosophy of Science Association, East Lansing, Michigan, pp. 163–175.
16. Duffy, J.: 1982, 'The Physician as a Moral Force in American History', in this volume, pp. 3–21.
17. Fox, R. C. and Swazey, J. P.: 1978, *The Courage to Fail*, The University of Chicago Press, Chicago.
18. Gauthier, D. P.: 1967, 'Morality and Advantage', *The Philosophical Review* 76, 460–475.
19. Gorovitz, S.: 1977, 'Bioethics and Social Responsibility', *The Monist* 60, 52–59.
20. Gorovitz, S.: 1982, 'The Physician As Moral Arbiter', in this volume, pp. 23–31.
21. Jellinek, M.: 1976, 'Erosion of Patient Trust in Large Medical Centers', *Hastings Center Report* 6, 16–21.
22. Klarman, H. E., *et al.*: 1968, 'Cost Effectiveness Analysis Applied to the Treatment of Chronic Renal Disease', *Medical Care* 6, 48–54.
23. MacIntyre, A.: 1975, 'How Virtues Become Vices: Values, Medicine and Social Context', in H. T. Engelhardt, Jr. and S. F. Spicker (eds.), *Evaluation and Explanation in the Biomedical Sciences*, D. Reidel, Dordrecht and Boston, pp. 97–111.
24. MacIntyre, A.: 1980, 'Regulation: A Substitute for Morality', *Hastings Center Report* 10, 31–34.
25. Macklin, R.: 1977, 'Moral Progress', *Ethics* 87, 370–382.
26. Morris, T. and Friedman, E. A.: 1979, 'Dialytic Therapy for Irreversible Uremia', *New England Journal of Medicine* 301, 1321–1328.
27. Morison, R. S.: 1980, 'On Ethics, Gyroscopes and Radar Sets', *Hastings Center Report* 18, 26–28.
28. Munson, R. (ed.): 1979, *Intervention and Reflection: Basic Issues in Medical Ethics*, Wadsworth, Belmont, California.
29. Nozick, R.: 1974, *Anarchy, State and Utopia*, Basic Books, New York.
30. Parsons, V.: 1978, 'The Ethical Challenges of Dialysis and Transplanation', *The Practitioner* 220, 871–877.
31. Passmore, J.: 1974, 'The Objectivity of History', in P. Gardiner (ed.), *The Philosophy of History*, Oxford University Press, Oxford.
32. Putnam, H.: 1962, 'What Theories Are Not', in E. Nagel, *et al.* (eds.), *Logic Methodology and Philosophy of Science*, Stanford University Press, Stanford, California, pp. 240–251.
33. Rachels, J.: 1980, 'Can Ethics Provide Answers?', *Hastings Center Report* 10, 32–40.
34. Ramsey, P.: 1970, *The Patient as Person*, Yale University Press, New Haven, Connecticut.
35. Rawlinson, M. C.: 1982, 'Health, Justice, and Responsibility', in this volume, pp. 87–102.
36. Rawls, J.: 1971, *A Theory of Justice*, Harvard University Press, Cambridge, Massachusetts.

37. Rescher, N.: 1969, 'The Allocation of Exotic Medical Lifesaving Therapy', *Ethics* 79, 173–186.
38. Rescher, N.: 1982, 'Moral Issues Relating to the Economics of New Knowledge in the Bio-medical Sciences', in this volume, pp. 35–45.
39. Rettig, R. A.: 1977, 'End-Stage Renal Disease and the "Cost" of Medical Technology', Rand Paper Series, P-6029, 1–15.
40. Scriven, M.: 1975, 'Causation as Explanation', *Nous* 9, 3–16.
41. Shapere, D.: 1971, 'The Paradigm Concept', *Science* 172, 706–709.
42. Siegler, M.: 1981, 'The Doctor-Patient Accommodation and its Relationship to Theories of Health and Disease', in A. Caplan, *et al.* (eds.), *Concepts of Health and Disease*, Addison-Wesley, Reading, Massachusetts, pp. 627–644.
43. Suppe, F.: 1977, *The Structure of Scientific Theories*, University of Illinois Press, Urbana, Illinois.
44. Towers, B.: 1982, 'Rights and Responsibilities in Medical Science', in this volume, pp. 77–85.
45. Veatch, R.: 1973, 'The Generalization of Expertise', *Hastings Center Studies* 1, 29–40.
46. Veatch, R.: 1977, *Case Studies in Medical Ethics*, Harvard University Press, Cambridge, Massachusetts.
47. Wartofsky, M.: 1982, 'Medical Knowledge as a Social Product: Rights, Risks, and Responsibilities', in this volume, pp. 113–130.
48. Weissmann, G.: 1982, 'The Need to Know: Utilitarian and Esthetic Values of Biomedical Science', in this volume, pp. 105–112.

LAURENCE B. McCULLOUGH

BIOMEDICINE, HEALTH CARE POLICY, AND THE ADEQUACY OF ETHICAL THEORY

In the preceding essay Arthur Caplan [2] raises a series of criticisms of recent attempts to apply ethical theory to moral problems concerning emerging biomedical technologies and health care policy concerned with the funding and allocation of those technologies: He begins his criticism with a review of the "ethics backlash", the response of some within the scientific and medical communities to debate concerning the ethical dimensions of their enterprise. Since that debate resulted, in the latter portion of the last decade, in a series of federal regulations concerning the conduct of biomedical research involving human subjects, it is not surprising that the backlash was quite severe. While it now seems to have subsided, that backlash was not without its effect, for it called into question the adequacy of ethical theory to the complexity of the ethical problems posed by revolutionary advances in biomedicine. Caplan's criticisms, then, focus on questions concerning the adequacy of ethical theory to advances in biomedicine and the challenge of those advances for health care policy.

1. THE STANDARD ACCOUNT

A dominant view in bioethics, according to Caplan, is that with respect to ethics, bioethics is nothing new. The passage he quotes from Clouser's landmark essay in the *Encyclopedia of Bioethics* captures this point of view nicely: there are well-understood moral rules and principles, along with their attendant ethical theories, that can be applied to problems in medicine and health care policy in a rather straightforward manner [3]. The skills that are called for are those of application — analysis, critique, and argument — and not those of the philosophical theorist. If there are any adjustments needed in theory, they are presumed on this view to be minor in nature — perhaps a clarification here or a rephrasing there in order to make ethical theory and its application more accessible to those in the target audience.

Caplan aptly dubs this style of thinking the "engineering model" of bioethics. This model commits at least two serious errors, according to Caplan. The first is that it assumes the adequacy of moral theory and thus that theory can be applied in a ready way to whatever problems are served

169

William B. Bondeson, H. Tristram Engelhardt, Jr., Stuart F. Spicker and Joseph M. White, Jr. (eds.), New Knowledge in the Biomedical Sciences, 169–175.
Copyright © 1982 *by D. Reidel Publishing Company.*

up by the biomedical community to the high table of philosophical discourse. The second is that, in their naiveté, bioethicists undertake these applications in a vacuum. They view problems through a glass darkly, as it were, and fail to appreciate the full dimensions of many of the problems they wish to analyze.

Caplan illustrates how both of these errors occurred in much of the recent analysis of the ethical dimensions of allocating scarce resources. In a penetrating analysis of his own, Caplan walks us back through what many would take to be wholly familiar territory, the funding and allocation of renal dialysis machines. What we discover as a result of his analysis is that the standard account has been wide of the mark, inasmuch as it has systematically ignored key features of the problem at hand: the politics surrounding competing medical technologies, the imperative need for a technology that is efficacious, the high, capital-intensive costs of introducing a new technology, and the social and economic dimensions of advancing a medical technology from the research to the therapeutic setting. These factors, Caplan correctly argues, should have as much to do with the shaping of our understanding of the ethical problems as should questions of equitable access to and allocation of a life-saving medical technology. By focusing only on the latter sort of considerations, in blind devotion to the engineering model, key issues have been misunderstood, for example, the exclusion of certain groups (the aged, let us say) because of the demands on producing a physiologically efficacious treatment rather than on grounds of social worth or standing.

On Caplan's view, then, key matters of fact must be well understood before the application of ethical theory begins. If they are not, we may commit egregious errors in our understanding of the character of the ethical issues we might face. As Caplan puts it, "Without such knowledge, ethical analysis is seriously hampered, both in method and legitimacy" ([2], p. 165). No simple engineering model therefore will do. Thus, the task of the ethicist is made considerably more difficult.

2. THE APPLICABILITY AND ADEQUACY OF ETHICAL THEORY

In general I am in agreement with Caplan's account. At the same time, though, I believe that he does not take his analysis far enough. More serious questions still can be raised about the relationship between ethics and emerging biomedical knowledge and its application in new technologies.

In raising these questions, I want first to distinguish the applicability of ethical theory from its adequacy. The notion of applicability means that theory can be successfully applied in analysis of problems presently at hand. Adequacy, on the other hand, demands that theory be such that it can be applied to any problem that might occur in the domain of concern. Thus, the notion of adequacy places demands of completeness and coherence on a theory that exceed those of applicability ([12], pp. 4 ff). On both counts there are problems for the application of ethical theory to the medical uses of new knowledge.

Consider applicability. When we distinguish it from adequacy we can see that the force of much of Caplan's critique is to the effect that the applicability of theory is a demanding task, requiring that we first get clear on the complex political, social, and economic context of problems, especially those concerning public policy governing new uses of medical knowledge.

Caplan does an effective job of revealing the dimensions of such problems. He does, however, miss a key point. Let us look again at his example of renal dialysis. Given his strong emphasis on the social, political, and economic dimensions of the ethical and policy problems posed in a paradigmatic way by dialysis, it is surprising that Caplan does not turn a critical eye on one such key dimension: scarcity or limited resources. Ethicists and others often simply take for granted that policy questions concerning the allocation of new medical technologies are raised in a context of scarce or limited economic resources, as if that scarcity were a phenomenon of nature, i.e., outside of the domain of human will to change ([4], [10]). Surely, though, such is not the case. An environment of scarcity is itself created by a history of political and social decisions whose character is far from inevitable — unless one takes so-called economic laws to have the status of natural laws. Thus, prior to questions about the just allocations of scarce medical technology, we need to raise still more basic questions about whether the scarcity itself is a just or fair social or political state of affairs. It is hard to imagine how answers to the latter sort of questions will not have a bearing on the former sort, with important consequences for the development and implementation of health care policy.

This sort of problem and those to which Caplan devotes so much of his attention, however, should be distinguished from problems concerning the adequacy of ethical theory. On this score Caplan's critique is more serious, for he challenges the view that ethical theory, as it were, is whole and entire and thus applicable, even in his demanding terms, to whatever ethical problems might occur in the development and application of new medical knowledge. It is as if, by implication from Clouser's view, ethics has nothing to learn from medicine. The peculiarities of medicine, on this sort of view, do not constitute lessons for ethical theory. In the middle portion of his essay Caplan challenges this view. In the remainder of my response to his essay I would like to extend those criticisms in some greater detail. I will do so at both the micro- and macro-levels of the uses of new medical knowledge.

3. MICRO- AND MACRO-LEVELS OF THE ADEQUACY OF ETHICAL THEORY

A key concept in ethical theory is autonomy: the right of persons to be self-determining both with respect to the values that give meaning and purpose to their lives and with respect to actions based on those values. In the recent bioethics literature, it has been argued by many that respect for autonomy is a key ethical consideration in a wide variety of contexts, including biomedical research, consent for treatment, and refusal of treatment, to name but a few. There seems to be a common assumption in much of their literature, namely, that an individual either is or is not a person. As Stephen Wear puts it, the paradigmatic account of autonomy is that it is binary: it is either/ or in character [11]. In my own view this is a legacy in ethics from Western metaphysics whose substances, monads, or actual entities were one and all robust. They can never suffer illness and the multiple assaults on one's humanity so accurately analyzed by Edmund Pellegrino [8]. The upshot of this realization is that illness does affect autonomy, diminishing it to one degree or another ([8], [11]). Thus we are not all at once and completely persons but only more or less so, a feature of the human condition well known to health care professions. As bioethics comes increasingly to appreciate the bearing of this feature on how professional responsibility should be understood, I want to suggest, it becomes necessary to modify ethical theory in a substantive manner. The recently-drawn distinction between strong and weak paternalism, which must acknowledge the importance of recognizing degrees of autonomy, is one important lesson forced upon ethical theory by medical theory and experience ([5], [6]).

Thus, Caplan is correct to note that "it is not at all obvious that moral theories have concocted an adequate set of moral theories" ([2], pp. 158–159). This is not simply because some have proved to be unworkable or that they are subject to some of the same problems as have been found to characterize philosophy of science. It is also because medicine has become for ethics a distinctive source of experience and wisdom of which it has been necessary to take account in ethical theory. Resort to "the same moral principle and rules we would appeal to, and argue for, in ordinary circumstances" ([3], p. 113), will thus fail the test of adequacy required for the successful application of ethical theory to problems occasioned by advances in medical knowledge.

At the macro level serious questions can also be raised about the adequacy of ethical theory to health care policy. These go beyond Caplan's insistence on an adequate *knowledge* base to conceptual matters having to do with ethical theory. Consider, for example, the proposal of some to employ a lottery to allocate scarce life-saving medical technology among candidates of otherwise equal standing [4]. On its face this seems a decent solution to a tough problem. But is a lottery method of allocating scarce resources a moral decision in the full sense?

Consider the problem of professional responsibility for the health care professionals utilizing this method of allocating the technology in question *and their services in support of that technology*. Full moral agency demands that one take responsibility for one's actions and decisions. A necessary condition for doing so is that one's actions and decisions be one's own. And decisions and actions are one's own, in part, if and only if one can give reasons for those decisions and actions. This is so because reasons bind agents and their acts together, so that we can trace the latter to the former and thus assign and assume responsibility. These are key concerns in the health care setting where the assumption of responsibility *defines* one as a *professional* physician, nurse, or whatever [8]. These are also complex matters in health care delivery, where team care diffuses responsibility. The problem with a lottery method is that, while it might appear to be fair, it dissolves responsibility, since — as a random and thus absurd assignment of opportunity — it is no decision at all. Use of a lottery thus becomes a subtle way to abandon the burden of moral decisions and with it responsibility for the consequences of decisions. The consequence, of course, is to leave health care professionals with the very problem which they faced to begin with: how to understand professional responsibility in allocating scarce life-saving medical services, including their own time and effort. To argue that the problem is really one of health policy and not for physicians and other health professionals to make will not do here. This move simply shifts the locus of the problem; it does not alter its character. On this analysis, then, a key concept in ethical theory is found inadequate to a basic feature of the problem it is meant to help analyze and resolve.

There is another, more systematic problem concerning the adequacy of ethical theory that Caplan identifies. This is what Caplan characterizes as the "theoretical incommensurability" ([2], p. 160) between seemingly opposing points of view, e.g., deontology and consequentialism. He suggests that this problem may be akin to one in the sciences where a structuralist approach would tend to ignore "the actual history and practices of scientists" ([12], p. 160). I want to follow up on this suggestion and reflect for a moment on the sociology and politics of ethicists and their discipline.

My concern here focuses primarily on the way ethicists learn their trade. The typical approach is first to array the great schools of theory and then carefully analyze their distinctive elements. Consequentialism is thus distinguished from deontology as if the two were wholly self-contained and adequate, hermetically sealed one from the other. Thus, what arguably began as convenient ways of capturing the primary emphasis of particular moral theories [1] was, in my view, transmuted into theories, themselves thought to be whole and entire. A more vivid example of Whitehead's "fallacy of misplaced concreteness" ([12], p. 11) in the history of ethics is difficult to imagine. Yet even a cursory review of major textbooks in bioethics shows that the fallacy persists. What is called for is a fully nuanced account of moral principles, such as that of Rawls [9], rather than the one-sided and thus truncated theory of a Nozick [7]. As long as philosophers persist in this error, they will condemn their theories and their attempted applications to the trashbin of inadequacy, inviting yet another "ethics backlash".

4. CONCLUSION

In the preceding Sections I have attempted to take seriously Arthur Caplan's criticism of the application of skills in ethical reasoning in attempts to understand those distinctive ethical problems occasioned by the development and new uses of medical knowledge. I regard his criticisms as sound. I thus took it as my proper task to expand the purview of that criticism. As a first step, I attempted to refine the focus of that criticism by distinguishing problems of the applicability of ethical theory from its adequacy. I then suggested how, with respect to both, the critical enterprise undertaken by Caplan could be extended still further. My intention in doing so has not been to wholly disarm ethical theory. Instead, it has been to urge the cogency of the view that, as we join ethics to the disciplines of biomedicine and health care policy, ethical theory has as much – if not more – to learn as it has to teach.

Georgetown University
Washington, D.C.

BIBLIOGRAPHY

1.   Broad, C. D.: 1930, *Five Types of Ethical Theory*, Kegan Paul, Trench, Trubner and Co., Ltd., London, England.
2.   Caplan, A. L.: 1982, 'Applying Morality to Advances in Biomedicine: Can and Should This Be Done?' in this volume, pp. 155–168.
3.   Clouser, K. D.: 1978, 'Bioethics', in W. Reich (ed.), *Encyclopedia of Bioethics*, Macmillan, The Free Press, New York, pp. 114–116.
4.   Childress, J. F.: 1970, 'Who Shall Live When Not All Can Live?', *Soundings* 43, 339–362.
5.   Childress, J. F.: 1979, 'Paternalism in Health Care', in W. L. Robison and M. S. Pritchard (eds.), *Medical Responsibility: Paternalism, Informed Consent, and Euthanasia*, The Humana Press, Clifton, New Jersey, pp. 15–27.
6.   Dworkin, G.: 1972, 'Paternalism', *Monist* 56, 64–84.
7.   Nozick, R.: 1974, *Anarchy, State and Utopia*, Basic Books, New York.
8.   Pellegrino, E.: 1978, 'The Fact of Illness and the Act of Profession: Some Notes on the Source of Professional Obligation', in L. B. McCullough and J. P. Morris (eds.), *Implications of History and Ethics to Medicine – Veterinary and Human*, Texas A & M University, College Station, Texas, pp. 78–89.
9.   Rawls, J.: 1971, *A Theory of Justice*, Harvard University Press, Cambridge, Massachusetts.
10. Rescher, N.: 1969, 'The Allocation of Exotic Medical Lifesaving Therapy', *Ethics* 79, 173–186.
11. Wear, S.: 1980, 'Mental Illness and Moral Status', *Journal of Medicine and Philosophy* 5, 292–312.
12. Whitehead, A. N.: 1929, *Process and Reality*, The Macmillan Company, New York.

SECTION VI

CONCLUSIONS AND REFLECTIONS: PRESENT AND
FUTURE PROBLEMS

H. TRISTRAM ENGELHARDT, JR.

WHY NEW TECHNOLOGY IS MORE PROBLEMATIC THAN OLD TECHNOLOGY

As the essays in this volume show, the availability or the likelihood of new biomedical technology raises moral issues of costs and of control. As a number of the essays also indicate, there are reasons to believe that the costs (financial and moral) may be greater in the case of the development of new technologies than with the use of those already at hand. These costs are especially troubling when set in the context of the competition for scarce resources, and the special needs of the Third World for population control, the treatment of indigenous diseases, and the provision of sufficient food for its populations.

New biomedical technology is also troubling, for it raises the possibility of changing the cultures in which we live. The biomedical sciences already have a striking influence upon the ways in which we are born, make love, live, fall ill, and die. We are becoming cultures framed in terms of the technologies that sustain our ways of life. Moreover, the very presence of knowledge creates obligations which were unacknowledged in the past when we were more ignorant of the dangers associated with particular diets, particular chemicals, and certain styles of life. The pursuit of new biomedical technology is thus always a potential challenge to the integrity of a culture. One might consider, for example, what will inevitably be the result of the availability of cheap and reliable means of prenatal diagnosis coupled with inexpensive means of abortion unassociated with appreciable morbidity or mortality. At least one court has already suggested that the knowledge of such risks combined with the technology to avoid them could create obligations of parents not to reproduce or not to carry to term a pregnancy associated with a high risk of the birth of a defective infant [1].

Insofar as a particular culture appreciates such possibilities as challenging, it may attempt to avoid supporting their development. One might think back, for example, to the reflections of the Ethics Advisory Board of the Department of Health, Education and Welfare regarding governmental support of research involving *in vitro* fertilization and embryo transfer [4]. In part, such reflections involve decisions regarding the extent to which a society wishes to forward new modes of reproduction. Decisions not to provide support can be justified by appealing to opinions generally held in a society.

William B. Bondeson, H. Tristram Engelhardt, Jr., Stuart F. Spicker and Joseph M. White,
Jr. (eds.), New Knowledge in the Biomedical Sciences, 179–183.
Copyright © *1982 by D. Reidel Publishing Company.*

Individuals have a claim upon determining how their funds will be used, both as funds taken from them, and as funds held by the society to which they belong. However, it will be difficult, if not impossible, for a free society to justify forbidding the pursuit of such research if privately undertaken. It will as well be difficult to justify forbidding the use of the fruits of such research. To do so would be to use common force to impose the views of a majority upon an innocent peaceable minority. One might think, for example, of countries such as Ireland which have endeavored to forbid by law the importation of contraceptives. One might interpret the Irish as attempting to defend the character of their society. Yet, such a defense is incompatible with the notion of a peaceable community, one not based upon the use of unconsented-to force [2]. In addition, given the allure of many technologies, it may in fact be very difficult to control their spread. For example, as in the past, when it has been impossible to prevent individuals effectively from acquiring contraceptives and abortions, it would likely prove impossible to prevent the use of prenatal diagnosis from becoming a routine part of prenatal care. And, as suggested, such a development will alter our culture's understanding of the rights and responsibilities of parents, and of the nature of parenthood. One will have become responsible not only for the number of one's children, but for their quality as well. One will no longer simply be able to accept one's children innocently as gifts of God.

Such technological developments are alluring, for they offer a mode of extending our control over ourselves and over the surd forces and patterns of nature. The triumph, for example, of the contraceptive ethos lies in its offering to individuals the ability to have their reproductive natures conform to their choices. In that it allows people to choose how often and when to join the reproductive with the recreational elements of sexuality, it simply augments without constraint the liberty to pursue one's own reproductive choices. The availability of effective prenatal diagnosis only increases this freedom.

More generally, biomedical technology offers a means for making our human nature conform to our chosen goals. It allows our personal choices to triumph over the surd forces of human nature. Biomedical technologies thus presuppose a distance between us as persons, as moral agents, and the peculiarities and particularities of our nature as members of a particular biological species (i.e., as humans). It suggests as well why it is natural for us as persons to manipulate our nature and to render ourselves our own product. What we do that is unnatural by the canons of the usual courses of human biology, may be strictly in accord with our nature as rational beings, as persons choosing our own destinies. To be a person, a rational free agent, is to envisage more congenial embodiments than what we possess from the present deliverances of human evolution.

Medical technology is thus not simply a means to restore the usual courses of human nature, but more fundamentally a means to achieve those courses that we may decide are best in accord with our chosen goals. Here again, the case of contraception is helpful. One may concede that contraception is unnatural (e.g., that it thwarts the usual courses of human biology), though yet in another sense quite natural (i.e., in accord with the rational choices of persons). Tensions between these senses of what is *natural* are occasioned by the development of modes of genetic engineering, as well as by already existing techniques such as organ transplantation and by pharmacological interventions that alter the usual character of human biological responses. Biomedical knowledge supports technological advances that forward the dialectic between persons and their embodiment in which persons render their bodies their own, less subject to the impersonal forces of biology.

As a result, a culture which may have come to terms with the usual courses of nature will find that it is confronted by biomedical technologies which change its value-structures. The habits of character and virtue which were once needed in order to live well as humans can be rendered unnecessary by a technological means of avoiding the problems which had provided the occasion for being skilled in such virtues and marks of character. For example, the virtues and character needed to care for the handicapped may become generally less important when physical and mental handicaps can be avoided either through treatment or selective abortion. When such liberations from the usual constraints of nature occur in a tolerant, pluralist society, the changes in ethos may be startling. It is such technological changes, and the possibility of yet further advances, that have evoked much of the contemporary interest in bioethics (e.g., organ transplanation and genetic engineering).

Bioethics has emerged as a secular framework within which to assess the costs, benefits, and jeopardies to rights due to biomedical technologies and biomedicine generally, and which no particular religious or cultural tradition has secular authority to mediate. Without denying the contributions of particular traditions, a secular bioethics offers a free pluralist society a neutral matrix for the analysis of ethical issues occasioned by biomedicine. However, insofar as a secular bioethics is framed in a peaceable, tolerant society, respect of freedom in negotiating moral rules will have precedence over particular claims for content for such rules. Respect of freedom has priority as a constraint upon actions in that it requires the fewest presuppositions: it is the condition for the possibility of the ethical community as that community which is not based on unconsented-to force.[1] Beyond that it will be very difficult to show that morally deviant ethical sentiments are morally wrong, for such will require an appeal to a common notion of a proper moral sense, which will not be shared in any great detail by a pluralist society.

As a consequence, the development of new biomedical technologies evokes procedural answers to its controversies, bureaucratic attempts to frame proper uses of such technologies by creating answers where none can be discovered. The moral accent then falls upon proper procedure in the creation of rules rather than upon the content of the rules created. Such rules, for example, must be fashioned in order to decide what diagnoses or treatments will under what circumstances be paid for through public funds. This issue is examined by Mary Ann Gardell, for instance, in her examination of the Dynamic Spatial Reconstructor (DSR). How are warrants for public subventions of the costs for uses of the DSR for particular patients to be established? What is troubling about such questions is that they force us to acknowledge the fact that we create the answers. We establish the indications for the use of particular diagnostic and therapeutic modalities, and for the public subvention of the costs of their use, by considering alternate ways of expanding common resources. The fact that we find such decisions troubling is disclosed by the concern that we ought not to develop medical technologies that cannot be equitably distributed.

Such reticence to gamble on the possibility of cheaper than expected technologies reflects a reluctance to face the responsibility of stoically creating lines between what will count as unfair, versus what will count as unfortunate distribution of scarce medical technologies. The development of new biomedical knowledge challenges us to face the brutality of the natural lottery which constrains us to make choices regarding which sufferings and foreshortenings of life due to disease we will blunt through biomedical technologies, thus expending our scarce resources, and when (and under what circumstances) we will not intervene, and instead employ our limited resources towards the pursuit of the evanescent pleasures of this life.

New biomedical technologies force us to take responsibility for our biological natures and for our socio-technological responses to our biological natures. We must decide what we ought to manipulate or change, and the extent to which we wish to create social entitlements to such technological interventions. New biomedical technology increases our responsibilities by increasing our powers. This involves a loss of innocence and an appreciation of knowledge as power, as Ross Kessel and William Bondeson argue in their essays. New biomedical knowledge is thus especially perturbing, for it is unsettling to lose one's innocence and to acquire new obligations.

Georgetown University
Washington, D.C.

NOTE

[1] This involves a suggestion of how one could give a more developed grounding of Robert Nozick's respect of freedom as a side constraint versus freedom as a value [3]. I have explored this in some detail elsewhere [2].

BIBLIOGRAPHY

1. *Curlender v. Bio-Science Laboratories*, 165 Cal. Rptr. 477 (Ct. App. 2d Dist. Div. 1, 1980).
2. Engelhardt, H. T., Jr.: 1980, 'Personal Health Care or Preventive Care: Distributing Scarce Medical Resources', *Soundings* 63(3), 234–256.
3. Nozick, R.: 1974, *Anarchy, State and Utopia*, Basic Books, New York.
4. U.S. Department of Health, Education, and Welfare, Ethics Advisory Board, *HEW Support of Research Involving Human In Vitro Fertilization and Embryo Transfer: Reports and Conclusions* and *Appendix*, 2 vols., Department of Health, Education, and Welfare, Washington, D.C., May 4, 1979.

ROSS KESSEL

THE USES OF BIOMEDICAL KNOWLEDGE: THE END
OF THE ERA OF OPTIMISM?

Optimism, n. Doctrine ... that the actual world is the best of all possible worlds; view that good must ultimately prevail; sanguine disposition; inclination to take bright view [5].

The optimist proclaims that we live in the best of all possible worlds; and the pessimist fears this is true [3].

In requesting that I prepare a concluding essay for *New Knowledge in the Biomedical Sciences*, the editors assigned me the title "The End of the Era of Optimism!" indicating, or so I presumed, that the papers being presented required tempering with the heat of realism. Having reviewed the manuscripts making up this volume, I have concluded that their authors are well aware of the crises facing medicine today, and are little in need of having their attention drawn to the limitations of a too optimistic view of their disciplines. I have therefore taken as my tasks an analysis of their reasons for believing that the current history of the acquisition and use of biomedical knowledge has reached a period that might be described as pessimistic, and, in a limited way, a presentation of some modest reasons for maintaining that a modicum of optimism is nevertheless in order.

The papers making up the current volume fall into three groups dealing with, first, the special roles of the physician and the biomedical scientist in the making of moral choices; second, some moral questions arising out of the pursuit and use of biomedical knowledge; and third, some questions regarding the just ways of distributing the benefits of new knowledge. While there are clearly many overlapping concerns, I view the presentations of Duffy, Gorovitz, and Towers (and to some extent that of Rawlinson) as falling into the first group, those of Weissmann, Wartofsky, and Schaffner into the second, and those of Rescher, Zaner, Beauchamp, and Rawlinson into the third.

My thesis will be that it is increasingly difficult to maintain an air of optimism as one moves from the realm of individual decision-making, through the issues raised by the acquisition and use of new knowledge, to those related to the distribution of scarce resources.

185

William B. Bondeson, H. Tristram Engelhardt, Jr., Stuart F. Spicker and Joseph M. White, Jr. (eds.), New Knowledge in the Biomedical Sciences, 185–191.
Copyright © 1982 by D. Reidel Publishing Company.

1. THE PHYSICIAN AS MORAL AGENT

I take the fundamental pessimism concerning the state of the profession as a moral enterprise, and the institution of individual practice in particular, to revolve around the loss of professional autonomy [13]. It is this, I sense, that lies at the heart of Towers's cry against those who "seem intent on destroying not only the evident advantages that modern technology has provided for the common weal, but also the potential for future advantages that will accrue to mankind" ([2], p. 77), and Weissmann's that society "should impose no pre-emptive restrictions on the *kinds* of new knowledge to be sought", even, apparently, "certain investigations on human subjects" ([2], p. 111). Towers deplores the loss of a humanistic approach to medicine, and at the heart of his concern (or at least his lack of optimism) is the view that there is a "rejection by many people of all authority figures or parental models in favor of self-sufficiency" ([2], p. 79). The " 'parentalist role' that physicians have traditionally played" ([2], p. 79) is declining. One suspects that he views the change from a more covenantal to a more contractual relationship between physician and patient as retrogressive and against the best interests of both.

The assumption of a moral role for the profession of medicine, while clearly of ancient origin, was not received with any great credibility until recent decades. As John Duffy has clearly demonstrated [2], the profession has followed rather than led, it has supported the prevailing mores and attitudes of the societies in which it is practiced rather than formed them. I would suggest this to be a continuing characteristic of the profession. As Duffy points out, individual physicians supported many of the popular movements of the Reform and the Progressive Periods of American history, and I would expect many physicians will follow the egalitarianism of today's times.

Contrary to Towers, I would see at least a glimpse of optimism in what he views as crisis. As Gorovitz points out [2], a more sophisticated public is beginning to view the physician's assumption of moral authority, and his frequent overriding of the patient's interests, autonomy, rights and dignity, as less than appropriate for a pluralistic society such as ours. Recognizing that patients walk in fear and that physicians have power over them, we need, as Rawlinson emphasizes ([2], p. 100), to define careful limits for the kinds of decisions we allow physicians to make. The reality that medicine is coming to recognize is that the practice of a secular profession in a complex society calls for the foregoing of the role of moral arbiter, a role which, as Gorovitz points out ([2], p. 28), the physician has neither the training nor the expertise to assume.

2. THE PURSUIT OF KNOWLEDGE

The beginnings of the era of optimism in the biomedical sciences can be dated fairly firmly to the late 1930's, although its roots clearly grow from the last years of the 19th Century. Lewis Thomas has dramatically described the intellectual impact of the first effective antimicrobial drugs. "Overnight, we became optimists, enthusiasts. The realization that disease could be turned around by treatment . . . was a totally new idea just forty years ago" [14]. Growing out of the applied sciences of bacteriology and industrial chemistry, the discovery and use of antibiotics has been viewed as an archetypical example of the advantage of supporting unfettered research. This ideology of science [5] was developed by Jacques Monod [10] into an Ethic of Knowledge, and used to support a utilitarian calculus to justify the expenditure of logarithmically increased amounts for medical research over the last three decades (see [12] and Rescher in this volume).

Whether or not we agree with Weissmann's assessment ([2], p. 106) that "there is ample support for the idea" that pure as opposed to applied research gave us streptomycin, the Salk vaccine and the rational treatment of leukemia, it clearly stems from the view that this assessment is properly made by the scientist himself. That ownership over biomedical knowledge is his rather than society's. It is from this anxiety, expressed in his quotation from Ayer [1] (ethical terms are calculated to arouse feelings and so to stimulate action), that Weissmann's desire to see the pursuit of knowledge uncontrolled by the laws and regulations that aim to codify society's ethical values stems. He is not optimistic that such a pursuit will be possible in the future, even if one could assume that it ever was in the past.

While sympathetic to Weissmann's view of the artistic nature of the scientific enterprise ([2], p. 106) I must surely agree with Jonas [9] and with Gorovitz [6] that science exists for the benefit of society, a view explored by Wartofsky in this volume [2]. It is difficult to disagree with his description of medicine as a cognitive practice in which knowledge is acquired in a social context and used to a social end, or not to agree that this demands social control (Wartofsky's "communal ownership") over the acquisition and use of biomedical knowledge ([2], p. 127). The difficulty, as Schaffner so eloquently points out ([2], p. 138), is in identifying the network of actors who participate in the acquisition of biomedical knowledge and the values that need to be weighed in deciding such questions as "What new knowledge is desirable?"

I would argue that there is room for optimism in believing that such questions can be answered in a moral manner, a manner that would attempt to accommodate varying views of the best interest with those of freedom and autonomy. The use of Institutional Review Boards to oversee the use of human subjects in research may well serve as a model for the identification of the network to be consulted, and the values to be considered, in answering questions of research priorities, the means of acquiring new knowledge, and its application and use.

3. DISTRIBUTING THE FRUITS OF BIOMEDICAL KNOWLEDGE

The third set of moral issues discussed in this volume revolves around questions of how we ought to distribute resources for the acquisition and use of biomedical knowledge; resources which are in short supply and which, if we follow Rescher, will increasingly continue to become scarcer. Both Rescher [2] and Beauchamp [2] would, in the end, adopt an utilitarian standard; the former arising out of considerations of economic theory, the latter from considerations of justice. It is not within the scope of this essay to examine all of the issues presented by Rescher and Beauchamp, and indeed their presentations are accompanied by extensive commentaries by Zaner [2] and by Rawlinson [2] respectively. I will limit my consideration to the fundamental economic question raised by Rescher. Is technological escalation, and hence escalation of cost, built into the very structure of scientific research, and does the rise of such high technology inevitably spill over from research to therapy, thus escalating the cost of the latter? The moral dimensions flowing from Rescher's thesis are clearly delineated in Zaner's commentary, which follows Illich [8] in arguing that a highly technological health service may well heighten and complicate sickness. Zaner suggests that this will, of necessity, call for an immediate redefinition of "the very best" that we have traditionally believed patients deserve ([2], p. 51).

Rescher's argument is that scientific questions inevitably get harder to answer, that this always leads to increased costs, and that a process of declining yield operates to raise the cost-benefit ratio. I will argue that this will hold only as we allow the technologically-based scientists to define the terms of the discussion, and that a more optimistic view is at least thinkable if we change that frame of reference. I will follow as examples two diseases cited by Rescher: tuberculosis and cancer.

Are today's problems more intractable than yesterday's? I seriously doubt that the question "What are the causes of tuberculosis?" is more difficult to answer today than it was to the physician of 1880 [4]. Indeed that question of 1880 bears more than a superficial resemblance to today's question "What are the causes of cancer?" Whether or not "latter-day problems tend to become more intractable than earlier ones" ([2], p. 36) surely depends on who is defining "the problem".

Does finding a cure for today's catastrophic disease demand a technological escalation? I would argue that the answer will only be "yes" if we accept a purely reductionist view of disease, and not even always then. Any list of today's "catastrophic diseases" will certainly reflect the values of the list-maker. I am by no means certain that the top end of such a list might not include alcoholism, arthralgia and other chronic pain syndromes, depression, and gonorrhea, entities whose reduction appears to be more amenable to socio-political impact than the "big three": cancer, atherosclerotic heart disease and stroke. Towers's criticism that "the vast sum of money that has been poured into biomedical research has gone into research . . . (within a) . . . bioengineering model of disease" ([2], p. 81), certainly bears upon this point of view. Even under the rubric of reductionist medicine, however, it is by no means self-evident that costs will always rise. To take only one current example, I would cite the employment of "hybridomas" (hybrids of two cells, one of which provides a wanted product, the other the capacity for cellular division). This simple and inexpensive technique, which can now be employed world-wide [11], will render obsolete the hoards of mice, guinea pigs, rabbits and horses used in the past to produce vaccines and other biological molecules. An example, among many, of technical de-escalation.

Does basic research draw resources away from therapy? Here the answer must surely be "yes and no". To return to the treatment and control of tuberculosis before the advent of chemotherapy, it is evident that the resources going into medical care were at that time enormous: construction of specialized hospitals, long periods of hospitalization, extensive nursing care, etc. The resources then being expended, professional as well as financial, "at home" could be considered reduced by research carried on "at the frontier" of microbial antagonism, even when it was apparently unlinked to a therapeutic outcome.

While this analysis may cast some doubt on what Zaner terms Rescher's Principle of Necessary Escalation ([2], p. 47), it in no way detracts from his thesis that conditions of scarcity always exist and that moral questions therefore always arise as to the distribution of resources. It does, perhaps, allow a little room for optimism as to whether Zaner is right in fearing that we are in a time when achieving the very best may well be little more than stuff for nostalgia ([2], p. 52).

4. CONCLUSION

Is there, then, any reason to believe that we will be able to make moral use of new knowledge in the biomedical sciences? Surely the answer is a qualified, but by no means resounding, "yes".

In the broadest area, that of decisions governing public policy, there is perhaps the least possibility of optimism. If any is to be derived, it is from the realization that philosophers are heeding Beauchamp's plea that those "interested in public policy would do well to start in the midst of policy problems" ([2], p. 60). The present volume shows that they are doing so.

In the realm of the pursuit of new knowledge, clarification of what Schaffner terms the Net of Biomedicine ([2], p. 141) will certainly lead to a richer consideration of the values involved in decision-making. The loss of professional autonomy which the biomedical scientist and physician will suffer should be well worth the price of admission.

It is, however, in the area of individual practice that I believe the greatest optimism is warranted. The "crisis" of changing relationships between physician and the society in which he operates is likely to lead to a brighter moral climate less characterized by a damaging paternalism and more respectful of the dignity of all the individuals involved.

All in all, then, I have rejected the editors' request that I write to the title "The End of the Era of Optimism!" Although I might have preferred "The End of the Era of Innocence", I hope that the title that I have chosen reflects at least a modicum of faith in the brightness of the future to be gained.

University of Maryland
Baltimore, Maryland

BIBLIOGRAPHY

1.   Ayer, A. J.: 1936, *Language, Truth and Logic*, Gollancz Book Company, London, p. 78.
2.   Bondeson, W. B., Engelhardt, Jr., H. T., Spicker, S. F., and White, J. M.: this volume.

3. Cabbel, J.: 1929, *The Silver Stallion*, Macmillan and Company, London, p. 26.
4. Dubos, R. and Dubos, J.: 1953, *The White Plague: Tuberculosis, Man and Society*, Little, Brown and Co., Boston.
5. Fowler, H. W. and Fowler, F. G.: 1911, *The Concise Oxford Dictionary of Current English*, Fourth Ed., Revised by E. McIntosh, 1951, Oxford University Press, Oxford, p. 833.
6. Gorovitz, S.: 1977, 'Bioethics and Social Responsibility', *Monist* 60, 3–15.
7. Holton, G.: 1960, 'Modern Science and the Intellectual Tradition', *Science* 131, 1190–1192.
8. Illich, I.: 1976, *Medical Nemesis: The Expropriation of Health*, Pantheon Books, New York.
9. Jonas, H.: 1976, 'Freedom of Scientific Enquiry: The Accountability of Science', *The Hastings Center Report* 6(4), 15–17.
10. Monod, J.: 1971, *Chance and Necessity*, Knopf Publishing Company, New York, pp. 140 *et seq.*
11. Nabholz, M. and Lambert P-H: 1980, *Hybridoma Technology*, UNDP/World Bank/WHO, Geneva.
12. Pawles, J.: 1973, 'On the Limitations of Medicine', *Science, Medicine and Man* 1, 1–30.
13. Pellegrino, E. D.: 1977, 'Society, Technology and Professional Expertise', in B. A. Boley (ed.), *Crossfire in Professional Education*, Pergamon Press, New York, pp. 1–17.
14. Thomas, L.: 1979, *The Medusa and the Snail*, The Viking Press, New York, p. 67.

MARY ANN GARDELL

THE BEST IS YET TO COME

Nicholas Rescher in "Moral Issues Relating to the Economics of New Knowledge in the Biomedical Sciences" [6] and Richard Zaner in his "Only the Best is Good Enough?" [8] call the pursuit of medical progress into question. Rescher tells us that as progress and advancements are realized in science and medicine, there is a marked increase in the over-all resource cost of realizing new scientific findings. Presuming such an inexorable and intractable trend, Rescher is impelled to ask these "very difficult and uncomfortable" moral questions ([6], p. 42):

1. Given the economics of research, should there be a deployment from research to therapy?
2. Should we redeploy resources from complex and expansive high-technology intervention to a lower level technology and, above all, to preventive medicine?
3. Should we abandon the prevailing moral precept that "Only the very best is good enough?"

In reaction to Rescher's essay, Zaner suggests that the resolution of the moral questions that his colleague raises depends on the redefinition of the sense of "the very best". Zaner notes the similiarity between Rescher's understanding of the relationship between science and technology, "Technological progress is an imperative of scientific progress" ([8], p. 47), and the view held by Hans Jonas, "Science is technological by its nature" ([3], p. 198). He accepts Rescher's analysis of scientific and technological evolution: scientific progress and technological development are related dynamically and dialectically, together increasing with time in sophistication and economic cost. The implications of this evolutionary trend are evidenced in the sociocultural growth and change taking place within the medical community. This trend is characterized by the following: an increasing use of the limited resources, such as money, personnel, and time. As a result, there has been an increased recognition of the scarcity of these necessities and of an increasing number of patient complaints and illnesses. And, as individual patients come to depend on sophisticated and expensive technological diagnosticians, an increased sense of personal alienation and decreased personal autonomy follows.

193

William B. Bondeson, H. Tristram Engelhardt, Jr., Stuart F. Spicker and Joseph M. White, Jr. (eds.), New Knowledge in the Biomedical Sciences, 193–197.
Copyright © 1982 by D. Reidel Publishing Company.

Here Zaner shares Rescher's insight, that the goal of this evolutionary trend, "the very best", might not be "optimal". He urges a reconsideration of the medical community's "very best" along with its reevaluation, possible abandonment, and replacement by a more "optimal" sense of "the very best" which may be "less" than "the very best".

However, the terms "optimal" and "very best" are ambiguous. One might consider, for example, a recent high technology contribution to optimal care – the Mayo Clinic's Dynamic Spatial Reconstructor (DSR) [1], [7]. The DSR is a new-generation scanning device which promises to provide a great wealth of diagnostic information on the heart, lung, and circulatory system to both physician and patient. Funds for this diagnostic tool were partially provided by the National Institutes of Health and totaled about 5.2 million dollars. Clearly, this highly sophisticated piece of biomedical technology had obtained political as well as social support.

One can appreciate and perhaps even share the Star Trek-like excitement over the DSR following even a brief description. It is this intellectual excitement which leads William Bondeson [2] to emphasize that we are the successors of Bacon and Hobbes, seeing knowledge as power which enables mastery over nature and its use to our benefit. The DSR is designed to increase insight into physiological and patho-physiological interrelationships between physiological structure and its corresponding function. This is accomplished by the complex interplay between its four units: (1) a DSR gantry mechanism which includes a 15 ton, 20 ft. long data acquisition device with 28 X-ray "guns"; (2) a video image storage system; (3) a reconstructor computer; and (4) a display and analysis system. When operative, the DSR gantry unit encircles the supine patient and its 28 X-ray "guns" fire in rapid succession, repeating its sequence 60 times each minute. A three-dimensional picture of the motions of the heart, lung, or a major blood vessel at any desired angle or chunk, and at any selected location is processed. The DSR's machinery and its capabilities are "the very best" compared to its well-known counterparts in the sense that it offers a three-dimension X-ray image of the human body's interior with accurate measurements of magnitude, rate, and volume of body blood and blood gases, with data acquisition 1000 times greater than those of commercial computed (CT) scanners. Upon completion its data processing ability promises to be "the very best", performing 3×10^9 arithmetic operations each second.

Herein lies the "theatrical appeal", as Bondeson calls it, of the use of technology in the therapeutic setting. The DSR makes possible a reified oxymoron, "noninvasive vivisection". It offers the scientific and medical community the opportunity to "see" entire organs, such as the heart, lung, kidney, brain, or segments of the vascular system, without performing invasive surgery. Similiarly, it becomes possible to section, cut, slice, or cube those intact organs of particular interest without the use of surgical apparatus. For the patient, the DSR offers a diagnostic procedure which is painless and involves little inconvenience. Most exams are completed in seconds and the patient is exposed to less ionizing radiation than is traditionally used in the diagnostic radiographic procedure.

How, then, would its use raise moral questions? In what respect is it not the case that the DSR supports optimal treatment? Consider a hypothetical case study: a middle-aged man visits his physician and wants to know the status of his heart. No particular complaint has brought the patient to seek his physician's advice beyond his anxiety of a future heart problem. Following a DSR diagnosis, the physician visualizes the heart wall, the coronary arteries, and the major blood vessels of the beating heart. The questions which come to mind follow: What criteria should the physician adopt in deciding what quantifies and what qualifies as an insufficiently nourished heart wall or a "moderately" or "greatly" narrowed coronary artery warranting surgical intervention? Realizing the technical nature of the DSR diagnostic data, can the physician expect the patient to be able to provide a free and informed consent to treatment? In the face of this difficulty, should a physician's more frequent use of therapeutic priviledge be condoned? Even prior to the DSR's use, what conditions are necessary and sufficient to warrant the use of the DSR? What values are presupposed by the arguments to establish such warrants for use? If used routinely, should other 20 million dollar equivalents be built all across the country? If so, who should pay? And should the same agency pay for the inevitably increasing number of surgical operations? How should one warrant use in order to contain costs?

Quite tenably, the unit price of the DSR could deescalate with time as has the price of electronic calculators. Nevertheless, conflict between competing moral values would remain. An increased use of the DSR in the clinical setting, for example, could possibly result in the "over medicalization" of an increased number of patient complaints, leading to an expansion of the number of persons adopting the sick role, and greater medical costs to the patient and community. Its use, whether routine or optional, would provide another piece of sophisticated technology that invites physician and patient dependence. This dependence may add to a decreased sense of the autonomy on the part of both physician and patient as well as an increased sense of alienation by the patient from his physician, and *vice versa*. Moreover, the

DSR's increased use may add to the disparity between a "reasonable" standard of health and an ideal, unattainable standard. As Zaner sees it, the patient, "presumably the focus of all this high-powered technology", the recipient of "the very best", consequently stands to "lose" ([8], p. 51). However, as Weissmann indirectly suggests, such technology may augment our feeling of autonomy by expanding our sense of control over ourselves and our bodies, and by enhancing our capacities to achieve our chosen goals.

This case study discloses the battleground on which different senses of "optimal treatment" conflict. The conflict springs from a tension among incommensurable values and among competing value hierarchies within the thought structure of the medical community. Reasons for this battleground have been suggested by Thomas Nagel [5]. In his "Fragmentation of Value", he underscores five fundamental types of value as the source of moral conflict: (1) specific obligations to other people or institutions; (2) constraints upon action deriving from general rights of persons; (3) issues of utility; (4) claims of perfectionist aims or values; and (5) commitment to one's own projects or undertakings. Consider, for example, the conflicts that arise when each of these values compete with another: (1) the physician's obligation to administer optimal treatment, in the sense of including a DSR diagnosis, to each patient vs. the patient's cost; (2) the right of citizens not to be taxed in order to support the use of the DSR with indigent populations vs. the right to receive a DSR diagnostic opinion when the "need" is evident; (3) the benefits, e.g., better treatment of heart disease, available to the patient community vs. the cost involved with the use of the DSR; (4) the value of scientific, technological, and medical achievement provided by the DSR vs. the financial and other social sacrifices; (5) the value of personal achievement familiar to the individuals intimately involved working on the DSR vs. society's "preferred" values or goals. It should be recognized that underlying a seemingly single value such as "the very best", one finds competing values.

Nagel argues that no unitary system of priorities is to be found since "different types of values represent the development and articulation of different points of view ... " ([5], p. 291). He warns against adopting a fixed hierarchy or priority of values. Instead, he recommends the use of "sound judgment informed by the best argument" ([5], p. 294) on the moral issues which generate conflict. Only by approaching conflict resolution in this way, i.e., by admitting the need for a theory of ethics which recognizes an essential fragmentation and plurality of values, can an "optimal" sense of treatment be negotiated and stipulated for a pluralistic society.

Both Rescher and Zaner invite the insensitive to take a closer look at the problems which arise in the therapeutic setting from the adoption of a simple or single sense of "the very best". I support Bondeson's admonition: "[t]he fire of Prometheus is not only warm, helpful, and comforting but there is the grave danger that we might be blinded by its light" ([2], p. 203). Yet, I share Ross Kessel's optimism that we might be able to articulate the moral use of new knowledge in the biomedical sciences. However, as Nagel suggests, there will not be one sense of moral "success" or "failure". An account of "the very best" will be far more complex and equivocal than Zaner acknowledges.

Georgetown University
Washington, D.C.

BIBLIOGRAPHY

1. Anderson, G. L. *et al.*: 1979, 'The Dynamic Spatial Reconstuctor', *The Mayo Alumnus* 15 (1), 1–47.
2. Bondeson, W.: 1982, 'Scientific Advance, Technological Development, and Society', in this volume, pp. 199–203.
3. Jonas, H.: 1966, *The Phenomenon of Life: Toward a Philosophical Biology*, Delta Books, New York.
4. Kessel, R.: 1982, 'The Uses of Biomedical Knowledge: The End of the Era of Optimism?' in this volume, pp. 185–191.
5. Nagel, T.: 1977, 'The Fragmentation of Value', in H. T. Engelhardt, Jr. and D. Callahan (eds.), *Knowledge, Value, and Belief*, The Hastings Center, New York, pp. 279–294.
6. Rescher, N.: 1982, 'Moral Issues Relating to the Economics of New Knowledge in the Biomedical Sciences', in this volume, pp. 35–45.
7. Ritman, E. L., *et al.*: 1980, 'Three Dimension Imaging of Heart, Lung and Circulation', *Science* 210, 273–280.
8. Zaner, R.: 1982, 'Only the Best is Good Enough?' in this volume, pp. 47–52.

WILLIAM B. BONDESON

SCIENTIFIC ADVANCE, TECHNOLOGICAL DEVELOPMENT, AND SOCIETY

To talk about the moral uses of new knowledge in the biomedical sciences is to talk about the ways in which the processes of the acquisition of knowledge and the processes by which ways are found to apply that knowledge can be made more sensitive to the individual and social consequences of these activities. We are faced today with an enormous range of problems which cry out for a solution and a fair number of them require advances in the sciences.

In order to make sense of these issues, we must first distinguish between the acquisition of knowledge on the one hand and its application on the other, the old distinction between basic science and technology. We can easily distinguish, for example, between that scientific knowledge which helps us to understand the structure of genes and the use of that knowledge via genetic splicing to produce human insulin. Although the distinction is a good one and often holds in the practice of science, it is a fundamental mistake, in my judgment, to believe that there will not always be pressures to take whatever basic knowledge we have and to try to put it into practice.

We may believe with Aristotle, as he states in the opening lines of the *Metaphysics*, that men, by nature, desire to know. That statement is one about human nature and its essential characteristics when the appropriate potentialities are realized and, of course, they are not realized, or even partially realized, in every human being. That statement is not an empirical generalization in my view; rather, it is a statement of the essence of human nature, as Aristotle sees it, and it describes the normative criteria for the ascription of that term. It is a statement about what human beings can become rather than what they are. But, given Aristotle's assumptions that knowledge was not only finite but completable, the problem about knowledge was not so much how it is discovered but rather how it should be ordered and, with the additional assumption of Aristotle that all of knowledge is easily attainable and equally valuable, it should be clear to almost anyone that Aristotle faced a world far different from our own.

In many ways we are not so much the children of Aristotle as we are the children of Bacon and Hobbes. Their approach to knowledge in any area of inquiry was not one of organization, of normative regulation, nor of structure; rather, their approach was based on the assumption that knowledge is

William B. Bondeson, H. Tristram Engelhardt, Jr., Stuart F. Spicker and Joseph M. White, Jr. (eds.), New Knowledge in the Biomedical Sciences, 199–203.

fundamentally power, power to give men a mastery over nature, power to enable men to bend nature to their will, power to mold and shape and not, as Aristotle would have put it, simply to understand.

Thus, a corollary must be added to Aristotle's statement that men, by nature, desire to know, i.e., that once men have knowledge the temptation to put that knowledge into use is virtually overwhelming. Since Aristotle thought that knowledge was essentially a theoria, i.e., a seeing, a vision, and a contemplation, it never occurred to him, given his distinction between the theoretical, the practical, and the productive sciences, that theory and practice, knowledge and its applications, science and technology, might have problems intricately intertwined with one another.

If, with Bacon and Hobbes, knowledge is the power to transform both nature and ourselves, then theory is no longer just theoretical, it is praxis. Knowledge is no longer easily attainable in all of its detail. Rather, the tragedy of our choices, as many have used the phrase, is the tragedy of needing to know so much, but not being able, for all kinds of reasons, and many of these as I will argue are economic, to know all that we want or need to know. Thus, a "pure" science is a theoretical goal but a practical impossibility. And this point is especially valid in the case of the biomedical sciences; there will always be the desire to use advances in these fields for the apparent or real benefits of patients out of the genuine desire, as Zaner has put it, to give them "nothing but the best". In terms of the myth of Prometheus, fire is not only the symbol of knowledge, but it also stands for the use of that knowledge to benefit the human condition.

But science in the last half of the 20th century is categorically different from all previous science in that it is no longer in the hands of the individual entrepreneur, either as scientist or as technologist. Without massive social and financial support, whether in terms of institutional, state, or federal help, science these days would be simply impossible. And the same kind of support is required in the private sector as well.

As Rescher has pointed out in his essay, it is taking larger and larger amounts of funds to produce ever smaller increases in our knowledge, and the magnitude of those funding requirements makes it imperative that the social character of support for the sciences be considered. Linear accelerators and renal dialysis programs have required enormous amounts of funding and, in both cases, the requirements have been so substantial that only federal support has been a possibility. But these projects raise the considerations of social benefit and distributive justice. What are the best means for insuring that new knowledge and new technologies can be used most appropriately?

Some have suggested the creation of a science court at the national level made up of both scientists and lay persons, which would set national priorities for funding projects in basic scientific research and in technological development. Others have argued that such bodies constitute a control upon the necessarily free activities of scientists and would restrict the range and scope of scientific inquiry. Both sides miss some crucial points.

First, given the structure of American science at least, there are numerous review mechanisms in which both peer and lay judgmental mechanisms are incorporated. And thus there are "courts", albeit low level ones already in existence. And there are also larger decision-making bodies, i.e., legislative ones, which set the funding patterns for federal agencies.

But second, the scientist still has the freedom to propose topics for research and even begin some initial work within his or her own institutional setting. But, if Rescher is right, then future advances in the sciences and in technology will require ever-increasing social scrutiny insofar as the funds used for these advances will compete with funds for other social programs. I cannot accept Weissmann's argument that the social support for science should be done on purely aesthetic and cultural grounds nor can I accept his view that the great cultural monuments of the past were produced for purely aesthetic reasons either. Wartofsky is far closer to the mark in his views about the social character of the scientific enterprise and the social obligations which devolve upon scientists, given the public character of their work both in terms of its sources and in terms of its consequences. Surely the principle of the freedom of the scientific enterprise can be defended on utilitarian grounds without the claim that all of scientific activity must have immediate and practical application. But, to return to Rescher's point, then one, and perhaps the primary, mechanism for the regulation of science and technology will inevitably be financial support from federal sources.

But there is another dimension to the issue of the social control of science and technology as that issue applies to medicine and medical technology. In an article in *Science* ([1], pp. 570–575), Richard A. Knox writes about current discussions in the Department of Health and Human Services concerning the merits of using Medicare and Medicaid funds for new medical technologies. The focus of the discussion is a study originated by a former secretary, Patricia Roberts Harris, concerning the criteria which new technologies must meet in order that their application can be funded by Medicare and Medicaid. By statute, Medicare is required to pay only for "reasonable and necessary" medical expenses without any definitions of those terms. The medical technology chosen for assessment as to whether it is "reasonable and necessary" is one of the most dramatic and aggressive, i.e., heart transplantation.

Leaving aside the issues of the benefits of the operation to the patients, the additional knowledge that might be gained about immunosuppressive mechanisms, the preservation of donor hearts and other kinds of knowledge gained by these procedures, the question remains as to whether or not public funds should be expended for this purpose. The Health Care Financing Administration has estimated that the first year costs of a national heart transplant program could range from 212.2 million dollars to 3.2 billion dollars depending on whether 2000 or 30 000 transplant operations were performed ([1], p. 571).

The high sophistication and consequent high cost of this technology make it impossible for it to be applied, except in a limited and experimental way, on any other than a national funding basis. And funding may once again be the most effective way in which decisions about technologies can best be implemented. However, this leaves the issue of the methods of assessment as well as the public policy decisions resulting from that assessment still to be determined.

Since all citizens have an interest in support for basic science, the development of new technologies, and the consequent application of those technologies, some social mechanism which takes the interest of justice and social benefit into account seems inevitable. Whether it be through a science court or through a National Center for Health Care Technology, only recently established, public policy discussions can and must deal with these issues. Should we, as a nation, spend several billion dollars on a program of heart transplants which will benefit 30 000 people annually or should we use those funds for a massive program to immunize the elderly against pneumonia, for example? And these are only two of many alternatives competing for a limited pool of resources. Thus some mechanism for assessing new technologies is imperative and this assessment is both a scientific and non-scientific task. To believe that technologies can be developed and understood by scientists and then turned over to others for an assessment of their social values is to commit the old philosophical blunder of a rigid distinction between facts and values. The outcomes of technology are best determined by those with knowledge of its detail. But this discussion also requires a contribution from those best able to assess the social impact and distribution of technological goods. My concern is that technology, especially medical technology, has sufficient theatrical appeal in American society these days that it will fare better in the pursuit of federal funds than will less dramatic, but equally costly, preventative measures. The fire of Prometheus is not only warm, helpful, and comforting but there is the grave danger that we might be blinded by its light.

University of Missouri-Columbia
Columbia, Missouri

BIBLIOGRAPHY

1. Knox, R.: 1980, 'Heart Transplants: To Pay or Not to Pay?', *Science* **209**, 570–575.

STUART F. SPICKER

THE LIFE-WORLD AND THE PATIENT'S EXPECTATIONS
OF NEW KNOWLEDGE

As the wisest of his race, Prometheus created man's
body from clay and water, and formed them in
the likeness of gods. Zeus, having decided to ex-
tirpate the whole race of man, spared them only
at Prometheus's urgent plea; for Zeus grew angry
at man's increasing powers and talents. Also angered
by Prometheus's actions, Zeus withheld fire from
mankind. Athene, who had breathed life into
man's body, offered aid to Prometheus, who
having gained secret entrance to Olympus, hid a
glowing charcoal — a fragment broken from a
lighted torch, since extinguished — and stole away
undiscovered by Zeus. Whereupon Prometheus
gave fire to mankind.[1]

1. INTRODUCTION

The essays which constitute the present volume tend to raise and clarify
issues from the perspectives of the physician, the biomedical researcher and
even the technologist and technocrat. Problems made thematic when turning,
as this volume does, to the moral uses of new knowledge in the biomedical
sciences, fail to be adequately raised, however, if we ignore the patient's
perspective. It may prove useful, prior to construing persons *as* patients (a
particular social role we should be reminded), to draw a sketch of our contemporary social world, not one depicted through the sociologist's categories
and jargon, but one penned by the philosopher's hand which takes its point
of departure from the patient's scientifically naïve standpoint.

2. THE LIFE-WORLD

In the simplest terms, following the later work of Edmund Husserl, the life-
world is the world that is constantly pregiven in everyday experience. Every
human purpose and activity presupposes it, but it is not a purposeful structure
itself. Furthermore, everything developing and developed by mankind — e.g.,
science and medicine — originates from the life-world. Particular goal-directed

205

*William B. Bondeson, H. Tristram Engelhardt, Jr., Stuart F. Spicker and Joseph M. White,
Jr. (eds.), New Knowledge in the Biomedical Sciences, 205–215.*

lives — that of the scientist's or physician's life-vocation — including their specific communal existence, belong to the life-world. This, of course, is also true of the philosopher's life-vocation. Each of these "worlds" has its particular universality determined by the end of the particular vocation in question. Though the biomedical scientist, physician, and technologist, as part of the "race of mankind", share a common life-world, they, once living in the "world" of science, medicine, and theory, *wish to accomplish something new*: Theory is to be substituted for nature, theory which, in the end, promises to lead to unconditionally, universally valid knowledge. This *new knowledge*, then, becomes the "domain" of the biomedical scientist, physician and technologist, and new questions are eventually posed and often answered.

The life-world comprises the sum of mankind's involvement in everyday affairs including our present knowledge and future hopes for further knowledge. "Consciously we always live in the life-world; normally there is no reason for making it explicitly thematic for ourselves universally *as* world" ([3], p. 379).

The life-world is, generally speaking, the social and historical world prior to scientific or mathematical conceptualization; it is the world oriented to human activities; it is an intersubjective world in a particular ever-changing and transforming historical context. This is the world in which consistent events take place with typical regularity — e.g., when an object is dropped it always falls toward the earth. The changing seasons occur with regularity and constitute an element of the life-world. The life-world, then, reveals an approximated, typical regularity. This life world is contrasted with scientific conceptualization in which certain regular events are compared against some mathematically ideal measure. In the life-world things can be described fairly approximately. This is our quintessential reality.

Modern science is therefore *only* a particular view of our life-world. In terms of the 20th century, technology, *not mathematical* physics, insinuates our life-world. In the life-world there is an absence of mathematical exactness. (It should be noted that only a few men/women participate in the world of science. It is crucial that we not generalize from the relatively few who participate in the world of modern science to all mankind.) The overall view and conception of the life-world contrasts with the scientific view shared by the scientific community, who attempt to account for the world in terms of idealized mathematical entities. The universal end shared by scientists, researchers, physicians, and technologists presupposes the common life-world; and the particular end of *knowing* the life-world in "scientific truth" presupposes this life-world as well. Furthermore, biomedical scientists (one might say with Husserl) "have eyes for nothing else but their ends and horizons of work" ([3], p. 383). No matter how much the life-world is the world in which physicians, biomedical scientists, and technologists live, and on which they found their theories, the life-world is *not* their direct subject matter. The biomedical scientist is man-in-the-scientific-attitude, working through a particular vocational interest. But the life-world is itself the foundation for all particular interests. To further complicate the matter, the life-world undergoes continuous transformation, however gradual the process. On certain though rare "occasions" a particular scientific theory may be assimilated into the meaning of the life-world. This is a very important point and one worthy of elaboration.

3. SCIENTIFIC THEORY AND THE LIFE-WORLD

A classical illustration of the modification of the meaning of the life-world is paradoxically revealed by way of two competing theoretical conceptions of celestial and terrestrial phenomena. That is, scientific theories — though originally theoretical projects disclosed by men-in-the-scientific-attitude — may themselves become assimilated into the general and typical meaning structure of the life-world. Thus we should distinguish (1) the universally shared life-world (which we rarely if ever need to explain to a child) and (2) the particular theoretical activity of men-in-the-scientific-attitude.

Moreover, scientific constructs can themselves become insinuated into the ever-so-slowly changing meaning of the life-world, as when a patient suffering tuberculosis in the 19th century came to "see" the tubercle bacillus in his expectoration; or, when a patient with adrenocarcinoma, a glandular cancer, has an operation and "imagines" it has micrometastasized, having "spread" to form tiny "nests" of cancer throughout his body. An even more striking example from the history of science illustrates the transformation of the life-world between 1600 and 1750. Consider, for example, the significance of Galileo Galilei's claim that Copernicus's heliocentric theory furnished a *better explanation* of both celestial and terrestrial phenomena than did Ptolemy's geocentric account. After all, Galileo was claiming, against the common sense meaning of the life-world of his time, that the earth was in motion (surely unexperienced and unobservable then) and that the stars did not revolve around the earth once a day (though the populus "saw" and believed that they did).

The implications for theology of this new conception, made possible by observational astronomy coupled with a radical "cognitive revolution", are legend and need not be belabored here. The important point for us is that Galileo was claiming that his notion of explanation compelled mankind's new *conviction*; and this conviction, though it required many years to deepen (even among scientists!) is now accepted as certainty by all of us and is comfortably insinuated into our 20th-century space-travelled life-world.

It is clear that we, at least, are convinced as to the reasonable adequacy of Copernicus's and Galileo's heliocentric cosmography. We no longer take the stars to be revolving around the earth (though for the romantic among us the Ptolemaic celestial world reappears every so often). Nor do we believe the earth is at rest – two quite counter-intuitive claims given our everyday visual and kinaesthetic experience, which is quite rightly Ptolemaic (at least this is the case for those of us who have yet to experience space travel first hand).

Why turn to the Ptolemaic conversion by Copernicus and Galileo, the reader might inquire? Simply stated, the scientific and theoretical world of contemporary biomedicine, which is seen as the foundation for clinical medicine, as well as the world of bioengineering and technological invention, have dramatically affected our life-world. Thus *we* live during a period in which another such "occasion" is taking place, however subtle the transformation of our life-world may appear to those presently living. The contemporary world of biomedicine and the so-called "new biology" of the day is itself, as a complex human activity rooted in the life-world, being assimilated into the everyday meaning of the life-world of mankind. This "assimilation" is not quite analogous to that which resulted from the genius of Copernicus and Galileo, but, "assimilation" of the conceptual theories and models of contemporary biomedicine it is nevertheless. This is most clearly revealed in the ways in which fundamental models of biology, through the media and public talk, become part of mankind's self-understanding. It occurs quite dramatically when persons adopt the patient or sick role. When the patient with some understanding of micrometastasis, for example, construes his own body as so "invaded", the disease "spreading" in small "nests", it is because such pseudo-scientific accounts have gradually been assimilated into the life-world. Many other examples could serve to highlight the essential point. But an even more significant (and perhaps dangerous) transformation and modification of our life-world is occurring which makes the above examples trivial by comparison.

4. THE EXPECTATIONS OF NEW KNOWLEDGE

The contemporary life-world, for patients or the healthy, is founded on radical and heretofore unimagined advances. Consider:

(1)   current advances in the curative and palliative powers of the present medical armamentarium and pharmacopoeia;

(2)   current understanding of the structure, function and influence of chromosomal and genetic materials;

(3)   recent ability to control the processes of conception and reproduction;

(4)   very recent successes with *in vitro* fertilization of human ova and the techniques required for embryo transfer to assist infertile females;

(5)   very hopeful signs that the "major killers" will soon be controlled through advances in biomedicine and bioengineering;

(6)   an ever-increasing anticipation that human aging processes will be inhibited, or at least dramatically retarded, e.g., to eliminate wrinkling of the skin and greying of the hair;

(7)   an ever-increasing likelihood that infants will be less and less likely to be born with anomalies and "defects";

(8)   the hope that epidemiological measures will be discovered to forestall the onset of, if not entirely prevent, numerous and deadly diseases.

All of these advances lead quite naturally (by a kind of "cognitive slide") to anticipations and expectancies as the future is protended or anticipated within the immediate present. Projected toward a future with its horizon of expectancies and anticipations, mankind no longer lives in quite the same material universe as did its ancestors. One single, but striking example, is that the essence of the material-organic universe has undergone transformation within the life-world. Matter is no longer a blunt, irreducible ultimate, as it was for Descartes and the Cartesians, but is construed as an always-reopenable challenge for further penetration and exploration. New knowledge is to be found in the "world" of sub-cellular reality, a world originally quite different from the life-world, but now assimilated to it by virtue of at least three hundred and fifty years of scientific activity.

The point of underscoring some of the domains where new knowledge is about to come to the fore is that we do not forget the fact that scientific theories and models are *very special ways of looking at the world*. Their adoption among more and more of us has already affected our generally-shared beliefs and expectations and how we shall henceforth reconstitute our living reality, the ever-present yet always changing life-world.

5. EXPECTATIONS, ARROGANCE, AND THE REMEDY OF FEAR

It is not without significance that the myth that surrounds Prometheus reminds us that he assisted Zeus with the birth of Athene from Zeus's head. And Athene instructed him in medicine and other useful arts, which he passed on to mankind. Prometheus's name, "forethought", though it may have originated in a Greek transformation of a Sanskrit word,[2] is not unrelated to "foreknowledge" and "expectation".

The contemporary life-world reflects the public's arrogant expectancy that what was once attributed to the independent powers of the gods (who like Zeus often resented mankind's power) is now to be *required* of mankind. For no longer are the unwelcomed outcomes of human reproduction, advent of sickness, insanity, and aging acceptable structures within the human life-world, but are resented as failures of scientific men in general, and physicians and biomedical scientists in particular. After all, the mythographers remind us that Prometheus, the maker of men, stole the source of power, fire, from Zeus on Olympus. Is it not true that the power once attributed to the gods is now transferred to mankind's menial medicine? How many of us in this pluralistic, secular world any longer blame the gods or God for the misfortunes of illness, insanity, disability, aging, and even death? Blame, which many believe has an appropriate place in contemporary moral consciousness, is now placed on men-in-the-scientific-attitude by the rest of us. We now take health, sanity, youth, and perpetual life as the expected and anticipated norm. Nothing less will do.

As my colleague Joseph M. Healey, Jr., has eloquently remarked:

Many patients have come to regard health as a static entity given by the physician to the patient. It is regarded as something which modern medicine can assure. This erroneous, yet prevalent, concept of health has led many patients to assume that undesirable health outcomes are avoidable, and, therefore, when they occur, they are the responsibility of the physician. The flaws in this line of thinking are clear, yet its popularity is increasing not decreasing ([2], p. 39).

Gradually, over the last decade, we have witnessed a popular disquiet to which the expectancies of new knowledge have given rise. The common word for those among us who anticipate nothing short of perfection from health professionals is, of course, *arrogance*. In a posthumous essay, the late

Franz J. Ingelfinger, M.D., focused his attention on charges of arrogance made against bioscientists, molecular biologists and parascientists in medicine — the physicians. The public's response has, of course, led to the fear among men-in-the-scientific-attitude, that arbitrary limits would be placed on mankind's search for new knowledge ([4], p. 1507). Dr Ingelfinger's thesis is that an "arrogance of ignorance" as well as an "arrogance of expertise" should be underscored more often, for both are devastating. But a third form of arrogance is now with us — *the arrogance of unreasonable expectations*, expectations of new knowledge and impeccable medical practice. Although it is true that the arrogance of ignorance is hardly ever mentioned, even less so is the arrogance of unreasonable expectations, that is, the public's new demand that physicians and biomedical scientists provide perfect resolutions to all health and health-related problems.

Lewis Thomas captured the spirit of these unreasonable expectations:

But there is something else going on that I do *not* understand. There is a tendency for people to become not just dissatisfied but positively apprehensive when simple imperfections in the system turn up: things that are clearly self-limited, that are going to get better in a day or two, now cause more anxiety than they used to — respiratory infections, gastrointestinal upsets, a headache, various pains and aches that are part of normal living ([1], pp. 173–174).

In short, the public has reconstituted the life-world in a new way: health, youth, sanity, and extended longevity are no longer mere idealizations. They are *expected to prevail*. Hence Dr Ingelfinger underscores the medical backlash, now a pervasive idea, "that the failure of medical ministrations is the patient's fault" ([4], p. 1510) and thus physicians accuse patients of being noncompliant; patients, on the other hand, expect physicians to be omniscient and omnipotent, at least when they fall seriously ill. It seems, then, that we are confronted not only with the "arrogance of scientific expertise", but with the public's "arrogance of ignorance" and the "arrogance of unreasonable expectations". What, if anything, can serve as a remedy?

Dr Ingelfinger suggests we consider the virtue of sophrosyne, that is, prudence or temperance, a virtue which in traditional ethical theory could counterbalance the vice of hubris. But I think this is inadequate. That is, Socratic temperance, though it surely tempers arrogance, will not turn us from the arrogance of unreasonable expectations with regard to our health and its maintainance, our forestalling of aging, and our longevity. I think we will need to be quite literally afraid. With Hans Jonas, I share the view that a psychology of fear, in spite of its disadvantages, is more appropriate for our life-world than mere prudence and skepticism. The spectre of this psychology of fear occurred when I attended, a few years ago, a California meeting of the Commission for the Protection of Human Subjects of Biomedical and Behavioral Research. The Commission's agenda for that meeting was primarily occupied with the ethical dimensions which surround psychosurgical research — also seen by the scientific community as a therapeutic modality for various behavioral disorders.

Notwithstanding the promises of biomedicine and psychiatry, as well as the technical-surgical sophistication of our time (or perhaps even in spite of them) the public made its views quite clear. I recall the placards:

"HANDS OFF OUR BRAINS"
"PSYCHOSURGERY IS LAUNDERED LOBOTOMY"
"STOP BRAIN MUTILATION"
"DON'T FUCK [3] WITH MY HEAD"
"BET YOUR ASS WE'RE PARANOID"
"SMASH THE THERAPEUTIC STATE"
"PSYCHOSURGERY IS A CRIME AGAINST HUMANITY"
"PSYCHOSURGERY IS SPIRITUAL MURDER"

The message was quite unambiguous. And it is "messages" like these that no doubt lie behind Hans Jonas's argument in 'Responsibility Today: The Ethics of an Endangered Future' [5]. This particular essay, published in 1976, is quite unique in the way it relates psychology to ethics (at a time when most philosophers are insisting on the separation of logic from psychology and psychology from ethics). I do not here refer to Jonas's arguments, those arguments that underscore mankind's responsibility to the biosphere and his future survival (what Jonas calls the "ethics of survival"), nor the intimate bond which his philosophy of organism reveals between humanity and nature. Specifically I refer to his "heuristics of fear", the psychological state which he implores us to adopt in order to be led to our true duties and responsibilities regarding biomedicine and bioethics. He urges us to take seriously the fact that "moral philosophy must consult our fears". Our era of modern technology, as he construes it, justifies such fear as a rational tactic. There is, of course, security and danger in this prompting. The danger in working to secure an all-pervasive psychology of fear with respect to modern biomedical technology and its potential is the risk (say) of early mortality, which we could all too easily come to accept as the norm. Had such an all-pervasive fear been at work, say in 1970, some time after the development of the trivalent oral polio vaccine, no parent may have consented to have his or her child swallow that "foreign" immunizing substance, itself a product of modern technology.

6. CONCLUSION

A few years ago, while a passenger in a New York cab, Mr Manny Auslander, the driver, expressed his concern about the serious nature of the drought then being experienced by Californians. He was hopeful that, as regards to rain, "they will make it". He suggested to himself, as well as to me, that "it was just a matter of time". Thinking that felicitous thought through, Manny (uninterrupted by me) interrupted himself. He remembered reading (asking me if I did) about an attempt to make rain which proved abortive. "Do you mean to say", he asked rhetorically, "they can't make rain?" The expression on his face was one of disillusionment. He had thrown into question what "they" (really the scientists and technocrats) could do, even given time.

Mr. Auslander may well be one among us who is beginning to question the longstanding belief in the prospect of salvation, presented and reinforced by today's cryptic images of modern technology. Manny may not yet have had the notion of apocalypse which, in this case, is a vision of the end of this planet; he may not have even asked himself whether he must make sacrifices, like restricting his use of fuel and water, which has heretofore been seen as plentiful, the notion of surplus being so easily furnished by modern technology. But Manny has surely come to see that the prophecy of doom now takes precedence over the prophecy of bliss, irrespective of the praise we daily offer to technology. It may be some consolation, then, to know that the distance is shrinking that heretofore separated the aristocrats from hoi polloi. It may, in fact, come to pass in the not too distant future, that those who work in the mean streets and those who cross them on their way to classrooms in edifices of steel and stone, share the thought of a common fate and the necessity to tread ever so carefully on the pavement of false hope. Brought together in that fashion, philosophers who have cherished and cared for the treasure trove of culture may come to accept their role of messenger, transmitting that heritage, which is now in danger of annihilation, to the streets. This is the most recent formulation of what Hans Jonas has called the practical uses of theory, a radical alteration of values with which we will now have to cope. For scientific, theoretical and speculative enterprises, heretofore of value for their own sake, are now merely a luxury our world may not easily allow even, perhaps, for the selected scientific few. All we can do, perhaps, is strike a bargain with the Devil, like Faust, and be prepared to live in constant fear of the future, while at the same time men-in-the-scientific-attitude are permitted to reconstruct, through theoretical activity, the one and only reality, which is nothing less than the eschatology of the life-world in all its concreteness.

University of Connecticut School of Medicine
Farmington, Connecticut

NOTES

[1] See Robert Graves's *The Greek Myths*, Vol. I, first printed in 1955, Penguin Books, Middlesex, England. Especially Chapter 39 "Atlas and Prometheus", also pp. 34–35.
[2] *Ibid*. p. 148. The Sanskrit word noted by Graves is *pramantha*, meaning fire-drill.
[3] The editors wish to note the origin of this now overused word. To begin with, it employs a word which, according to at least one dictionary, could not be printed in full anywhere within the British Commonwealth until late 1961. The roots of the word are, however, ancient. There does not appear to be strong evidence to substantiate an often-offered derivation of the term as an acronym for "for unlawful carnal knowledge". It appears rather to be drawn from the Latin *futuere*, which in its roots seems to be strikingly similar to a pictorially suggestive Egyptian hieroglyph, *petcha*. The Latin, *futuo, futuere, futui, futata est*, originally meant only a man swiving with a woman. Quite clearly, the word has not only been liberated, but has been given metaphorical force in non-academic disputes concerning issues in bioethics. For further information on some of the issues of derivation please see Eric Partridge, *Origins: A Short Etymological Dictionary of Modern English* (Routledge & Kegan Paul: London, 1966), p. 239.

BIBLIOGRAPHY

1. Bernstein, J.: 1978, *Experiencing Science: Profiles in Discovery*, E. P. Dutton, New York.
2. Healey, J. M.: 1977, 'The Patient Viewpoint on Malpractice', in D. J. Self (ed.), *Social Issues in Health Care*, Teagle & Little, Inc., Norfolk, Virginia, pp. 35–41.
3. Husserl, E.: 1970, *The Crisis of European Sciences and Transcendental Phenomenology*, (transl.) D. Carr, Northwestern University Press, Evanston, Illinois. Originally published in 1962 as *Die Krisis der europäischen Wissenschaften und die transzendentale Phänomenologie*, (heraus.) W. Biemel, Martinus Nijhoff, Haag. Based on Edmund Husserl's manuscripts of 1935–1936. See *Beilage* XVII, pp. 459–462, written perhaps in Winter, 1936–1937.

4. Ingelfinger, F. J.: 1980, 'Arrogance', *The New England Journal of Medicine* **303** (26) (Dec. 25), 1507–1511.
5. Jonas, H.: 1976, 'Responsibility Today: The Ethics of an Endangered Future', *Social Research* **43** (1), 77–91.

EPILOGUE

As these essays have shown, we live in the expectation of new technological breakthroughs in medicine that will occur on the basis of new biomedical knowledge. Such an understanding of reality has become a taken-for-granted element of the ways in which we live our lives. As a result, we do not often appreciate the extent to which it is bound to the post-Renaissance West's belief in progress. However, when we contrast it with periods in our past when we saw history as more cyclical, our character as a future-directed culture is more plain. We see ourselves on the ascending curve of ever-increasing knowledge and increasing technological powers. This general aspiration of Western intellectuals became a part of common biomedical expectations with new surgical techniques abetted by antiseptic techniques, the "miracle" breakthroughs of modern medicine with antibiotics, and the new computer-assisted modes of diagnosis and treatment that provide us with CAT-scanners and our contemporary intensive care units.

This point must be stressed, for it determines the character of decision-making with regard to health care, both by physicians and by patients. Physicians in general expect that new antibiotics will be developed, for example, to provide defense against strains of bacteria now gaining resistance. On the other hand, patients will often engage in risky health habits, hoping that when they are faced with the consequences, successful treatment will be available. Thus, a patient may continue smoking in the expectation that by the time he or she is afflicted by bronchogenic carcinoma of the lung, a reliable treatment will have been developed. The expectation of new knowledge and its consequences frames our understanding of health care. To some extent, this includes suspicions, fears of the advent of a brave new world, concerns with *in vitro* fertilization, and widespread genetic engineering. However, for the most part, the promise of a brave new world of greater medical knowledge and abilities is sought and affirmed. Thus, interferon may be regarded as a beneficent promise of better treatment due to recombinant DNA technology.

Modern health care and the moral issues it raises can only be understood against this background and possibility of new medical knowledge. These background expectations can often intrude in unexpected and even unreasoned

217

William B. Bondeson, H. Tristram Engelhardt, Jr., Stuart F. Spicker and Joseph M. White, Jr. (eds.), New Knowledge in the Biomedical Sciences, 217–218.

ways. For example, the prospect of ceasing the aggressive treatment of a terminal patient may be criticized on the basis of a hope that there may yet be a "miracle" breakthrough for this patient and his or her disease. We experience illness, disease, and health in terms of an expected future of greater knowledge and greater capacities. Undoubtedly that expectation is itself heuristic. It drives us to seek new knowledge and to develop new applications of that knowledge. It drives us as well to the puzzles that have framed this volume: reflections concerning the proper roles of physicians, the proper distributions of scarce resources, and the proper allocations of responsibilities for controlling and shepherding knowledge. That is, such expectations have engendered the philosophical reflections that have framed the contemporary character of the discipline of the philosophy of medicine and its special province, bioethics.

When a society becomes a free, pluralist community of individuals subjected to rapidly changing capabilities and ever new possibilities for realizing the human condition, philosophical reflection is inescapable. It is sought as the standpoint from which to judge the character and probity of our self-transformations. Philosophy is, after all, a child of crisis. It flourishes in times of intellectual ferment. And to live in the expectation of new knowledge is to live on the edge of possible crisis and in the ferment of an open future. One never knows when new biomedical knowledge and technology will provide for a change in the very character of the human condition. This uncertainty brings a culture to engage in an auguring of the intellect, reading the roots of its conceptual commitments, and of its understandings of itself and of its powers. This auguring *is* philosophy. The possibility of new biomedical knowledge encourages us to philosophical reflection. This volume has, thus, in exploring the implications of new knowledge, searched to the very roots of contemporary bioethics.

NOTES ON CONTRIBUTORS

Tom L. Beauchamp, Ph.D., is Senior Research Scholar, Kennedy Institute of Ethics, and Professor of Philosophy, Georgetown University, Washington, D.C.

William B. Bondeson, Ph.D., is Professor of Medicine and Philosophy and Co-Director of the Program in Health Care and Human Values, University of Missouri-Columbia, Columbia, Missouri.

Arthur L. Caplan, Ph.D., is Associate for the Humanities, The Hastings Center, Hastings-on-Hudson, New York, and Associate for Social Medicine, College of Physicians and Surgeons, Columbia University, New York, New York.

John Duffy, Ph.D., is Priscilla Burke Professor of History, University of Maryland at College Park, College Park, Maryland.

H. Tristram Engelhardt, Jr., Ph.D., M.D., is Senior Research Scholar, Kennedy Institute of Ethics, and Rosemary Kennedy Professor of the Philosophy of Medicine, Georgetown University, Washington, D.C.

Mary Ann Gardell, B. S., is Research Assistant, Kennedy Institute of Ethics, Georgetown University, Washington, D.C.

Samuel Gorovitz, Ph.D., is Professor and Chairman, Department of Philosophy, University of Maryland at College Park, College Park, Maryland.

Ross Kessel, M. B., Ch.B., Ph.D., is Professor of Medical Microbiology and Immunology and Acting Dean, Office of Graduate and Interprofessional Studies and Research University of Maryland at Baltimore, Baltimore, Maryland.

Laurence B. McCullough, Ph.D., is Assistant Professor of the Philosophy of Medicine, and Associate Director, Division of Health and Humanities, Department of Community and Family Medicine, Georgetown University School of Medicine, Washington, D.C.

Mary Crenshaw Rawlinson, Ph.D., is Assistant Professor of Philosophy, State University of New York at Stony Brook, Stony Brook, New York.

Nicholas Rescher, Ph.D., is Professor of Philosophy, and Chairman, Department of Philosophy, University of Pittsburgh, Pittsburgh, Pennsylvania.

Kenneth F. Schaffner, Ph.D., is Professor, Department of History and Philosophy of Science, University of Pittsburgh, Pittsburgh, Pennsylvania.

219

William B. Bondeson, H. Tristram Engelhardt, Jr., Stuart F. Spicker and Joseph M. White, Jr. (eds.), New Knowledge in the Biomedical Sciences, 219–220.
Copyright © 1982 by D. Reidel Publishing Company.

Stuart F. Spicker, Ph.D., is Professor of Community Medicine, University of Connecticut School of Medicine, Farmington, Connecticut.

Marx W. Wartofsky, Ph.D., is Professor of Philosophy, Boston University, Boston, Massachusetts.

Gerald Weissmann, M.D., is Professor, Division of Rheumatology, Department of Medicine, New York University School of Medicine, New York, New York.

Joseph White, Jr., M.D., is Director of Medical Education and Continuing Education, St. Paul Hospital, Dallas, Texas.

Richard M. Zaner, Ph.D., is Stahlman Professor of Medical Ethics at Vanderbilt University, Nashville, Tennessee.

INDEX

abortion, nineteenth-century view 14ff, 16f
Allen, Nathan 8
Andromeda strain 107
arbitration, moral 24, 28
Aristotle 126, 199, 200
Athene 210
Auden, W. H. 106, 110
Auslander, Manny 213
autonomy in scientific research 133
Ayer, A. J. 108

Bacon, Francis xvii, 199, 200
Beauchamp, Dan E. 58ff, 92ff, 98, 101
Beauchamp, Tom, xiv, xv, 55ff, 77, 87ff, 101, 161, 165, 185, 189
benzene and work-place safety 63
bioethics
    as moral engineering xvi, 161ff, 169
    as philosophical enterprise 155ff, 169ff
    inadequacy of 157ff
    secular framework of 181
biomedical knowledge
    acquisition of xi, 199
    application of 199ff
    distributing the fruits of 188ff
    expectations and xii, 209
    libertarian model 105ff, 131ff
    need for 105ff
    optimism and 185ff
    possession (ownership) of ix, xi, 113ff
    socialist model 113ff, 135ff
biomedical research
    and cost escalation 37ff
    and therapy 40ff
biomedical technology
    cost escalation 36f
    morality of 55ff
    new vs. old 179ff

obligation toward 57ff
social control over 55ff
biomedicine
    a complex schema 141ff
    controls in xv, 105ff
    economics of 35ff
    model of 143
    policy-making 145ff
    values in 131ff, 142, 145ff
Bloomer, Amelia 10
Boardman, H. A. 5
Bondeson, William xvi, xvii, 183, 199ff
Bonner, Thomas 6
Brill, A. A. 9
Brooks, Harvey 134
Burnett, Sir MacFarlane 41, 47
Burnham, John 11

cancer research costs 40
Caplan, Arthur xvi, 155ff, 169ff, 185
cardiovascular disease, research and costs 40, 195
Cartwright, Samuel A. 17
Celine, Louis-Ferdinand 109
Chandler, George 8
Chargaff, Erwin 110
Charleton, John 4
Chesterton, G. K. 105
chimaeras 107, 111
Clouser, K. Danner 157f
Coates, Joseph 56
collective action in biomedicine 60ff
commitment as value in biomedical science 105ff
Connolly, Cyril 109
contrast theory, ethics and 148
Copernicus, Nicholaus xi, 207, 208
cost-benefit analysis xiv, 61, 62ff, 88ff, 93ff
Crick, Francis Harry 144

221

The Philosophy and Medicine Book Series

Managing Editors

H. Tristram Engelhardt, Jr. and Stuart F. Spicker